Ao Dai

Ao Dai

My War, My Country, My Vietnam

Xuan Phuong

Danièle Mazingarbe

With a foreword by Frederick Z. Brown

☐ **EMQUAD**
INTERNATIONAL, LTD.

Published by EMQUAD International, Ltd.
P.O. Box 60, Great Neck, New York 11022
www.emquad.com

Originally published as *Ao Dai: Du couvent des Oiseaux à la jungle
du Viêt-Minh*, copyright © 2001 by Editions Plon, Paris, France

This edition copyright © 2004 by EMQUAD International, Ltd.
All rights reserved.

Translated from the French by Lynn M. Bensimon
Edited by Jonathan E. Myers

Library of Congress Cataloging-in-Publication Data

Xuan Phuong, 1929-
[Ao Dai. English]
Ao Dai : my war, my country, my Vietnam / Xuan Phuong, Danièle
Mazingarbe ; with a foreword by Frederick Z. Brown — 1st American ed.
    p. cm.
Translation of: Ao Dai, Du couvent des Oiseaux à la jungle du Viêt-minh.
ISBN 0-9718406-2-8 (hardcover : alk. Paper)
1. Xuan Phuong, 1929- 2. Vietnam—History—1945-1975. 3 Vietnam—
History—1975- 4. Revolutionaries—Vietnam—Biography. I. Mazingarbe,
Danièle. II Title.
DS556.93.X84A3 2004
959.704'092-dc22

2004050695

Printed in the United States of America on acid-free paper

FIRST AMERICAN EDITION

EMQUAD and its colophon are registered with the U.S. Patent and Trademark
Office. All rights reserved.

Contents

Map of Vietnam

Editor's Note

Throughout the text, metric units of distance (kilometers), weight (kilograms), and volume (liters) have been left unchanged, but units of area (hectares, square meters) have been converted to acres or square feet, and temperatures (degrees Celsius) to degrees Fahrenheit.

Foreword

In *Ao Dai*, Xuan Phuong recounts a harrowing half-century journey through revolution, war, personal deprivation, and, finally, victory. The "peace" she finds after 1975 turns out to be far from Ho Chi Minh's dream of a Vietnam "ten times more beautiful,"[*] but Phuong clings to her faith in her country, and she perseveres. She tells how the North Vietnamese summoned the determination and blood to defeat the government of South Vietnam and the United States, and unify Vietnam under a communist government. On another level, *Ao Dai* is the story of a woman swept along by the tide of history, one human being trapped in the coils of the "cold war." In that sense, *Ao Dai* is the story of all of Vietnam.

From the 16th century onward, European explorers had scouted Vietnam's coast, seeking colonial footholds for Christianity and commerce. In 1627, a French Jesuit priest, Alexandre de Rhodes, landed at Faifo (now Danang), a Portuguese trading station in central Vietnam, and revolutionized the Vietnamese language by transcribing its Chinese ideographs into the Roman alphabet. Bibles could now be printed in *quoc ngu* ("national language"). In 1787, Bishop

---

[*] Ho Chi Minh, "Testament," quoted in William J. Duiker, *Vietnam Since the Fall of Saigon* (Athens, OH: Ohio University Center for International Studies, Southeast Asia Studies Series Monograph Number 56A, 1989).

Pierre Pigneau de Behaine carried the French flag forward by escorting Nguyen Anh, a contestant in one of Vietnam's imperial power struggles, to the court of Louis XVI at Versailles. A treaty aligning France with the Nguyen Anh faction was signed, and in 1802 Nguyen Anh was crowned Emperor Gia Long. France's subsequent colonial conquest of the entire country met sporadic, often violent resistance from many Vietnamese, but in 1861 French forces captured Saigon and a French governor-general was appointed for Cochinchina. In 1883, France declared a "protectorate" over Annam and Tonkin, the central and northern areas. The Nguyen Dynasty endured until 1954; its last emperor, Bao Dai, was more at home on the French Riviera than in his palace in Hue. During this colonial period, a Vietnamese elite—landowning, relatively prosperous, in many cases Catholic—grew up around the French presence.

Xuan Phuong was of aristocratic blood, born in Hue, the royal capital of Annam. While growing up in privileged circumstances at a time when French colonial power in Indochina was at its apex, she feels the stirring of nationalism. She is unable to reconcile the admirable qualities of French civilization with the inequities of France's colonial rule and the indignities inflicted daily on the Vietnamese. In 1920, just nine years before Phuong's birth, Nguyen Ai Quoc (later, Ho Chi Minh) had denounced French imperialism at a congress of French socialists, and joined the French Communist Party and the Third Communist International, headquartered in Moscow. In 1930, Ho founded the Indochina Communist Party and then skillfully blended Vietnamese patriotic, anti-colonial aspirations with the ideology, organization, and discipline of Marxism-Leninism. The foundations were laid for a struggle that would endure throughout much of Phuong's life.

The Second World War was a cruel time for Vietnam. In 1944-1945, the Franco-Japanese government requisitioned the entire rice harvest, and two million Vietnamese starved to death. Phuong and her teenage peers, radicalized by the brutal treatment of their society and sensing the disintegration of the Japanese occupation and French colonial power, were drawn into the Resistance. In Phuong's poignant account of leave-taking from her family on March 10, 1946 to join the guerillas at the age of sixteen, one sees the culmination of the internal conflicts in which Phuong's sense of duty to family and the lingering influence of her elite, quasi-Western upbringing clash with her desire to join the fight against foreign domination. "Resistance," Phuong comes to realize later, would also entail a wrenching social upheaval.

Phuong spent nine years in the jungles of North Vietnam along the border with China. As we read about the hardships Phuong suffered during this period and her personal accomplishments, we should also recognize the turbulent international environment in which events in Vietnam were unfolding. The Second World War ended in August 1945 and with it the Japanese occupation. The war in Europe had already come to a close. The "cold war" between the United States and the Soviet Union that emerged from this period would—tragically for Vietnam—determine the course of events in Indochina. The future of the French colonial empire in Africa and Asia, and particularly Indochina, had become a contentious issue between Paris and Washington, with the French adamant that they must retain their Indochina colonial possessions. President Franklin D. Roosevelt had strong reservations about permitting the French to reestablish colonial control and favored either a firm timetable for Vietnamese independence or some sort of United Nations trusteeship.

With Roosevelt's death in April 1945, American concerns about Vietnam's independent status were eclipsed by the urgent need to resurrect the shattered economies and infrastructures of Western Europe. France, an American ally, was left to negotiate Vietnam's status with Ho Chi Minh's resistance movement, the *Viet Nam Doc Lap Dong Minh* or Viet Minh. Initially, the Vietminh had included Vietnamese noncommunist nationalist elements as ardent for independence as were the communists; by 1946 these nationalists had been outmaneuvered and crushed by Ho's cadres. Elsewhere during this post-war period, the Soviet Union had managed to install pro-Soviet communist regimes throughout Eastern Europe. Berlin, isolated inside the Soviet sector of Germany, remained a flash point for confrontation between East and West. In 1949 Mao Tse-Tung's Communist Party of China defeated the U.S.-supported Chiang Kai-Shek regime, thereby giving the resistance a vital source of "fraternal" material assistance directly on the northern border. It was across this border that the Vietminh would transport the artillery pieces that sealed the doom of the French forces at Dien Bien Phu in 1954.

With the breakdown of negotiations between France and the Vietminh in 1950, the United States was faced with either supporting France's attempt to reestablish its control by force of arms or acquiescing in a gradual assumption of power by Ho's Vietminh guerilas—the "Resistance" that Phuong had chosen to join. Events in Europe and Asia during the previous five years, and especially North Korea's invasion of South Korea in June 1950, had confirmed the United States' view that international communism, headed by the Soviet Union and China but buttressed by communist insurgencies in Indochina, was a threat to the security of Thailand and the newly independent states of the developing world, such as Malaysia, Indonesia, and the Philippines (the famous "domino theory").

From 1950 onward, it was this identification of the Vietnamese communist movement with the cold war agenda of Moscow and Beijing that drove Washington's hostility to North Vietnam. Vietnam's nationalist struggle for independence and Ho Chi Minh's links to the international communist movement could not be disassociated from each other. Vietnam had become a function of the cold war.

From Phuong's account of those years we cannot discern if she was aware of the seismic developments taking place beyond Indochina that were to shape events. In May 1954, the defeat of the French garrison at Dien Bien Phu was the cataclysm that shattered France's grip. Under the Geneva Accords of July 1954, Vietnam was divided in half at the 17th parallel. A million Vietnamese took part in a population migration reflecting their political preferences and expectations; Vietminh partisans moved from South to North but many more Vietnamese (including most of the Catholic population) fled from North to South to avoid inclusion in the communist Democratic Republic of Vietnam, the DRV. A significant number of Vietminh cadres remained in the South, going underground as future "Viet Cong" to pursue the revolution against Ngo Dinh Diem's Republic of Vietnam, the noncommunist government created in the South by the United States in 1955. Many families, Phuong's included, were split in two. At the heart of the bitter military conflict that would wreak such destruction for another 20 years was this deep division between those Vietnamese who moved South and those who chose to stay in the North.

For Phuong, the years after Dien Bien Phu and a new life in the DRV were as hard as the nine years of survival in the jungle. Faced with suspicion because of her refusal to join the Communist Party—she felt she had no need to prove her devotion to Vietnam's independence—Phuong states, "I never could have imagined that this time of peace would be so hard to bear" and wonders "How could the country have come to that?" From 1955 to 1957, North Vietnam was racked by the Party's campaign to stamp out "bourgeois elements" in the society and to force a land reform and collectivization program that would bring the agricultural sector to ruin. The parallel with what had happened in the Soviet Union and China is striking. In the Vietnamese Communist Party's attempt at radical social engineering we see echoes of Stalin's campaign against the *kulaks* (rich peasants) in the 1920s and Mao's "Great Leap Forward" in the late 1950s which caused the death of millions of Chinese and set back China's economic develop by decades. While Phuong would survive this awful period, so vividly described in her chapters "Everyone to Dien Bien Phu" and "The agrarian reform," many of her resistance comrades who had also become members of the "undesirable class" and had decided to remain in the North were ultimately devoured by the revolution they had served.

During the decades of the 1960s and 1970s, Vietnam was the knife-edge of a global proxy war—in Vietnam the war anything but "cold"—between the United States and the Soviet Union and China. The massive American military intervention in Vietnam was by all measures the most destructive of several other overt and covert confrontations in the "third world." From 1968 to 1973, the United States and the two opposed Vietnamese governments attempted to negotiate an arrangement whereby the United States could depart "with honor" and leave the Vietnamese parties to settle their affairs. Today, it seems bizarre to realize that in 1972, while President Nixon was in Moscow to negotiate an arms control agreement with the Soviet Union, the North Vietnamese "spring offensive" was slashing across the DMZ and waves of B-52 bombers were striking Hanoi for days and nights on end. For

Phuong—a pawn on the global chessboard—such events could only be reflected in deaths of friends at the DMZ or in Hanoi. In 1973, the Paris Agreements ended direct U.S. military involvement, and in 1974 Nixon was forced to resign from office in disgrace. In effect, the Watergate scandal had spelled the end of viable American support for the Saigon government.

Phuong changed remarkably during the "American war"; she became a successful motion picture director and established relationships in the Soviet Union and in Eastern and Western Europe. The collapse of the South Vietnamese regime in 1975, the humiliating exit of the United States, and the reunification of Vietnam under a communist system are all fascinating parts of her tale. But for Phuong, like so many Vietnamese on both sides of the struggle, the rise and fall of governments and the arcane geopolitics of the "Great Powers" were really incidental to discovering the fate of their divided families and seeking their reunion. It is in the final chapters of her book and the Epilogue that we see so clearly the astonishing qualities of this woman, Phuong, and at the same time the durability and intrinsic strength of the Vietnamese people from both North and South. What we do not see, except for the impact on Phuong's immediate family members, are the sufferings of those Vietnamese on the losing side after 1975, particularly in 1976-1978 when the Hanoi government, repeating its errors of twenty years earlier in the North, attempted to wipe out the southern private sector and to collectivize agriculture. Nor do we sense the pain of Hanoi's forced "reeducation camps" that embittered the South Vietnamese and made post-1975 reconciliation difficult.

How can we grasp the rich complexities of this extraordinary book? Phuong was born into the resistance struggle against the French. She was certainly idealistic but apparently not devoted to Marxism-Leninism, believing only that Ho Chi Minh was a leader who could gain Vietnam's independence. In 1954, she resented her treatment at the hands of a new dominating elite. She was disgusted by their mismanagement of the national economy, and was in effect disenfranchised. Nonetheless, she fought for her country for another two decades of the "American war." By 1975, Phuong and her peers had become a "lost generation"—overjoyed by liberation and unification in 1975, yet cynical and disaffected by the draconian aspects of the new government of a unified Vietnam.

Xuan Phuong represents a bridge between the Vietnam of the war years and the Vietnam we see today in her Lotus Gallery, in the thousands of Hondas on Ho Chi Minh City's bustling streets, and in a Vietnam that is at peace with its neighbors and that has moved from the dogma of Marxism to an expanding market economy—a Vietnam that has literally joined the world. Let us also appreciate Phuong as a bridge between the two million Vietnamese who live abroad (the *Viet Kieu*) and the 81 million who still live in Vietnam. But Xuan Phuong's own words offer the best appreciation: " ...I have always had the confidence that Vietnam would become the country of our dreams. Even if, today, injustices and unacceptable living conditions prevail for many, it is the role of the Vietnamese, themselves, to determine their destiny."

FREDERICK Z. BROWN

Associate Director, Southeast Asia Studies Program
SAIS/The Paul H. Nitze School of Advanced International Studies
The Johns Hopkins University
1619 Massachusetts Avenue, NW
Washington, DC 20036

Prologue

The wide, stone steps that make their way down to the river between clusters of bamboo lead to the Eo Bau ferry, which crosses to the opposite bank and continues on to Hue. At five o'clock in the afternoon, it is already cold along the water's edge.

March 10th, 1946. I am 16 years old.

That very morning, when I announced my intention of leaving home, my mother's strong opposition to my plans only served to reinforce them further in my mind. Nhan, my little sister, begged me to stay. My brother sobbed. My father's reaction would have been even more violent, but he was in Phan Thiet, one hundred twenty kilometers from Hue, and in those times of war we had no means of communication. My heart was heavy as I folded some clothing into a bag.

My comrades of the Resistance were waiting for me on the other side of the river. I climbed aboard the ferry, shivering, clad in the purple *ao dai** that I wore to school, my white pants, and equally white sandals. My long hair was

---

* The *ao dai* (pronounced *ao zai* in the North and *ao yai* in the South) is a traditional garment. This very tight tunic, open on the sides and worn over baggy pants, symbolizes the Vietnamese woman, though it may also be worn by men.

pulled up into a bun, and I was without a coin in my pocket. I turned around and saw Xuan Ba, my third brother, who was waving his hand, but my thoughts were already far away. I would never see my father again, as he died in Los Angeles in 1981. My family had relocated in the United States after leaving Saigon in 1975. In fact, I was to enter the city on the heels of the North Vietnamese liberation troops, only two hours after they left on that very same day. But in 1990 I was to see my mother again. At Charles de Gaulle Airport in Paris, she didn't recognize me. Forty-four years had drifted by, nine of which I had spent in the jungle—the duration of the war of liberation against the French. It was the most difficult and the most exciting period of my life.

In Hanoi, I experienced the early days of communism and the dark period of the American bombings. I gave birth to three children, changed occupations several times, without ever leaving Vietnam. It occurred to me that telling my story would allow me to render homage to the companions of my youth, those whose examples I followed: physicist Ton That Hoang, who became my husband; Dang Van Viet, the "grey tiger" of Colonial Route No. 4; Ha Dong, founder of the Vietnamese Air Force; Do Duc Duc, artisan of anti-aircraft missiles; and all my comrades from Hue, many of whom sacrificed themselves for their country. I also wanted today's youth, especially the Vietnamese for whom uncle Hô is only a historical figure, to understand the suffering that our generation endured. Finally, I wanted to explain to my newly reunited family why I had made those choices that had separated us from each other for so long.

Ao Dai

Ten girls are not worth a boy

My mother, Nguyen Thi Xuan Oanh, was a descendant of a Hue royal family. Custom had it that she should give birth to her first child in the house where she was born. That house belonged to my maternal grandfather, Nguyen Xuan Han, a Mandarin of the Court in Hue.[1] My father, Nguyen Xuan Can was kept away from the event.

From then on, it was the midwife who inherited the most important role. That is why she was chosen—for her authority and, equally important, for the reputation of her family, which necessarily had to be a closely-knit one. My mother gave birth to me in an isolated room, which was carefully sealed off from the world. The bed was covered with a brocaded quilt that served to fend off evil spirits. She was to remain in bed for a month with the baby she was nursing, looked over exclusively by the mid-wife and my grandmother.

---

[1] Mandarin: a title that is acquired through competitive examinations. The maternal grandfather of Xuan Phuong, Nguyen Xuan Han, after having brilliantly passed his exams at the Temple of Literature in Hanoi, was named "Tri Huyen," a mandarin title which allowed him to direct the administration of the District of Nam Dan at Nghe An. He married the daughter of a princess, who, in the order of royal hierarchy, was the aunt of the King of Annam. Thus, Nguyen Thi Xuan Oanh, the mother of Xuan Phuong, is a royal princess on her mother's side.

During this period, nobody else was allowed to enter the bedroom out of fear of bringing ill luck to the child.

According to tradition, each member of the family was to give the baby an old article of clothing. Here, it would be sky blue, the color suited for girls. It was required, as well, that the garment come from a healthy child and thereafter be handed down to yet another newborn. Finally, my grandmother took care of burying the placenta in the garden, at the foot of a longan tree that continues to bear fruit to this day.

Like so many families, we keep a list of possible first names, spanning generations. For girls, they are names of birds. My mother therefore did not have to come up with one. For me, the name was to be Phuong, "the phoenix." For nothing in the world would one risk giving a name that had already been used. That would have been considered a very bad omen for the child.

According to a Vietnamese proverb, "ten girls are not worth a boy." In other words, ten girls are worth nothing. My father was very disappointed in having had a daughter. In order to be consoled, my mother assured him that the second child would be a boy. The following year, my brother, Phat, was born.

I never learned what the astrologer had said on the day of my birth, December 15th, 1929, under the sign of the Snake.[2] For my tenth birthday, another highly revered astrologer came to the house. When it was my turn, he looked at me for a while and then nodded his head. "It is she who will often be caught between life and death." My mother was furious. "Ours is a

---

[2] At birth, even in poor families the parents want to know the fate that has been allotted to their child. The Vietnamese horoscope uses the principals of Chinese astrology, with twelve animals corresponding to the twelve lunar months. The sign of the Snake is the sign of intellligence, and of endurance, but it is always prone to numerous injustices.

well-to-do family. Why should such a thing happen to my daughter?" The man continued: "During her youth, she will be confronted by many dangers, and she will experience the worst nightmares. It is only afterwards that good things will come her way. But she will not be at her parents' deathbed." For us, not being with our parents at the end of their lives is the worst thing that could come our way. He continued: "She is going to leave her family very early in life." Then, addressing my mother: "Madame, I am very fearful for your daughter." He looked next at my younger sister, Nhan: "This is the one who is going to feed you, not your older daughter. She will not provide for you one single day. She will not pay back your kindness."

My mother was twenty years old when I was born. She had been married for two years. My maternal grandfather, who wanted his seven daughters to be perfectly educated, sent my mother, who was the fourth in line, to the very renowned Dong Khanh Middle School in Hue. That is, until the day when a revolutionary named Phan Chu Trinh wrote to the French government to denounce torture in prison and a very strong support movement started within the establishment. A strike followed, in which pupils and students participated. Many were thrown into prison. My mother, being the daughter of a mandarin, was simply dismissed. Upon returning to her native village, scarcely a month afterwards, she met my father, Nguyen Xuan Can. Son of a mandarin, too, he was living in Phan Ri, deep in the middle of Cham.[3] He very quickly asked for her hand in marriage. She spoke French and she was one of the first women to be able to drive a car and to ride a horse.

---

[3] Cham: the kingdom of Champa was at its height between the 11th and 15th centuries, before being destroyed during the expansion of the Viets towards the South. About 60,000 Chams still live along the coast today, in the region of Nha Trang and in the Mekong delta.

The following year she was to have taken her graduation exams, but she would obtain her diploma only later, once she had been married.

My father, appointed by the French government, was school principal at Dalat and regional Inspector of Schools.[4] His first position had been in the heart of Annam, and then, from 1930 for the next twelve years, in Dalat. This city resembled no other in Vietnam. Everyone spoke French. With its comfortable climate of seventy to eighty degrees Fahrenheit year round, it was the preferred vacation spot for civil servants. They occupied houses built in the French regional styles, all different one from another, and they met in each other's shops, such as the bakery called *Michaux*, and the hairdresser *André*, run by Madame Suzanne.

My father supervised the schools of the city and its surroundings. He was in charge of the only elementary school as well as responsible for censorship of the local newspapers, which consisted of noting all the articles that were hostile to France. He often travelled around for his inspection tours, by railroad or by car. Our black Citroën, always perfectly polished, did not go unnoticed in Dalat. Dressed most of the time in a blue, green, or black brocade tunic, white trousers, leather slippers, and a turban on his head with an ivory plate bearing his name, my father would ride in the back seat. It was Bay, our chauffeur, who drove him around.

In Dalat, there were only two mandarins: the Executive-Director of the Province and my father, the Inspector of Schools, known as "*Monsieur*, the Revered Director."

We lived in a very big house that belonged to the French government, on the *rue de l'Ecole*. It was on the same hilly street near the local market where my father's school was

---

[4] Annam had been a French protectorate since 1887. The Resident-General was the head of the Vietnamese civil service.

located. The large reception room was decorated by my mother with numerous Chinese antiques, notably many huge and magnificent blue urns, and statues bought by my father from dealers who visited him regularly to propose their objects.

The servants lived in quarters situated on the other side of the courtyard. They used to be light-hearted and could be heard laughing. As children, we liked to go over to see them. But our parents put a stop to that. There was Lap who pulled the rickshaw and Duong, who was in exclusive charge of ironing my father's clothes. In return for his good and loyal services, the latter asked the *Résident supérieur* of France to grant him the title of *petit notable*. We had an excellent chef, Bac Bep, "uncle cook," who was rewarded with the ninth grade of *notable du village*. There was also Nguyet, the gardener, and several others whose precise tasks were never revealed to me. There were twelve of them altogether, plus a nanny for each child. My Chinese *amah*, A Cam, spoke only Cantonese, which I learned by being with her. It was something my grandfather did not like at all because, for him, the only real language was Mandarin.[5] He ended up insisting that she leave and that a Vietnamese nanny take her place. As far as living quarters were concerned, brothers and sisters were segregated from one another. Although each of us had a private bedroom, there were only two bathrooms. Here, we bathed ourselves in running water, but, despite the separation, we still had to keep our panties on. Furthermore, even our laundry was never to be hung up in public.

---

[5] During the ten centuries of Chinese domination, the bourgeois class of the *Annamites* had of necessity to learn to read and write the Chinese letters. Next, all the candidates who participated in the triennial competition to select the Mandarins of the Court or the Provinces, organized by the kings of Annam, had to learn by heart and be able to write down the works of the great Chinese poets. The Mandarin dialect is the Chinese language of the elite.

My mother's day began very early. She was the first in the family to get up, at the same time as the servants, and she would say her prayers in the room reserved for the altar of our ancestors. An imposing Buddha, which had been commissioned personally by my father, had pride of place there. I got out of bed when I heard the bells that marked the end of prayers. Then my mother met with the chef to decide upon the daily menus and the other servants followed suit to be given instructions for the day's work. Everybody called her *"Our Gracious Lady."*

At home, she would always be dressed in natural ivory silk with many bracelets on her wrists. She had very long hair, which almost reached her feet. To wash it, she needed help from two people; to let it dry, she had to climb up on top of a ladder and wait. I loved to keep her company because she would tell me stories.

Every Saturday, at home, my parents would hold a ball. Early morning, the servants would spread talcum powder on the wooden boards of the reception room, and rub it in to polish the floor. Then a buffet would be set up with huge quantities of various dishes. We also had a well-furnished bar, with bottles of every imaginable color tended after by two older cousins who were living with us during their studies. Whether French or Vietnamese, my father's tennis partners or his hunting companions gathered for this event. On a gramophone brought over from France, with records ordered from the department store *Le Bon Marché*, we played European music such as rumbas and tangos. For these evenings, I wore one of my blue or pink dresses with balloon sleeves, which were set aside for these occasions and of which I was very proud. The children were called to present their greetings before the beginning of the ball. Sometimes we were even allowed to stay and dance. But after the dancing, we had to go to bed. The adults would then settle down to play *mahjong*. My parents, as well as their friends, were crazy about that game. Sometimes, they would even remain at the table from Saturday afternoon to Monday morning, playing with tokens that would later be exchanged for money. When I opened the door to look at them, my father would wave me off: "Go away! This isn't entertainment for you." Later in life, I never dared to play, from fear of also catching the vice.

Planning for these evenings, my parents had a dance teacher come to the house. He was a Tonkinese with a small moustache, always dressed in a cream-colored tussah suit and a bow tie, who worked evenings in a bar. His elegance enchanted my mother, as it did me, and just as it did the teacher at my father's school who developed the habit of joining us for these lessons. We were insatiable for tangos, waltzes, and fox-trots.

Our parents also taught us to sing French songs, like those of Tino Rossi or Josephine Baker. Only my mother knew the traditional Vietnamese melodies that she could marvelously play and sing despite their difficulty. We spent entire evenings in the small study listening to her. It was during these particular moments that we had the feeling of being close. When, on occasion, my parents had terrible rows, my mother would confide in me. On one of the evenings when my father had been unfaithful she insisted that we go together to the house of a certain Madame Tung. Through the lighted window, my father could be seen dancing in close contact with that woman. My mother was even capable of hiring the services of someone to beat up her rival. But I prefer to put all of these stories out of my mind.

Not even for the balls would my mother wear anything other than her *ao dai*. She always dressed in the Vietnamese style, never as a European in the way my father sometimes did. Although she was a very modern woman, compared to others of her generation, she kept on dressing in the traditional style of the women of Hue.

Two seamstresses came weekly to the house, but this did not prevent us from being faithful customers of *Le Bon Marché,* whose catalogue we received regularly in the mail. I had bed sheets printed with scenes from the adventures of *Bécassine,*[6] which had come with a free bonus album, *Bécassine in the Snow.* I didn't understand the entire text, but it became my favorite book. Regarding clothes, my father insisted that all his children be dressed in the same way, which meant that most of the time we wore a kind of overalls—a one-piece pants and shirt outfit—whose model he had found in a French newspaper. My brothers and sisters didn't protest, but I hated them. I was mortified when I heard people's comments as we passed by in the street: "There go the children of *Monsieur l'inspecteur.*"

---

[6] *Bécassine*: the name of a classic French comic book series that portrayed the adventures of a young provincial girl.

Uncle Hien, the revolutionary

My paternal grandfather hated Dalat because it was the city of "blue eyes and hooked noses." He also disapproved of our way of dressing and only my mother escaped criticism in that matter.

He was a tall and stately figure, with sharp eyes and a long, white beard. He always dressed in a blue or black brocade robe[1], worn over white pants, with black slippers and a turban. Whenever he came to see us he would merely sigh. If, however, we happened to have French visitors at the house, he shut himself off in his large bedroom overlooking the garden, closed the shutters and waited for them to leave. Should we visit him in Phan Ri, we had to dress in the Vietnamese style. The women, who included my sisters, my cousins and myself, were not allowed to use the main entrance of the house. Only the men had the right to pass in front of the altar of our ancestors. We had to use the back door.

I was quite afraid of my grandfather because he was always blaming me for not seriously studying the Chinese language—something that all well-educated people had to do. Being the oldest child, I was supposed to carry on the family tradition. A former laureate at the Court of Annam, my

---

[1] Gold brocade was reserved for the Emperor, purple for the high-ranking mandarins, and blue for those of a lower grade.

grandfather could not understand how one could refuse to learn Chinese. He regretted the passing of days gone by. The period when Chinese literature was studied and *song* calligraphy[2] used. One evening—it was the fifth day of the new moon—he wanted to show me the sky: "Listen to this verse of the *Song* Dynasty that evokes the moon's beauty. 'By whom was this golden nail etched across the western sky?' Do you not find it infinitely more beautiful than your descriptions of the moon where it is forever invariably round?"

My parents did not share the same opinion since a powerful movement that started at the beginning of the century was setting a pace and encouraging the population to write in Vietnamese. But they dared say nothing. As soon as my grandfather looked like he would be spending a month in Dalat, my Chinese books resurfaced. As soon as he had gone, I breathed a sigh of relief and closed them again, for I found that language very difficult.

My parents spoke in Vietnamese with each other and with us, but only French with their friends. They were very westernized. They read the French newspaper, *L'Annam,* which was published in Hue and mailed to Dalat, as well as other French publications whose titles I have forgotten. My father also used French to write the speeches that he had to address to his pupils. In school, however, he first delivered them in Vietnamese, and only afterwards in French.

I have no memory of ever hearing politics discussed at home. At least, until the day Hien, my first uncle on my mother's side, came to live with us. The day of his arrival, my mother solemnly gathered all of us in my father's study. "I ask you not to mention the presence of your uncle to anyone. If you do, the French Bureau of Investigation might put us all in

---

[2] In China, the *Song* Dynasty (960-1279) was a period of high cultural learning.

prison." Hien refused to live in the main house, preferring the servants' quarters. It was just as well because this way nobody could suspect him of hiding in our house. One morning, Hien took me aside in the courtyard: "Phuong," he said, "look at these people who work for your family. This situation can no longer endure. They, too, have the right to be happy and go to school. We are going to change all that." I did not really understand what he meant, but I felt very proud that he was trusting me, and his words have remained engraved in my memory.

The following week, it was my father's turn to gather us together in his study. In our presence, he addressed Hien directly: "You must leave for the plantation now. If you are found here, you will be arrested and the safety of the whole family will be in jeopardy—even more so as I work for the French Administration. In Laba, you will serve as foreman and watch over the work of the coolies." The next day, Hien set out for my father's coffee plantation, seventy kilometers from Dalat.

The following vacation, we went to join him in *Laba*. In that magical place, surrounded by forests, we were lodged in houses built on piles. We went horseback riding all day long. On the plantation, there lived a great number of dark-skinned people, the *Moïs*[3]. These men and women wear only loincloths and their teeth are filed down to their gums. For them, on the contrary, we are "dog-people" on account of our bite. They also have pierced ears and every year they widen the holes by adding thicker rings. They do this until the day the entire earlobe rips off, which then calls for a huge celebration. I must

---

[3] *Moï* means "wild one" in Vietnamese. The French called them "mountain dwellers." They belonged to one of fifty-four to sixty ethnic minorities (depending on sources), living principally on the high plains and in the mountainous regions of the North.

have been eight or nine years old when a woman came up to me with a basin full of water that she had fetched in the creek. Her two enormous earlobes were swaying back and forth and I was scared out of my wits. Later on, we got to know her and found that she was, indeed, very gentle and kind. One evening she wanted us to hear the trumpeting of the elephant calls. Just in front of our house, two boys belonging to her family made a cup with their hands around their mouths and let off a loud bellow. They were answered first by the echo and immediately afterward by the elephants. In those times, the forest was still very dense—an authentic primeval forest full of enchanting mysteries.

From this time on, it was my Uncle Hien who supervised the work of the *Moïs*. I often went along with him during his rounds. "The French gave this plantation to your father," he confided in me one morning, "with obligation for him to use the *Moïs*. That is what is known as exploitation." Another time, seizing the occasion of my parents' return to Dalat, Hien took me to see a *Moï* dwelling. These were shacks so precariously built on piles that when you walked the flooring partially gave way under your weight. An old man with very swollen knees and a gaping wound on one thigh was squatting by a fire. "This man cultivated coffee for your father," my uncle told me. "Now that he is ill, he earns nothing and he does not even have medication for treatment. That again is exploitation," he added. "Unfortunately, he is not an isolated case on the plantation. Another family suffering from malaria doesn't get the least medical care, either. The French behave in this way on their plantations. Your father follows their example."

I would not have dared mention that conversation to my parents for anything. But I managed to obtain a first-aid kit, anyway, by raising the possibility that I might get snake or insect bites. It contained, among other things, Mercurochrome and permanganate that we had sent over from France and, thus, with my uncle, we were able to tend the old man's wounds. When it was over, his entire family got down on their knees to thank us.

During that vacation, some friends of my father's came with their children to visit us. In the evening, we sang French songs. Outside the window, small, dark faces were watching us, which left me with a very strange impression.

The taste of ginger

My father's native village, Phan Ri, was three hundred kilometers from Dalat and certain mandarins of the province preferred sending their children to his school because its reputation was the best on the High Plains. Thus, there were twelve boarding students with us, which made seventeen children in all.

Three whistles would sound out every morning and, impeccably washed and dressed, we had to line ourselves up in the dining room at exactly half-past eight. However, we were not allowed to sit down as long as our private tutor did not give us permission to do so. Furthermore, if we did not stand up straight, he would tap us on our backs with a copper-banded, wooden teak ruler in order to correct our bad posture—and, believe me, that could hurt an awful lot! The tables were square and accommodated only four of us.

As our parents were with us at the meals, suitable behavior was mandatory. Manners were to be respected, like serving oneself first with a spoon before using chopsticks to eat. However, the worst show of disrespect was talking during the meals. In light of these rules, it was not surprising that we avidly sought out the servants' company. At least with them, we enjoyed ourselves. Finally, before leaving the table, it was also forbidden to leave one single grain of rice in our bowls. If we did, that evening we were deprived of supper. Such strict practices would remain with us forever.

Our parents had the privilege of being served special dishes prepared by the chef, and a simple servant took care of the children's food. I liked everything that my father would not allow me to eat. He forced meat and fish on me, although I was a vegetable-lover. Apparently, only the poor eat vegetables and the rich eat a lot of meat.

In spite of the presence of servants, it was unheard of for a woman not to know how to cook. As a child, my mother had already sent me into the kitchen to observe the preparation of meals. Besides the traditional dishes, it was necessary to know how to make candied fruits, which was a tradition particularly in Dalat. At the end of every lunar month, every household in Hue offered elaborate meals. It was the moment to show off how well educated the girls were and how far they had mastered the art of cooking. Recalling those feasts is enough for my mouth to start drooling again: kumquats, mandarins, and tamarinds, whose delicate skin had to be removed in such a fashion that, once candied, the fruit would look exactly like one ripe on a tree. But ginger, in particular, was special! My mother took me personally along with her to the market in order to choose it. I learned that ginger should neither be too fresh, nor too dry, either. Then, she would show me how to peel it, how it should be boiled several times so that it wouldn't be too potent, and, finally, how to cook it. The "hand of ginger" had to be as translucent and golden as amber so as to impress our guests. "There, please enjoy!"—All the ladies in Dalat could have testified to my good education. But my work did not stop there because I still had to bake fruitcakes with rice flour and various other ingredients.

At home there was also a fine tradition of vegetarian cuisine. It was quite possible to get to enjoy a meal consisting of about fifty different vegetable and fruit dishes without ever realizing that they did not include any meat. The chef was particularly successful with cherry tree flowers fashioned out of lentil paste. Indeed, they looked so much like natural flowers that they could have been easily confused with real ones. Contrary to practicing Buddhists, who are vegetarians, we only refrain from eating meat on the first and the fifteenth of the lunar month. For that reason, we kept two distinct sets of kitchenware, and god help whoever used the wrong bowl! To put my mother beside herself took nothing more serious than the dipping of chopsticks meant for ordinary soup—the one containing meat—into a bowl reserved for the vegetarian version. As for boys, they were not allowed in the kitchen as it was considered a disgrace. It was preferable for them to play soccer.

Everybody was frightened of my father. As soon as we heard his chauffeur shifting gears on the incline leading to the house, we used to run and hide behind the pillars of the building. Suddenly, there was no more laughing or playing, and nobody except my mother dared contradict him. Needless to say, idle chatter with him was also out of the question.

A "behavior log" containing seventeen leaves—one for each pupil—was used to watch over us. Scrupulously kept by our tutor, nothing would escape his reporting: "Eight o'clock: Phuong is not working. Nine o'clock: Phuong is out for a walk down the street." Fortunately, though, he was a Ping-Pong fanatic, and, since we owned a table, we used to play with him, losing the games deliberately so that he would not tattle on us to my father about our mischief—especially me, as I was a regular tomboy and loved to play even more than the others. Actually we had three different tutors who were students in my father's graduation classes and whom we called "my elder brother-tutor." Our fate was thus in their hands, for every week my father would check the log, examine all the entries, commenting all through: "Phuong! All right. Phat, you were still playing at that hour? Lay down! ..." When he was finished, he would then take a very long stick and deliver one blow of it for every misbehavior committed. It was extremely painful and it took us a full week to recover. The most serious moment of all, though, was when my father summoned one of us into his study and we dared not open our mouths. I was convinced, however, that he really liked us, in his own fashion.

With my mother, we could do anything we wanted. Whenever there was a *matinée* for children, she was the one who paid for our seats at the "Dalat," a movie-house on the main square, next to the market. They showed movies with Shirley Temple, Danielle Darrieux, Clark Gable ... and we went all together once a month on the average, sometimes escorted by a tutor, sometimes not. If we needed money to go to the theater more often, there was only one solution: pulling out some strands of my mother's white hair. Ten of them gave you one ticket, but I found a means of making them go a long way further by cutting them in half. When there were no white hairs left, we had to say goodbye to extra movie sessions. We were fortunate, however, because we could still use toads of which she was extremely scared, even if there were two of them carved out of jade in the reception room. I would hide one in my hand and call my mother. As soon as she was close enough I would suddenly spread my fingers and the toad would look at her with its big protruding eyes. Terrified, she hit me two or three times on the head but also gave me enough money for all of our tickets. Actually, once over the first shock, she burst into laughter.

At night, when we were in bed, she came to kiss us goodnight. I really found her beautiful with her light-colored silk pajamas, and her long hair undone. She told us stories and poems; and she played the sixteen-string guitar.

My father was someone who never laughed, never hugged us, and always kept his distance. Looking back, I believe he felt some pride in being that way. Later in life, he would write to me on numerous occasions in verse, to which I equally replied in poetic form. After our long separation, I was no longer frightened of him. In 1981, when he was very ill he confessed: "Phuong, I'm suffering from an incurable kidney disease. What scares me most is having my old bones buried in the cold California soil." But he was too wary of the Vietcong to return home.

Outside our house, down the street on the right, there were several Chinese shops. One had a yellow sign with the letters *R.O.* and another had one in blue, reading *R.A.* They respectively stood for *Régie Opium* and *Régie Alcool.*[1]

We often went to the *R.O.* because all sorts of candy could be found there and we enjoyed watching the Moïs purchase their salt and dried fish. It was called the *Old Man's Shop* because the owner was an old Chinese man in a black skullcap, a green robe with brown brocaded sleeves, and a long pipe. His son was a pupil at my father's school and he would often say to us: "Greetings, *Monsieur l'inspecteur's* children."

Each time I went there I would see very thin and pale people come in. On the counter, there was a funny little copper thimble and the customer would hold it out to the shopkeeper who, then, took a round can, also made of copper, put it upside down above the thimble and pressed. From a hole made in the lid, a black liquid poured out into the thimble and filled it. Then the customer paid and left. In fact, the whole process was

---

[1] *RO & RA* signified State-authorized shops that legally carried opium and alcohol.

very intriguing. We soon had an explication from the Chinese woman who sometimes escorted us there who told us that it was opium: "They smoke it and then it is like flying up to heaven. The problem is that in the long run they come back down and must smoke again to go back up." My uncle gave me an altogether very different explanation: "It is a poison which is going to kill off the entire Vietnamese race if they keep at it. The French approve of it because it is the best method not to have opponents. With one thimbleful of opium, it is five or six months of the user's life that vanishes up in smoke. And once they have started, they find it impossible to stop."

One of my uncles, my father's brother—the one whose sons were living with us—was a serious alcoholic. When he came to see us in Dalat, he refused to have a drink of claret or any of the liqueurs that were offered him by my father's French friends: "They're women's drinks," he said, preferring the *choum-choum,* which was a forty proof rice liquor not available in the R.A. We did not have to be asked twice to go along with him whenever he needed some, being quite content to get into the forbidden shop. He never forgot to introduce himself as he entered: "I *am Monsieur l'Inspecteur de l'enseignement's* brother." Someone invariably answered: "Yes, we know that. What can I do for you?" My uncle then explained: "I want very strong liquor. But you must let me taste it first so that I can be sure yours is really worth it. If not, I'm going to go elsewhere." When it came to paying, the Chinese man did not dare take the money that was being offered to him: "If that's the way it is, put it on my brother's account," he retorted.

In Dalat, it was customary for the shopkeepers to ask for payment at the end of every month. Although my father was furious when he received my uncle's bills, he refrained from saying anything for fear of losing face. On more than one occasion I heard my mother cry out: "Heavens! Look at how much your brother has spent again!" "Be quiet!" he said, "He has bought this liquor to offer to friends for a feast given by our father."

Later, I understood what this *Régie Alcool* was all about. Around Dalat, there were seven villages of about a thousand inhabitants all told, to each one of which a certain quota of liquor was assigned. It was the Mayor's task then to encourage alcohol consumption. The same was true of *Régie Opium*. Although the French encouraged its use, the smokers were generally very much looked down upon and forbidden from belonging to any administration. They were called the "flat-eared citizens," an allusion to the fact that opium addicts consecrated a great deal of time to lying down.

In 1945, opium would finally be banned. Furthermore, the pipes were confiscated in the opium dens and piled up into huge bonfires. But in fact, a good many people continued to smoke on the sly in the northern part of the country despite the risk of heavy sanctions. Years later, in 1975, while I was working as a filmmaker in the Cao Bang Mountains, I was struck by the incredible beauty of the poppy fields during the spring flowering. I told my cameramen: "Tomorrow morning, after sunrise we will film this blooming." We were lodged in a house built on piles by people belonging to a minority group. One of them was smoking opium and looked at us with a weird smile. Soon afterwards, when the sun had risen, we left, happy as larks to be treated to such a beautiful sight and we went out filming non-stop. All of a sudden, however, my head grew heavy, my knees began wobbling and, looking around, I saw that my two companions were lying down on the ground. Barely conscious, I sensed being roughly lifted up, transported then lain down in a house. Totally lethargic, I drifted into a deep state of half-bliss and half-nightmare where time had no more importance. Then, someone gave me some very hot soup to drink and suddenly I was in fit shape again. My two cameramen had gone through the same experience as myself. Our hosts just sat there laughing for we had remained unconscious for forty- eight hours.

In fact, nobody ever risks walking through poppy fields at sunrise because the fragrance causes dizziness. We could never have known that since in our families, fortunately, no one had ever smoked opium or even cigarettes.

On May 15th 1975, when I returned to Dalat, the old man was still there in his shop with his son who was selling Chinese medicine: "You are *Monsieur l'inspecteur's* daughter," he immediately said to me. "Wait a minute, I have something for you." He then handed me a pile of papers that he retrieved from the shelf above. "Here, take them as a souvenir." They were bills signed by my father.

In Dalat, life, too, was much more light-hearted than elsewhere. On some Saturdays, the cook prepared chicken and all sorts of *pâtés,* and on Sunday mornings, with other well-to-do families, we would go picnicking in the surrounding forests. My mother always brought along a burner, and eggs from our own hens for omelets; and under her surveillance we collected mushrooms that she added as seasoning. We exchanged dishes with friends, told stories, and laughed joyfully together.

Fifteen kilometers or so from Dalat, some French people had a farm where they kept wild deer—*katons*, as we call them here in Vietnam. Only once had my father authorized us to go along with him on a hunt. Stalking tigers was done at night, and he would go alone, accompanied by four servants and, on occasion, by one of his colleagues who shared his passion. One morning a servant came home yelling: "Madame, Madame, Monsieur has killed a Lord of Thirtieth!" A tiger was not called by its proper name—something that was supposed to bring bad luck. The carcass of the animal was secured to the rear of the car, we hopped in, and someone began to beat a drum to clear the road ahead. Thus, we set out, like a circus parade, around the market square and around the entire city. The snapshots that my mother had taken of the event have unfortunately disappeared.

My first school

When I was five years old, one year younger than the standard age, my father decided that I should begin attending his school. Too bad for me if the idea of leaving home and having a teacher was frightening: I was hardly old enough to argue the contrary.

My father laid down the rules to be obeyed: girls and boys were to be dressed in the same manner. Depending on the weather, it had to be a black tunic over white pants or white all over and wooden clogs instead of sandals. At that time we did not yet have the Party, but given my father's way of ruling over everything, it came to the same in the end.

In August, on the evening before school was to begin, he told my servant: "Tomorrow, wake up Phuong at six. She must go to school." When I heard that, I started crying and my belly ached. My mother showed me sympathy, but my father simply accepted calling the physician, Doctor Morin. I eventually fell asleep and the next morning, still in a drowsy state, I had to leave home. My father had forbidden my mother from going with me, but my servant accompanied me all the way to the school—which was right behind the house. At the entrance, there was a big drum and, at eight o'clock sharp, the attendant rolled twelve long blows followed by twelve short ones, which went on resounding for a long time. Immediately, the pupils lined up in the courtyard and I felt very left out, not knowing what to do. Fortunately, a very kind teacher came towards me and took me with her to her classroom. She was the one who was taking dancing lessons at our house, so, all things considered, that first day of school turned out to be fine in the end.

The first grade was modeled on the French school system, but taught in Vietnamese. I learned the alphabet and arithmetic. My teacher was the only female on the faculty and I remember her walking around the courtyard in her violet silk *ao dai* and a long silk scarf around her neck and her very long hair. Every body would look at her, particularly the other teachers. We only addressed her as "respected Mistress" and the other teachers as "respected Master" and would not have dared pronounce their names. And God help those who were reckless enough to blurt out: "Mistress So and So." We felt it to be so insulting that it would make us start to cry.

I must have been nine years old when my father took me to the Linh Son Pagoda, which was one of the most popular in Dalat. With about thirty other girls my age, we were initiated with devotion to the prayers of Buddha. Some of us were there for confession, others to find peace of soul again, to become better through good deeds, to be sheltered from material misfortune, or to help the dead depart serenely. For the beginning of prayers, we also learned how to handle the bell and the gong with its mallet made of jack-tree wood.

Every evening except Sunday, at about six, my mother gathered the whole household before the great imposing Buddha next to the altar to our ancestors. Once in a while, rather than intoning the prayers by herself, she allowed me to lead the ceremony. Very proudly then I would raise my voice to the ringing of the bell and the rhythm of the gong. On the altar, sandalwood was slowly consumed in a white jade perfume-burner that gave off intoxicating fragrances. Eventually my two brothers and youngest sister would end up drifting off to sleep, as they were quite young. When the final gong was heard, Duong, the servant in charge of ironing my father's clothes, would come and wake them up to take them to their rooms.

Le couvent des Oiseaux

I do not remember much about my early schooling except it having been a happy time. I had just completed my elementary school when my father ordered me into his office and said: "Phuong, you are still much too young to go to secondary school far from Dalat, so as I want you to be well educated you shall be a boarder at the *Couvent des Oiseaux*,[1] next year." Upon hearing the word "convent" I started to cry: "It is quite useless to try and oppose it," he continued, "I have made my decision. If you remain home, you will never be able to speak French properly."

My father, aside from other activities, taught Vietnamese at the *Couvent des Oiseaux* and had managed to get me enrolled there. It was the best of all the schools in Vietnam, and was founded by Princess Nam Phuong,[2] who had been a pupil at the eponymous establishment in Paris. In fact, it was still under direct Paris control. Besides the three hundred French girls, daughters of officials, bank directors and other

---

[1] *Le couvent des Oiseaux* (The Convent of the Birds): a religious boarding school for girls that was highly fashionable with the bourgeoisie until the 1970s.

[2] Princess Nam Phuong was the wife of Emperor Bao Dai. As a Catholic, she insisted on monogamy and, thus, Bao Dai became the only Annam Emperor to have but a single wife.

high-ranked executives, there could not have been more than a dozen Vietnamese, essentially the daughters of the great estate owners of the South and the three princesses, Phuong Mai, Phuong Lien, and Phuong Dung.

One week prior to the first day of school, my mother took me to *Chez André*, the hairdresser's next to the *Hôtel du Parc*. Madame Suzanne's mission there was to give me a permanent in the French fashion. The curlers were too tight and hurt, and I thought I looked perfectly awful with curly hair. However, the next morning, when I discovered by my bedside two black and white checked dresses, custom made at the *Ciseaux d'Or*, a French tailor's boutique, along with a hat sporting a knotted ribbon in the back, and two plain beige dresses which were to be my everyday uniform, my spirits picked up a bit. I was also fitted with gum-soled brown suede shoes that I was very proud to wear, despite the pain they induced. To this day, they have given me a strong aversion to new shoes.

When my father opened the car doors in front of the big school buildings, I remember a slight breeze like a caress on my face. The place was dazzlingly beautiful, standing in the middle of a large park at the top of a hill planted with pines. The heavy wooden doors of the school opened onto a hall paved with multicolored tiles. Nuns, all in black with just white edging around their faces, were coming and going busily. To the left side of the hall, there was the office of Mother Marie-Chantal, with large windows that allowed her to watch over everything.

My father took me directly to my classroom to be introduced to Mother Marie-Thérèse, who would be my tutor. Hardly had I sat down when I burst into loud sobbing, oppressed by the feeling that I had to face an unknown world. They had placed me next to a French girl, Juliette R., to stifle any temptation I might have had of speaking Vietnamese. In spite of her tireless attempts at solacing me, however, that first day was torture. I missed my mother, brothers and sisters, and the classes were given in French, which meant I had trouble understanding everything. Recess especially proved a nightmare: several pupils made a circle around me and found it funny to pull my hair and shout Poung, Poung, instead of Phuong. The nuns who kept an eye on us from a distance did not seem keen on intervention. I had to fend for myself. For some time I was their whipping girl, but after six months I was ranked first in the class and from there on in nobody dared touch me again.

That first evening I was so tired that I did not even notice what we were served for dinner. From the dining room, the girls went straight to their class dormitory rooms, which were under the responsibility of a Mother Superior who slept in an adjacent room. Like every other bed, mine had an image of the Virgin Mary hanging on the wall above it. I was given the number 12 locker. I slipped on my regulation nightgown—a long, cream-colored robe—and, before going to bed, went to the large bathroom lined with sinks to prepare for the night. Then came prayer time. I tried my best to repeat the words along with the others. Finally in bed, Mother Marie-Paule came to tuck me in and, when she was kissing me goodnight, I could feel the slight sting of her moustache.

At six o'clock, the shrill ringing of a bell woke me up. We all went to wash and pray again. The breakfast room opened onto the garden. The tables were already set with a glass of milk, bread, and one soft-boiled egg for each of us and, just like at home, we had to eat in perfect silence. When it was over, we went directly to our classrooms. Every girl wore the same beige uniform, and only the assorted ribbon colors on the collars made it possible to distinguish the age groups. The youngest, up to seventh grade, had white polka dots on blue, the middle-aged group sported deep chocolate brown, and the oldest, light brown. From then on, my name would be *Hélène,* a decision made by Mother Marie-Thérèse for the sake of practicality. I was in seventh grade and my curriculum included spelling dictations, grammar, English, and French history. That first dictation was entitled "A Cyclone in the Atlantic." I did not know what a cyclone was, let alone the Atlantic, so I spelled those words phonetically. When Mother Marie-Paule read my test, she burst out laughing: "Children," she said, pointing at me, "let me introduce you to a real character. I could never have imagined anyone making so many spelling mistakes. Tell me, Phuong, don't you know what a cyclone is?" "No, Mother," I said.

Actually, I did not know very much about anything, and was especially ignorant of the French behavioral codes. Suddenly seized by a violent need to go pee, I whispered to Juliette, my neighbor. "Hush!" she said, "you have to say 'Mother, I must leave,' and curtsey at the same time." By the time I had reached Mother Marie-Paule and started to curtsey, I could no longer control myself. Overwhelmed with shame, I hung my head low and just stood there. "This is extremely rude, what you have just done here, Phuong. Next time, try and control yourself better." I swallowed back my tears and murmured "Yes, Mother."

At four o'clock, it was snack time, with bread and bananas, and up to this day I have kept up the habit, to the utter dismay of my children who always wonder "How can you go on eating bread with bananas?"

Our English teacher, Thérèse F., was French, which explains my terrible accent. My father, the Vietnamese language master, was the only man allowed to have the honor of teaching at the *Couvent des Oiseaux* and each time he came the nuns would welcome him enthusiastically. I am convinced that some of this prestige rubbed off on me.

One third of our time was taken up by catechism that I did my best to learn by heart. Also mandatory were learning how to sew and etiquette—what type of curtsey to use under what circumstances, how to behave during birthday celebrations, how to greet our parents' friends. Every day, we used to curtsey at least a dozen times: Good morning, Mother, Good morning, Mother—each time was another curtsey.

My family had been Buddhists for several generations. But the fact that I had never been baptized did not prevent me from very quickly behaving like everybody else. I prayed, went to confession, and even to communion.

Whenever I had gotten good marks during the week, I was allowed to leave school with my father at noon on Saturdays, after he had finished his morning classes. Otherwise, I was kept at the Convent and it was all the more difficult for me, as I was not even compelled to work. On those Sundays, instead of being with my parents, worshipping at the Pagoda, I would go to the six o'clock mass. Afterwards, most of the time, all alone, I would wander in the park on the hill, or walk around the garden behind the school buildings. In late afternoon, at about five, organ music could be heard coming from the church. I would linger there, sitting on a bench, listening to the music and intoxicated by the fragrance of the white lilies that adorned the altar.

Rather quickly, I became a good pupil, although I did not like studying French very much. I was extremely enthusiastic about mathematics, which my fellow students had great difficulty in understanding. In fact, no sooner had the teacher begun to submit a problem to the class that I already knew what was entailed to solve it and where it would eventually lead. My homework was completed in a jiffy and I had no difficulty learning.

If only I had been allowed to go home every evening, I would have been perfectly happy. Except for the fact that very soon the attitude of the French towards the Vietnamese began to worry me. Every Monday we had the flag ceremony to attend. First came the French flag, and then the Vietnamese, after which we sang all together "*Maréchal, nous voilà!*"[3] It was already in my character to be very independent and I hated that moment. One morning, while we were singing, I saw my friend Juliette step forward from the ranks and jump up and down, over and over again, on the shadow cast by the Vietnamese flag. "Dirty Annam, dirty Annam," she kept repeating and I felt that her remarks were directed at me. How could she dare say that when she was living on our land? Why did she stay if she hated our country so much? Juliette immediately realized that I was furious with her. "What are you angry at?" she asked me, "This is not your flag: you are French, aren't you?" "No," I said, "I am not French. I am an Annamite. When you say 'dirty Annam' and you trample my flag underfoot, it is I you are hurting." From that moment on, I refused to speak to her, which, in fact, Mother Marie-Thérèse did not even seem to notice. When I mentioned the incident to my father, he ordered me to be quiet: "You must not speak that way. This is a period of friendship between the French and the Vietnamese, and if you were ever overheard it might get me into trouble. I am afraid you are being influenced by your cursed uncle."

From that day on, every visit to one or the other of my French acquaintances provided an opportunity to see how

---

[3] *Maréchal, nous voilà!* ("Field Marshal [Pétain], we are here!"): the best known song of the Vichy Government (1940-1944), sung on official occasions, in schoolyards (as above), and at political rallies.

contemptuous they were of Annamites—even my friend Claude, to whose house I was frequently invited. One day, her Vietnamese servant had placed a jar of strawberry jam on the table, but as we were talking I do not know how or why the lid fell to the ground and shattered. Claude immediately started yelling at the servant, abusing her with the words: "Dirty Annamite," which made me immeasurably sad.

It was shortly after my arrival at the convent that I witnessed another of the memorable events of my youth: the inauguration of Emperor Bao Dai's mansion in Dalat. My mother wore a velvet *ao dai* and a diamond necklace and my father, his most beautiful tunic. As for me, I was dressed in a blue velvet dress and patent leather shoes especially ordered from Paris for the occasion. We drove up to the foot of the hill where the mansion stood. From there, everyone was to walk up the main alley and through the park, and gather in the courtyard in front of the building. It must have been about six o'clock and there were about fifty people: mandarins with their families and the French. All of a sudden the huge white house lit up with two hundred light bulbs, according to my father. It looked like an ocean-liner. Then Emperor Bao Dai appeared on the balcony with his wife and the *Résident supérieur* of France. The crowd began applauding and shouting, "Long live his Majesty!" Then, the doors of the mansion opened and a French brass band played as we walked inside.

There, the light was blinding, vases were overflowing with flowers, and the sideboards in the main reception hall were teeming over with all sorts of dishes. My father told me that the Emperor had had chefs come over from France for this ceremony. The most impressive to me, though, were stands loaded with mountains of apples and cascading bunches of grapes. I hardly dared go near them or touch anything, as I was so overwhelmed by their beauty. Throughout the entire evening, people kept arriving with presents and at some point a very dark-skinned woman started to sing: it was rumored that she also was specially invited over from Paris for the occasion.

I cannot remember what time it was when we left, but I opened my eyes when my father picked me up in his arms to take me to the car. I probably had fallen asleep in an armchair.

The Emperor used to reside in this mansion rather frequently, as it was simpler and more comfortable than his palace in Hue. He was said to be often seen in the company of women other than his wife and there was a story about how the Empress had arrived one day when he was out hunting and, upon his return, had taken shots at him after chasing at his heels. Dalat was a very small town, so everyone was very quickly aware of the incident. This did not prevent the Empress from visiting quite often since her daughters were studying at the *Couvent des Oiseaux*. As I was a good pupil, she sometimes pointed me out to them as an example to follow: "See how *Monsieur l'inspecteur's* daughter has rapidly learned French. She is now perfectly capable of reading and writing it, whereas you ..."

One evening, I was invited to the mansion for dinner. At seven sharp, the French governess opened the door of the dining room and I was asked to sit down at the table. The princesses, wearing traditional brocaded *ao dais*, were already seated and I was placed next to Princess Phuong Mai. Then, across the room, the door opened and all the guests stood up: the Empress appeared in a yellow brocade dress, followed by Prince Bao Long, the heir apparent. She went to her place at the table and still standing, made the sign of the cross and said grace aloud, accompanied by all the company. Only when she had taken her seat did everyone follow suit and the servants then started coming in with dishes of French cuisine.

The rule was to eat in total silence and not to allow the knife to screech against the plate. Also, one had to sit up straight and to speak only if spoken to by her Majesty—that which she rarely did do. Even if I was used to this etiquette, both at home and at the convent, I was very shaky at the idea of doing something that might displease the Empress. In the course of another dinner, at which I had also been a guest, I can remember the Prince was behaving in a particularly bad manner, but his mother simply reminded him: "Never forget that you are Heir to the Empire."

Good-bye to childhood

We lived in Dalat from 1929 to 1942.

In 1940 came the Japanese invasion, of which I have kept but a vague memory since I spent most of my time at the Convent and stayed on the plantation at vacation time. It was only later, in Hue, that I would fully realize what that occupation had meant.

In 1942 a squabble broke out with the *Résident général* who blamed my father for having failed to censor two anti-French articles. Following this incident, my father asked to be transferred to Phan Ri, his hometown. From what explanations my mother gave me about these articles, it seems they had been published while he was away and he had been caught unaware. So, in Phan Ri, he continued to discharge his duties as School Inspector, but my mother could not get over leaving Dalat and all her friends. They were then in a quiet little town in central Annam, an area of seaside dunes, where the ethnic minority Chams lived. The weather there was very hot and dry, and the soil unproductive. Breeding an odd steer or two was just about all that could be accomplished.

At first, I had to remain a boarding-student at the *Couvent des Oiseaux*, far away from my family, and I felt very much alone. This period, then, marked the concrete beginning of the fortune-teller's prediction. Later on, I was able to move in with Madame Le, my first elementary school teacher, and live right next to the market. She had a sister my age, Kim Chi, and her family was also originally from Phan Ri, which was why my father had allowed me to board with them. It was from one of the windows of their house that, at the end of 1943, I witnessed the arrival of the Japanese soldiers into Dalat. They were wearing yellow uniforms, carrying long swords, and speaking an alien language that struck fear into our hearts.

From one day to the next, the *Couvent des Oiseaux* was closed down. Some of my French fellow pupils had already been repatriated. I did not understand much about politics but I felt that this was all very serious. Then, following the first days of the Japanese occupation, I left Dalat to be with my parents again in Phan Ri. I remember the trains being overcrowded, but at that time they were still running.

In Phan Ri there was no French high school. Consequently, I had to interrupt my studies. Fortunately, very soon after my arrival, my uncles and aunts in Hue wrote to my parents, insisting on my going to live with them in order to be able to resume schooling. I was delighted at the prospect since I was not so keen on waiting at home for a suitor to come and marry me, as did most young ladies my age. My father's parents opposed the project, but relented when my mother argued that I would be living in her sister's home.

There still remained someone to convince: the centenarian revered by all the family, my great grandmother. We went into the large room where she was lying on her bed, dressed in a golden *ao dai*. Three servants helped her sit up straight and we bowed down low to her. "I have ordered your father not to let you leave," she decreed, addressing me. "I beg of you," my father said, "Phuong was used to studying. Now she is bored. She would be perfectly all right in her aunt's home in Hue." My mother, in turn, went down on her knees to implore her to change her mind. My great grandmother just sat watching us for a long time and then dismissed us with a contemptuous flick of the hand, as if I were already a fallen woman. "Do as you please," she said, and with a deep sigh fell back onto her pillows. In February 1945 I was finally able to leave for Hue.

Before I left, my father ordered all of us into his office where we just stood, arms folded, not daring to meet his eye. "Your elder sister is leaving to go study in Hue. She will be living in the house of your sixth aunt. Phuong, you are to learn by heart what advice I am going to give you now. Never look a man straight in the eyes. Never spit. Never leave the house unless you are wearing your *ao dai*. Walk without making any sound. Do not drag your feet." With him it was an obsession, so much so in fact that half a century later, when I was reunited with my younger brother Phat, he told me: "At last we can drag our feet when walking down the street." Altogether, there was a score of recommendations, all of them laid down in superb calligraphy, as was his custom. With him, nothing was ever left to chance and I was quite enthralled with the idea of escaping such supervision.

I had to travel eight hundred kilometers to Phan Tiet where I took the train to Hue. I had never taken such a long trip on my own; the train stopped at every single station along the way. Just when I was just about to leave, an enormous sadness suddenly gripped me. My mother had prepared a huge suitcase that I could hardly manage to hoist into my compartment, and my father, although he had insisted on paying for a first class berth, preferred to stay away, leaving the chores of farewells to my mother. Could he possibly have been frightened of being unable to refrain from tears? He could not have known that we would never see each other again. The cars were crowded with Vietnamese passengers only—no French could be seen any longer in these parts. My mother made sure the conductor would watch over me and I felt safe in my berth. Later, watching the landscape flash by on the other side of the window bars, I was suddenly seized by a crying fit, as if I were having a premonition. But then I fell into a deep drowsiness. That journey seemed endless. At every stop, I saw Japanese soldiers walking back and forth on the platforms, but my provident mother had supplied enough food for me not to have to get off the train to find something to eat.

At Hue the station was buzzing with activity, but Uncle Phan Tay spotted me immediately. He was an engineer with a Franco-Vietnamese electric company, S.I.P.E.A.,[1] and his house opened onto a dirt alley. It was the first time that I was going to live in a workers' district—in a modest house amidst others just as modest. There was no bathroom, only a large basin where everyone had to take turns drawing water with a dried up half-shell of a cocoanut that was tied to the end of a stick.

In the room I shared with my three cousins, my lot was an iron box-spring bed with its head painted bronze-green and adorned with an angel, and a white pillow and sheets. Right next to it was a window overlooking areca palms covered with fragrant flowers. At night, once we had finally turned off the light after having completed our homework, their nice smell would fill the air in the room.

Aunt Tay insisted on my washing my sheets and pajamas, myself: "Otherwise you will never be able to get married," she used to say. So I rubbed Marseilles soap[2] into them at a small creek by the house. It was clear to me that people were living under much harsher conditions. There were

---

[1] *Société Industrielle pour l'Electricité en Asie.*
[2] Marseilles soap (*Savon de Marseille*): a pure household soap made with olive or palm oil.

women out selling cakes day and night, regardless of the weather. From the coziness of my bed, I could hear them calling to the passers-by: "Who would like a lentil cake?" When I conveyed my surprise about it to my uncle, he could not get over it: "Indeed Phuong, you don't know anything about real life."

Ever since famine had been afflicting the north of the country, and corpses had to be picked up off the streets in Hanoi,[3] my aunt insisted that we never leave one single grain of rice in our bowls. "Rice is the jade bestowed on us by the heavens," she used to say. If, however, there was any rice left after we had eaten, she went and gave it to the poor.

That was the beginning of a new life. In spite of the incredibly messy political situation and the omnipresence of the Japanese, I had a great feeling of freedom. Actually, I was living under the same roof with two uncles of mine. My aunt's younger brother, Tien Tich, "heaven's blessing," who was king of the house and was not interested in anything although five years older than me—later he would leave for France and work for the evening daily newspaper *France Soir*—and my uncle Tay, the engineer, who very quickly shared with me his need for independence.

"Life can never get better if we keep on being under other people's domination," he kept repeating. In the evening he sought every occasion to talk in private with me. He told me about the birth of the revolutionary movement, explained the *Viêt-minh*,[4] and why one could have trust in the revolution.

As for my aunt, she was an old fashioned woman: she cooked and waited on her husband's needs. Yet she understood

---

[3] Between 1944 and 1945, this famine would cause over a million deaths.
[4] Viêt-minh: contraction of *Viêt-nam doc lap dong minh hoï* (Alliance for the Independence of Vietnam), created in May 1941 by Nguyen-Ai-Quoc, later known as Hô Chi Minh.

his activities, even though she could not share all of his certainties about them. In my opinion, my uncle had preferred that she know as little as possible. I realize today how delighted he must have been to find me, a sort of virgin soil where the seeds of his ideas could be planted and eventually bloom. In any case, it was the first time I was being treated as an adult by anyone.

In the morning we all got up at five and, before having breakfast, did a few physical exercises together. Then my aunt would give each of us a ball of rice with meat or shrimp, which was to be eaten for lunch. Thus, I left for school carrying a wicker basket in which, besides the rice, there was a wooden box in the form of a notebook that held my pencils, fountain pens, and ink. Very often it included a flower, for the fragrance. Some of my fellow-pupils, whose parents had been abroad, carried satchels that were much admired by the rest of the school children.

A few houses down the dirt alley, Du caught up with me and, a little bit further on, two other girlfriends who went to the same school joined us. At about seven o'clock we caught sight of the big buildings standing near the River of Fragrances. The drums had not yet sounded and everybody was chatting. We were very few girls among hundreds of boys and I knew we were being watched with keen interest.

From my very first day at the Khai Dinh School—so baptized after the father of Emperor Bao Dai—I was struck by the excitement there. No one could resist such an electric atmosphere. Almost immediately, I found myself enrolled in the underground Association of Patriotic Students. As we would eventually find out, the *Viêt-minh*—of whom Phan Tu Quang was the representative within the school—would select the students they believed were deserving enough to be recruited. Our group at that time was about six or seven strong.

This was also when I first heard about someone named Nguyen Ai Quoc,[5] who was living in China and preparing the revolution. Little by little I was beginning to be aware of the extent of the anti-French movement. Nguyen Ai Quoc had decreed: "if we cannot become independent through negotiations, maybe we shall have to resort to armed struggle. This is why we need to be prepared." Then, in compliance with these prospects, we were given first aid instruction. Every one of us had to know how to improvise a stretcher from two lengths of bamboo and a jacket, and to deal with bandages. No practical aspect was neglected.

In the beginning, if my marks were not good enough, I stayed and worked at school on Sundays. Otherwise I went with the entire family to one of the pagodas, which, in Hue, were magnificent and incited one to the act of praying. Then we would wander over to the Royal tombs and until nightfall, among these majestic surroundings, I would review my lessons that I had brought along on the trip. It also happened on occasion that my maternal grandmother, who lived on the outskirts of Hue, lent us her junk. In this case, I would take along a few comrades and we would set forth all the way to the mausoleums to study, returning by moonlight and singing all the way home.

My friend Oanh Thuc—*the Virtuous One*—was always clad in white and would sit in the bow of the junk, bathed in moonlight, with her frail back perfectly erect. The landscape was magical. Whenever my uncle suggested I invite my friends, my aunt prepared a vegetarian meal which was a specialty from Hue. Based on fruit and soybeans, every one of the dishes was sheer delicacy. Then she laid the table under the grapefruit trees and the scents that the food gave off went to

---

[5] Born 1890 in *Nghe An* province to a family of intellectuals, he would become "Hô Chi Minh" in 1941.

our heads. My grandmother would come out to tell us to enjoy the meal, check that everything was as we fancied, and then vanish, leaving us to ourselves. After lunch, everyone went back to work. Those were the only quiet moments in the week. The school's quasi-official anthem was written there by a great composer named Luu Huu Phuoc: "Let's throw away our pens to go forth and conquer independence for the country." When I saw the movie *The Dead Poets' Society*, it reminded me of that period—there was the same enthusiasm, the same need for freedom. At that point, everyone was dubbing everyone else *"comrade"* but we had a hard time not calling our teachers *"Monsieur"* anymore. Among them, two were for the Vietminh and three for the French. "Remain quiet, my friends," our philosophy teacher used to say, "you are young; you do not know what you are talking about. France is a marvelous country." But I noticed he did not really dare pursue the subject. In fact, he might have been a little afraid of us. When it was time for his class, those like himself who were against the Vietminh, came to our classroom to ask whether we wanted to study or not. It was no, of course. The chemistry teacher, whom we called "CO_2", always insisted on teaching his class anyway, and we openly sighed and asked: "Will it still be much longer?" Once in a while a Vietminh official came: "Meeting at six, in the covered yard. Be prepared to speak." "And what am I supposed to do now?" the teacher complained, "How dare you treat me like this!" Upon which we all started to yell at once: "CO_2! CO_2!" Many of these teachers had to keep a dictionary close at hand for they had still not mastered the Vietnamese technical vocabulary. Some were still dressing in the European way, with a tie. One, the scion of a royal family, still kept wearing a velvet *ao dai* embroidered with the flowers of longevity, his head was topped by a turban, and he wore leather slippers on his feet. Each time this man came into our class, he looked down on us as if we were inferior beings. He addressed me as Thi Phuong, which means "girl Phuong" and not "Miss Phuong." For the boys, he used Tro, meaning "pupil." Whenever he came near one of us, he would dab his nose with a handkerchief scented with menthol, as if we were giving off a bad odor. Some of the teachers, too conspicuously pro-French, had to leave school altogether. Others still, like Mr. Hoang, supported the Japanese.

At that time, class instruction in civics was replaced by mandatory instruction in the Japanese language. One day, Mr. Hoang came to teach us the first syllables, but nobody would repeat after him. "If you do not want to learn, I will call the Japanese officer," he threatened. "Repeat after me ..." We started repeating the syllables all together but in great disorder. The poor man turned crazy, but the classes lasted two or three months, until the Japanese left. In fact, no one would study at school anymore. We only went there to talk.

From time to time, someone in the audience would stand up and speak: "Dear friends in the class, I have to say good-bye. Tomorrow I am to leave for the combat zone." Everybody then applauded; some started crying. In the evening, I hurried back home to tell everything to my uncle. I had a hard time falling asleep such was my excitement.

Among my friends, the only ones who refused to participate in the movement were those who belonged to families that had claimed French nationality, like Thérèse L., whose father was a civil engineer. In the beginning, just like me she had enrolled in the Association of Patriotic Students. Then, very quickly, she started to reproach us with betraying the French and began standing aloof. Most of my comrades—the majority, boys—were two or three years older than I was and they became my "older brothers." They wore black *ao dais* down to their knees, or European garb with khaki pants and a shirt. They were more mature than I was and had immediately started participating in the revolutionary movement. Among them was Dang Van Viet, who would become the hero of Colonial Route No. 4 during the war against the French. His father was Minister of Justice in the Bao Dai government and they lived in the Citadel. There was also Ha Dong, who would later create the Vietnamese Air Force. But at that time, they still were a merry group of deadpan boys who nobody could resist—especially Viet, with his bicycle. It was a very handsome bike, good enough for a prince's son, from which he had taken off the fenders and brakes, allegedly to make it more "chic," but in my opinion, rather to catch the girls' attention. All of them would later continue their studies at the school called the "Vietnamese Saint-Cyr,"[6] set up by the pro-Japanese government to train new officers to further their cause. The Vietminh's agents would succeed in rallying almost their entire class around their cause.

From the outside, these agents looked like any other student—they were just slightly older. They noticed the serious students who practiced their religion seriously, and they never left them alone. Quang, who was responsible for our group, was from Hue. He had started out studying in our school; then spent two or three years in underground training before returning as an instructor. Almost every evening, he held meetings to explain to us why we had to fight the French and why we had to fight the Japanese. It the beginning, those meetings were supposed to be secret but soon they were held overtly in private homes, with the speakers standing in the middle of the courtyards and everyone else sitting on the ground.

---

[6] Saint-Cyr: the prestigious French military college, equivalent to West Point.

We were intoxicated by this general movement for independence. All the humiliations I had had to suffer at the *Couvent des Oiseaux* came back to me, but at last we were to rid ourselves of our inferiority complex. Soon the school was deserted and the unfortunate who still wanted to work were looked down upon with utter contempt: "How dare you continue to study, when we are not even independent yet?" Of course, I shared this opinion. And shared it all the more wildly as I had met and fallen in love with a boy among Quang's disciples. In those times, it was not as it is now; we would look at each other and we knew we were in love. That was all. Simply holding hands would have been extremely improper.

I was fifteen; Nam was seventeen. After every meeting we figured out how to stay on alone in order to speak to one another in private. Nothing more. One day we spent the entire afternoon at the Pagoda of the Celestial Lady, two kilometers away from the house. The next morning, my grandmother had me summoned by a servant: "Who is that boy?" she asked. By luck, my uncle Tay was standing right behind my grandmother and I answered, looking straight at him, "I was with my uncle." My Grandmother turned around towards her son who confirmed what I had just said: "Yes of course, I was with Phuong yesterday." So she burst out laughing, relieved: "When I think this has kept me from sleeping all night! I was going out of my head worrying about the idea of Phuong being with a boy." Thank you, uncle, for having accepted to play the game. Otherwise, I am sure she would have sent me back to my parents.

Late one evening after a meeting, while Nam was walking me back home down the Road of the Sparrows, we passed people who were learning to walk in step and to fire guns. Then someone shouted at us: "Do you think this is really the moment?" Manifestations of love were rather badly looked upon at that time. It was better to show off one's patriotism, and suddenly we felt quite ashamed of our emotions.

Sometime later, Nam's mother came to ask for my hand in marriage. Then, his father paid a visit to my grandmother. Both our families seemed ecstatic at the prospect of our union. Although I would never have dreamed of asking Nam about the position his father held, my parents had managed to get the information. His family was one of the richest in Nghi Loc, a city situated in the center of the country, in the province of Nghe An, and his father was also the principal of a school. From then on, there was no longer any reason for us to hide. We did not leave each other's side, and my fellow-pupils never stopped teasing us. It was in the spring of 1946, right before I left to join the Resistance, that Nam went back to Nghi Loc. He was an only child, and he had chosen to remain with his family while participating in the village resistance movement, rather than leave everything behind, as I would soon be doing.

The other side of the bridge

From the earliest days of 1945 I began to hear my aunts' interminable discussions about the struggle of the populace against the Franco-Japanese rice requisitions.[1] From my grandmother's house, I could hear the rumbling of the drums echoing one another over the countryside. My grandmother lit incense sticks and prayed that Buddha spare us in these troubled times. Every evening at dinnertime, my uncle brought up the problem of that terrible famine that was taking a heavy toll all across the north of the country. At the time, I no longer had any news of my parents, or of the rest of my family in Phan Thiet.

It was then that my uncle began to have me actively participate in illegal actions. "Every day to get to work I have to cross a bridge," he told me. "Two Japanese soldiers armed with bayoneted rifles stand guard over this bridge and check everybody. I would like you to carry a package to someone at the market on the other side. If the Japanese question you, tell them that you are to deliver it to someone at the market, but you know neither the name of the person, nor the contents of the package." The first time, he gave me three or four pieces of folded paper that I slipped under the cover of a notebook. On

[1] Since 1944, rice had been confiscated from the populace and left to rot in Japanese-guarded warehouses (see page ix).

the bridge, my friends and I passed in front of the Japanese. There was nothing particularly suspicious about five young girls in white *ao dai* who were chatting away with each other. What would have happened if I had been stopped never even occurred to me. The next day, I started all over again, and again for many days afterwards. Then, my uncle taught me how to make propaganda leaflets. After having melted gelatin in the kitchen, I would hang it up to dry at my bedroom window. Next, I wrote the text that was prepared by my uncle with thick lettering in violet ink and applied the sheet onto the gelatine until the paper had absorbed the ink to finally print my leaflets. After this work, my uncle brought me red and yellow fabric. I stitched together small red rectangles with yellow stars, which represented the flag of the Vietminh, and delivered them to designated addresses. Without knowing it, I had become a liaison officer. The police never ventured into such a working class neighborhood, so no one could ever suspect us of wrongdoings.

In the middle of the night of March 9th, 1945, we were awakened by the sound of gunfire everywhere. The sky was glowing with pale strips of light. My uncle burst into the house: "The Japanese have just disarmed the French!" he cried out at us. Whereas of late, the Japanese soldiers had been kept in closed quarters in their barracks, they could now be seen everywhere in the streets, fitted out in their ear-muffed helmets and holding their bayoneted rifles. In the schools, too, the insurrection was beginning to be felt.

My uncle failed to come back home one evening, so I realized that he had joined the Resistance. I then went to live with my grandmother, whose house stood in the middle of an immense orchard on the outskirts of Hue. But I didn't stay there for long.

From that moment on, things started to happen in very quick succession. In May, my uncle's organization sent me off to Hanoi to study medicine in the company of four other female students from Hue. Here on in, as Quang said, we shouldn't be satisfied with merely studying out of books. It was better to master a useful trade in order to participate in the fight for independence. Why had it been us who were designated? That remained a great mystery. But we didn't even ask ourselves the reason why—what counted was the pride we felt in having been the chosen ones. It was only later that evening when I had returned to my grandmother's house that the impact of it all finally hit me. It meant leaving everyone once again—saying good-bye to my family and friends in Hue, and going off to live alone in Hanoi. From this angle, the perspective was much less enchanting.

I don't really remember how we made the trip, but I believe the train to the north was still functioning. I do remember, however, the sudden appearance of my mother on the eve of my departure. As elegant as usual, she was followed by a young boy carrying two huge suitcases. "Apparently you're going to leave for Hanoi?" "Yes, mommy." "And what for?" "To study to become a midwife." "Midwife? That isn't a profession for you. Your father wants you to be an agricultural engineer." My father and my mother had decided this so that one day I could run the family plantation. We talked all evening. Realizing how obstinate I was, she had to come to terms with my decision: with or without her authorization, I was going to leave for Hanoi. But I couldn't refuse as well the two suitcases full of clothing that she had specially brought for me. I don't know remember just how many *ao dais* and pants they contained.

In Hanoi we were lodged at the hospital and only allowed to go out on Sundays. Here again, the teachers belonged to a very privileged class. They kept the habit of communicating with one another in French, just as was the custom at the Medical Institute. They often found it difficult to express their ideas in Vietnamese and could not find the right words. Sometimes, we didn't even understand them at all and they had to repeat what they had just said in French. For them, we were just ordinary students—young girls from Hue with long hair, dressed in white *ao dais.*

The first time I entered the obstetrical ward I almost fainted at the sight of eighteen huge-bellied women all in the midst of screaming with pain from their beds. But there was no turning back, for one day I could be useful to the Revolution. The tramway stop was in front of the hospital. The first time we tried to board the carriage, we didn't know what end to get on and people made fun of us. Compared to Hue, Hanoi, with all its lights, seemed to us to be paradise. The *rue de la Soie,* the *rue des Broderies,* and all the others in the commercial district were overflowing with their goods.

One Sunday, on a rare occasion, I went to see a film at the *Philharmonique* Theater with one of my comrades. Compared to the women of Hanoi, so elegantly dressed in their lavender silk *ao dais* and their long fluttering scarves, we must have looked like little country girls in our white cotton outfits. All of a sudden I felt my hair being pulled. Turning around I saw two French soldiers. Having lived in Dalat with my French friends allowed me to be quite bold: "So is that what the French Legion is all about—pulling the hair of young ladies?" They then blushed and excused themselves for their rudeness.

In August of 1945, the situation in Hanoi became very critical. In the *rue des Vermicelles,* two kilometers from the center of town, French soldiers had killed some Vietnamese. Showing up suddenly, Quang gave us orders to go back home: "There is going to be fighting. You must return to Hue." Two days later, the School for Midwives closed. We then left, terrified at the idea of crossing paths with some of those fearsome red-beret legionnaires who had fired on the *rue des Vermicelles.* Quang made fun of us: "If they see you, they will swallow you alive like little *vermicelles.*"[2]

When I arrived back in Hue, I found my aunt and her three children living in a small house in my grandmother's garden. Ever since her husband had joined the Resistance, my aunt was living in fear.

On August 25th I witnessed the abdication of Emperor Bao Dai at the Citadel. The evening before the event, the red and gold Vietminh flag was hoisted throughout the city. There were huge demonstrations and the entire population was in the streets. There was no time for sleep. That Sunday I was supposed to take part in a scout outing.[3] We were to picnic in a small wood at the edge of town. On returning to Hue around five o'clock, we followed the wave of people who were advancing towards the Citadel.

On a platform in front of the *Porte du Ciel,* we caught sight of Emperor Bao Dai, dressed in a yellow robe and turban and surrounded by three Vietminh functionaries—easily recognizable in their modest clothing—and by several other people.

The Royal Family was grouped on the left-hand side of the courtyard. The crowd was thronging on the right. Suddenly a man's voice cried out: "From this day on, royalty is abolished in Vietnam. Emperor Bao Dai is from here on in the simple citizen Vinh Thuy. And now, citizen Vinh Thuy has

---

[2] vermicelles: Chinese noodles

[3] The scouting movement in Hue, as all over Vietnam, always had great influence in intellectual and scholarly circles. Even after the Revolution of August 1945, the Scouts' activities did not cease to expand. It was only after 1954 that this movement began to regress.

permission to speak." Next, Emperor Bao Dai who looked very young stepped forward. He addressed the crowd: "Citizens, let me be understood. I prefer to be a free citizen than an enslaved king."

The members of the Royal Family were weeping. The people cried out and applauded. Then the Emperor could be seen picking up the royal seal, which was wrapped in yellow brocade, and also his huge sword to display to the crowd for the last time before handing them over to the Vietminh functionaries. According to the man standing next to me, the men were members of a delegation of the people's government, which had come from Hanoi under the leadership of Tran Huy Lieu. The latter, in turn, waved the sword and the seal in the direction of the audience before putting them down again on a table. At that very moment, cannon fired twenty-one times. Someone took down the Emperor's yellow flag and raised the red flag with its yellow star. There were more cannon shots, and the tension reached its climax. People all around were crying. But the tears were not always of joy: it was easy to see that not everyone sympathized with the new leadership that was taking root. Lost in that crowd, I felt that I was a witness to a major event. I would have liked so much to talk about it with my parents. A few moments later, everyone scattered throughout the citadel and took part in an immense sacking.

That same evening, our leaders informed us of the Japanese capitulation following the atomic bombings of Hiroshima and Nagasaki. Then, on September 2nd, the day of the official Japanese surrender in Tokyo Bay on board the USS Missouri, President Ho Chi Minh, addressing a crowd from Ba-Dinh Square in Hanoi, declared our country independent.

Shortly afterwards, without any of us understanding what was going on, Chinese soldiers began to be seen in town.

They were clad in yellowish uniforms with wrinkled caps on their heads and enormous leg puttees. They were visibly starving and seemed hardly able to move. Some of them had features bloated by disease, explaining why they were immediately nicknamed "the Tau-Phu," meaning "the Chinese bloated by hunger." From one day to the next, the soup and cake hawkers disappeared from the occupied districts. One day, I saw two Chinese soldiers arrest a woman who was selling soybean cream. They opened the earthenware jar that contained the cream, added to it the whole bottle of ginger syrup that was supposed to accompany it, mixed the entire thing with their bayonets and, taking turns, proceeded to polish it all off. Having finished, they collapsed in the grass and remained there until nightfall, eyes shut, mouths hanging wide open as if they were dead. Soon, the Chinese had taken over the covered yard, as well as the rooms on the second floor, forcing us to find shelter on the third floor and share the space with people from other classes. On occasion, we would throw pieces of cake, or sweets from the windows to those unfortunate soldiers. Generally speaking, they behaved rather properly with us, but when the devastations they wrought in the markets became known, the candy stores and the restaurants closed down.

My aunt, who had a very hard time finding lentil beans and sugar, lamented "What evil times!" these were, and ordered us to make sure that the kitchen was always locked because "these Chinese will soon be swiping our rice pots from us." When the Chinese miraculously disappeared at the beginning of 1946, leaving mountains of garbage behind, the population in its entirety was hard put trying to give back to the city its former elegance. This was when the French soldiers, who had been lying low, suddenly reappeared and settled in the Mang Sa barracks right in the middle of Hue.

Why should my mother have chosen such a wild period to bring my brothers and sisters to live with my grandmother in Hue? I hadn't a clue. It was all the harder to fathom as my father had remained in Phan Ri. My feelings towards my family then were rather complex: I was happy to see them but regretted the fact that I could not tell them about what I was doing, nor share the enthusiasm awakened in me by the fight for independence. But, once again, our meeting was not to last very long.

In my Resistance group, there were three other girls and eight boys from the same social background who came to the meetings. Sung, our new group-leader whom we called "brother," was a short, kindly, but extremely convincing man. It was thanks to him that we finally got to understand the reason why we had to re-conquer our country. One evening, he called for a meeting and said: "Since you all speak French, you are going to go on a counter-propaganda mission, to explain to the French that they must not continue the war because they are going to lose it anyway." In other words, time had come for us really to join the Resistance.

Back home at my grandmother's, I hastened to go to bed but did not feel at all like sleeping. Should we obey? Should I leave my family, renounce every single thing that had been part of my life up to that point? The next morning I still hadn't managed to make a decision and when Sung arrived we remained in the garden to avoid being overheard. "You have to go," he repeated, "if we don't become independent, all of this is going to disappear." He was pointing to the house with its magnificent orchard. "Without independence, there won't be anything left of your family."

The next morning my decision was made. All around me, the young people of my generation were going away to participate in the revolutionary movement. I could no longer postpone my decision. I told my mother that I needed to have a talk with her. We sat outside on a bench and I told her I was going to leave and it was just as well since young women were likely to be raped by the French. I was just repeating what our leader had told me to say. But I had never expected such an outburst of violence as that which came from my mother. Although she never even once raised her voice, she refused even to hear what I had to say. My father was far away, so I would never know if he, on the other hand, could have managed to make me stay.

Towards five in the evening, I started down the track that led to the river. I boarded the Eo Bau ferry with my heart in my throat and when I turned around there was my younger sister, Yen, who was sobbing. I would then have liked to turn back, but it was already too late.

On the other bank, I met with three people of my group. That was the rule. We only moved in small groups of three at most, to avoid attracting attention. The leader immediately took us to a straw hut, deep into a very destitute area, where the only furnishing consisted in a large bamboo bed-frame. "From now on, you are part of the revolution," he said. We did not quite realize what he really meant, but were impressed by how formally he spoke. Very quickly, though, we felt as if we had landed in hell. It was pitch dark by then and we all fell asleep on the bed—twelve people in all, the boys on one side, the girls on the other.

In the morning, as soon as we opened our eyes, each one of us was given two fist-size balls of rice and sesame seeds, to be directly eaten out of our hands. That was to be the entire food ration for the day. Our first mission consisted in preparing propaganda leaflets to be handed out to the French soldiers who came to the market everyday. The girls had to be dressed as vegetable hawkers and the boys as bootblacks or cigarette dealers. "French soldiers, why are you staying here? You only know too well that we, the Vietnamese, are fighting for our independence." We all wrote our own leaflets in French, then proceeded to print them. In mine, which were approved by our leader, I explained that we came from well-to-do families, that we had relinquished everything to fight for our independence, and that we would struggle to the bitter end. Since the food sellers were mostly on our side, one of the vegetable ladies had offered to make me her salesgirl. Each time a French soldier bought green beans or potatoes, I put a leaflet in his bag. One morning, a soldier I had already noticed the day before came back and smiled at us. Cautiously, we refrained from slipping propaganda into his bag. The very next day, he returned and asked directly: "Where are the leaflets?" We answered in Vietnamese that we did not understand. According to our leader, that soldier was trying to trip us. After a few days, since nothing bad had happened, the leader allowed us to start in again with the leaflets. The same soldier came back, took one and, in French, told me he was in love with me. Far from laying traps, he had actually fallen for the salesgirl. He, too, would have preferred to go back to France and, even though I found him friendly, I really did not know what to do. Fortunately, he did not show up the next day and, in fact, we never saw him again.

It was at that point that I gave up my *ao dai* and started wearing black pants and a brown shirt. White, by then, was forbidden, as it was too conspicuous and too easily dirtied under our living conditions. In the house we occupied, there was only one water tap for everybody to use in turn. The boys were not really used to parading in their underwear before girls, and when we happened upon them so attired, they were just as uneasy as we were. I had still never seen a totally naked boy, and even girls did not let themselves be seen naked by one another.

What ended up taking its toll was not being able to wash my hair as often as I used to. It started to fall out, but I did not want to cut it short. Every month when I had my period, life became a torture. I had to find an old pair of pants, tear them into strips and wash those out at night—at the risk of being shot at—in a nearby canal. Often, the fabric would not dry and I had to use the strips still wet and cold. But I did not want to complain. I had already been reproached enough with being different from the others. That had started from the very first day when they had seen my bare feet: the others, who were used to walking without shoes had hardened calluses on their soles.

As we were nearing Christmas, Sung decided we should take advantage of the French feelings of nostalgia. So we wrote poems that we would read to them on certain evenings, using a megaphone. I am still rather proud of the following verse I had composed all by myself: "Listen to me *Frenchling*! Christmas without bells *chiming*, Christmas without midnight *feasting*—that is all the colonization's *doing*." Generally they simply answered with abusive language, until the day when we set fire to wet straw sprinkled with ground peppercorn in order to produce enough heavy smoke under their windows to choke the soldiers who were inside the *Hôtel Morin*. With one of my comrades, we started to yell out loud: "French soldiers, do you know for whom you are fighting?" They answered, "It is for you, *Mesdemoiselles!*" and started firing their guns at us. Luckily, we got out of that one unharmed. We were not even scared, so passionately involved in the fight we were!

One evening, as I was already lying down exhausted on the bed, someone called: "Phuong, your mother is here."

Outside, I saw my mother standing by a rickshaw and I ran to her and hugged her. She returned my kisses, crying. "You must come back," she implored. "The entire family is suffering without you. Grandma wants to die. I beg of you, come home."

"Mommy, try to understand me. If no one gets involved in the fight, we shall never become independent. I had to leave. I had no other choice in the matter."

"And your father, how am I to tell him?" she went on.

"You must explain to him that leaving was my decision, and mine alone."

I talked to my mother the whole night long and, at dawn, she left without once turning around. When I got back into the house, Sung was waiting there. He just gazed at me without saying anything because he knew that I had made up my mind.

We stayed in that house until December 19th, 1946. On that day, we had returned so exhausted from the market that we did not even feel like eating. All of a sudden, rifle and machine gun fire burst out in the distance. "There we are. It has begun!" Sung cried out. He then signaled for us to gather around him and he declared solemnly: "Up to this point, you have been actors in an unarmed struggle, a propaganda struggle. From now on, you are to be engaged in an armed conflict." In view of the fact that the agreements reached between the French and the Vietnamese had not been respected and Ho Chi Minh's call to President Léon Blum had remained unanswered, Sung explained to us that Ho had just launched an appeal for the reconquest of national independence. He then gave each of us a grenade—the first that I had ever seen. "If the French arrive, pull out the pin and throw it in their direction." As a Buddhist, I realized for the first time what was expected of us. "But I'll kill them!" I cried out. He had a stinging answer: "If they don't die first, then it is you who will die!"

Outside, it was pitch black and drizzling. After having left the hut, we went around the back and crossed over the railroad tracks in single file. All of a sudden, bullets hissed all about us. Terrified, I hung on to one of my comrades: "I want to go home." "Too late," he told me. By crossing the tracks, you have once and for all gone over to the other side." My whole body was trembling and I clutched the grenade in my hand. The bullet sprays seemed to increase as we continued to walk on in the dark. Finally, we arrived at a temple, at the entrance of which an officer was waiting for us: "We are the heavy propaganda unit of Zone 6," Sung announced. In the shadowy darkness of the interior were crowded at least a hundred people together with injured soldiers, all lying directly on the floor. That officer in charge, Xuan, was older than us and looked quite tough. We grouped ourselves around him in the gleam of light provided by the bamboo torches. "Who knows how to use a rifle?" Nobody answered. "You have been in the Resistance for several months and you don't know how to use a rifle?" One amongst us flew back at him that we had been in charge of distributing leaflets to the soldiers. "Useless!" Xuan yelled, erasing with one word everything we had been doing. "Tomorrow, I'll teach you how to handle a rifle." I had wrapped my grenade in the large mauve scarf that I was using as a belt. Throughout the temple, loud cries of pain could be heard. Right near us, a man had just had his two legs amputated without having been given anesthesia. This time for sure, we had really joined the Resistance.

We all slept on the clay ground, without mosquito nets. The smell was appalling, but nothing could have troubled our sleep since we were so exhausted. The next morning, we were entitled to our bowl of rice and, without losing a second, a soldier led us outdoors to teach us how to shoot. The rifles were long and very heavy, got jammed very often, and when they did, the bullet had to be extracted from the barrel before we could try again. I couldn't manage to fire. I was paralyzed at the idea that a shot would go off. Though I closed one eye and held the butt against my cheek, when the instructor cried: "Fire!" I didn't pull the trigger. "Comrade, I just can't. I'm too afraid." I would have had a hard time explaining that my Buddhist education strictly forbade killing. Fortunately, though, I was soon left alone and I watched my comrades practice. The second day, the soldiers led us to another straw hut in a district near Hue. It resembled a lot the one we had just left: "Here are your new headquarters. From now on, your mission consists in explaining to those Vietnamese who do not want war why we, on the contrary, do; and to the French that they must surrender." From that point on, we infiltrated the entire area every day in order to explain to the people the reason for our personal engagement.

One evening, the order came for us to go to the *Ecole pratique*, a school that had formerly been used for technical teaching. A unit of Vietnamese soldiers was being held under siege there, surrounded by the French. A hedge served as the outer boundary of the school, and behind it were a number of buildings. Three of them were occupied by the French, and two others by the Vietnamese. Our mission was to deliver the order to withdraw, an order without which they wouldn't otherwise have made a move. There were five in our group, each of us fitted out with balls of rice and dried fish in a belt around our waists. On our backs, we carried a container of water, bandages and Mercurochrome to treat the injured. We had to ford a river in order to get to the school located on the other side, climb a bank, and then cross a road before getting to the hedge. The French controlled the road from buildings that they were occupying. Once we had struggled up the bank, we were to wait for them to fire before crossing the road. I held hands with Le Khac Tinh, a boy in my class. He murmured: "At the count of three, go!" Together, we crossed the road and jumped into the hedge. I saw him double over and fall down. "Are you hurt?" He didn't answer. Something slimy began to drip on my hand and I understood that he had been killed. This death marked the end of my adolescence.

I really believe that Buddha accepted coming to my aid that night. Without knowing in which buildings the soldiers were hiding out, I took off towards the first wing. I knocked softly and was ready to flee if someone answered, "Who's there?" I heard a whining, and someone said something in Vietnamese: "Water. Give me water!" After I had identified myself and the door had opened a crack, I could smell an abominable stench. Inside, injured soldiers had been lying there for three days without food or water or any treatment. I had to chew the rice before putting it into their mouths; then I gave them something to drink. With the remaining water, I tried to clean their wounds and to bandage them with strips cut from my short-sleeved blouse. But they had to be moved, too. On crossing back through the hedge I could hardly see Tinh's body. Four of my comrades succeeded in evacuating the injured by constructing a makeshift raft out of bamboo. But not my dead friend: we would have had to come back and that would have been too dangerous.

Within several weeks, we were caught up in a swirl of events. Every day, the bombings followed one another and the number of casualties multiplied. Every day we had another mission to accomplish. The infernal chain of events worried me, as it did some of my comrades. It was so much the more worrisome in that certain notions of social class now began to interfere in our relationships with others—something that had not in the least way occurred earlier. In fact, since becoming a part of the army, comments about our integration multiplied:

"They are just petty bourgeois intellectuals." We could not have helped feeling rejected. When, for example, we were given orders that we didn't understand, we were the only ones who dared to ask for explanations. For the others, an order was an order. We had also begun to notice slight differences in behavior. When we were around, nothing much got to be discussed, particularly if it was of a political nature. All we knew was that Ho Chi Minh was at the head of the fight, but he seemed very remote to us, like some kind of religious image. He was in Hanoi, while we were in Hue and had no real idea of his intentions. We simply went about fulfilling the tasks that were assigned to us, with our typical enthusiasm and determination.

Our day began at four in the morning. We had three hours ahead of us to speak to the population before the French woke up. Fortunately, we were given food at the few and rare markets that still existed, which made our mission somewhat less trying. Next, we would all gather together at the staff headquarters: soldiers, partisans, guerrillas, and us, the "intellectuals," who were assigned to the liaison company. In the afternoon, we went from outpost to outpost, carrying messages, arms, or food. We would get back around six o'clock, as it was getting dark, to have our meal with the soldiers: the inevitable bowl of rice with shelled sesame seeds, which was our staple dish for months on end. Only afterwards, did we enjoy again a lost moment of our youth, for once back in our straw hut, we practiced our own music, sang songs, and acted out improvisations of plays. Revolutionary Vietnamese songs were followed by French ones, which we sung in low voices. Someone would begin: "Brave sailor, come home from war ..." and then all the others picked it up together. We might have been put into jail for doing that, or something even worse. In times of war, a rifle shot is quickly fired.

In January 1947, just after the defeat of the Vietminh in Hue, we left the city. Traveling by night, along with the heavy brigade unit from the Hue front, we went to Nghe An Province, three hundred thirty kilometers away, in the Fourth Zone. It was a forced march through forests, almost always by night, along Route No. 1, which was dotted with French outposts. Some of our comrades had already preferred to return to their families, which was something that we were still free to do.

From here on in, there were only twenty or so of us left in Group C from the district of Phu Cam. The trip seemed endless and, little by little, due to our fatigue, we lightened our loads of food and clothing. When we came across sand dunes, those of us who had preserved some little family mementos, preferred to bury them there. "Here is the tomb of our past," one of us uttered. Half asleep, we marched on at night and, on occasion, I would come to my senses thigh deep in the middle of a river. Our little group of partisans blended into the surrounding nature and would vanish behind the trees at the least alert. The army had given each one of us a pair of pants and a jacket. By then, I no longer had any sandals and I had begun to walk barefoot. I sometimes suffered so much that I wanted to cry and, had I done it, they would no doubt have been quick to accuse me of being a petty bourgeois. In the evening, we would soak our feet in salted water in order to relieve the pain. Then I would try to find a piece of cloth—a piece of anything—to protect my wounded feet during the night. Eventually, I even tore up my one and only brassiere. It was the getting up in the morning and having to remove the bandages, that was the most painful. Soon, when the soles of my feet had hardened, I was able to cross entire forests and trample paths teeming with leaches. That year, from 1946 to 1947, will forever remain for me the year of "painful feet."

To our great surprise, everything in the Fourth Zone had remained "as before." The contrast with the chaos that was reigning in Hue was enormous. There was electricity; there were inns and soldiers everywhere, and a perfectly organized army. From then on, we turned from liaison agents into a "propaganda unit for the Resistance of Central Vietnam and of the Fourth Zone."

Starting then, our role consisted of traveling about the provinces of the zone and acting out plays of our own creation in the different villages. In other words, we were to explain the war to the people and exhort them to aid the Resistance in supplying food and shelter to the soldiers. Without our really understanding why, certain villages accepted us, and others, especially the Catholic ones, did not. In the latter case, we would just pass by. In the former, we quickly improvised a stage and costumes, used charcoal as eye make-up and invited the people to come and see the show.

One of the recurrent themes of these plays was the story of a father whose daughter had joined the Resistance. The father, who was a landowner, preferred to watch over his rice fields until the day when they were bombed during an attack, and his house and fields were totally destroyed. The father then understood the reason why his daughter had joined the Resistance movement.

I played the role of the young girl. The father was played by my friend Tang Hich, who would become Vietnam's Minister of Culture between 1993 and 1998. With time and experience, we ended up improvising. One evening, Tang Hich walked onto the stage with half of a moustache. Doubled up with laughter I had to come up with lines that would send him backstage to add the other half. The villagers applauded and broke out laughing, too, without really knowing why. It was extremely satisfying to be able to bring a little bit of joy to these unfortunate people. When we spent several days in the same spot, we took advantage of the occasion to teach the alphabet to the children.

Sometimes, we had to journey more than fifty kilometers at once, barefoot and carrying a full load on our backs. In that region, the climate is hot and humid by day and freezing at night. Although we were in the free zone, there were occasional bombing attacks. We would hide in the forest as soon as we heard the planes, even if we had been careful to camouflage ourselves with creepers and leaves.

At night, we slept in the temples or in the pagodas. Some of our comrades were often so tired that they did not even have the strength to take off their make-up and it was really weird to see theatrical faces spring out of the dark.

Another particularity of that period was the constant hunger that ate away at us. When the villagers held out their cakes for sale, it was true torture because we hadn't one single coin to buy them. The organization provided us with just enough to eat once a day.

For a long while, we were accompanied by an orchestra of about twenty musicians who were fifteen or twenty years older than us. Times gone by, they used to live in the French barracks and it was they who played the "Blue Danube Waltz," among others of that period, at the parties in Hue. They had given up everything, joined the Resistance with wives and children, but suffered even more than we did from this new way of life since they were used to the amenities that the French civil servants had so much enjoyed. Monsieur Minh, the conductor, nicknamed "Monsieur Bugle," was a sergeant in the French army. His wife prepared his meals for him, and it was something to see her look for pieces of cloth to use as placemats when we ate with our fingers, seated on the ground. We ended up giving her what little money we had, and afterwards she gave us food: "That is all you have? It is only two portions." There were eight of us, but it was better than nothing. I remember the grilled rice that we scraped off the bottom of her pan. Nobody wanted it but us.

The hardest of all was having to take off again with our entire load, and never really being able to stay in the same place for long. When I was in the depths of despair, I would recall my former life, the happy moments with my family, and it was these recollections that helped me to go on. But soon, the orchestra dispersed. One day, Minh announced that he had decided to stay in that village with his wife and children in order "to open an inn." Our leader was furious: "Is it a salary you want? But what is money, anyhow? This is all rubbish. To save the homeland, you must stop always thinking of money. You are greedy people and you don't understand anything about anything!" "It is you who are too young to understand," Minh sighed. In turn, the saxophonist decided also to open an inn, in another village. Then, another musician followed suit. Soon, we were left to our own devices. In these already very poor villages, life was to become still more difficult. The population not only had to till the land to feed itself, but also to "cooperate." In other terms, it had to provide rice for the soldiers and furnish manpower for the army, for Ho Chi Minh had given an order to destroy everything in order to stop the advancing French.

The roads were put out of service, and even getting around on a bicycle was impossible. Ho Chi Minh also said that no shelter should be left for the enemy and people destroyed their own houses. In Vinh, not one single brick building remained standing. That was the movement someone dubbed "Let's Destroy Our Homes to Work for the Resistance."

The peasants would often ask us news of the front: "What is it like in Hue? Why have you retreated? Are the French going to arrive soon?" We were at our wits' end to answer their questions because we, ourselves, didn't understand much of the present overall situation.

There was a beautiful young girl in our unit, with magnificent eyes. The boys were all in love with her. She was the daughter of an important mandarin in Hue and we had both gone to the same school, Khai Din. She confided in me one evening: "Phuong, I can't go on. I can't stand seeing the peasants living like this anymore. I'm going to return to the city. I beg you to come with me." For me, there was no question of turning back, but I felt that she had made her decision. That evening, we stepped outside the pagoda where all the others were sleeping. She had brought out the guitar that had never left her sight since leaving Hue and she began to play.

There was a full moon that night and, together, we resisted the urge to cry. I had the feeling that we would never see each other again and I fell asleep with the sound of the guitar. When I woke up, she had already left. Somebody must have been waiting for her. She had left me a letter: "Dear Phuong, I am leaving. I worry a lot about you, but since you have decided to stay I pray that nothing will happen to you and that we will see each other again one day." By afternoon, everyone knew about her departure. Two or three days afterwards, the police of the Fourth Free Zone asked to see me. In theory, I had no reason to worry because these were people that we saw all the time. The superior officer was very stern: "Sit down!" he screamed." "What is this all about, Uncle?" "Don't look surprised," he continued in a wild voice. I have been told everything about it: I know that you organized your friend's escape. The evening of her departure you were outside the pagoda together." "That is true. She wanted me to leave with her, but I refused." All of a sudden, I realized that he thought I had stayed to spy on the unit. "Why did you refuse?" he continued, as if he had read my thoughts. "Because I see too much suffering all around me. I joined up and I prefer to stay on with my comrades." I had to reiterate my answer at least five times and then write it down. Two days later, I was called in again. "Write down what you said." Then two days later, again: "Write." I could not take it anymore. It had become an obsession. "If you continue like that, I will follow my friend. You are treating me as if I were guilty, although I have done nothing." Day after day, they continued to harass me so that I would confess.

After the episode, I began to get tired of that kind of life—walking incessantly, always putting on the same plays, being kept apart from everything, like my comrades. The others often took leave for mysterious reasons or formed groups for conversations amongst themselves. Why were we so set apart? Ever since my friend's departure, I had the impression that they were even more suspicious of me.

My suspicions were confirmed three or four months later, after having been summoned by the head of police security in Nghe An. When I entered his office, he had a wide smile and offered me some hard candies—rare food in those days. "Brave Phuong," he said to me, "We now know that you had nothing to do with what happened. I interrogated you because I couldn't do otherwise. As of now, the case is closed. Reassure yourself." "I had told you the truth. Why did you order me to write it down?" "In a similar situation, even I would have had to do it. You were with someone who escaped, so it was normal procedure to interrogate you." We continued our conversation until my unit head appeared at the door—all smiles as well. He took me in his arms: "You can't imagine how happy I am for you, Phuong."

The case might indeed have been closed, but I felt profoundly hurt that my word was put in doubt. I also began to understand why in certain villages, and not only in the Catholic ones, people had refused to let us put on our play. The villagers were weary of us, taking us for staunch communists, whereas we considered ourselves simple students who were struggling for the liberation of the country.

We knew that Ho Chi Minh was a communist. In order to save the homeland, he had been able to mobilize the forces of a whole people, so being a communist, then, was something admirable. But our theoretical knowledge stopped there and I recognize the fact that we didn't really look any further.

Upon the festivities of *Tet,* which marked the end of the lunar year, another incident occurred that further contributed to the strengthening of my determination. Throughout the Zone, every old village was protected by a bamboo fence, which was closed with a gate. That particular day, the villagers refused to let us enter: according to tradition, guests who are invited in on the day of Tet are supposed to stay on. Under the given circumstances feeding thirty or so persons was out of the question. We were therefore doomed to wander the countryside. It was a dark night, without stars or moonlight. We walked on, bent over with the weight of the supplies on our backs. Memories of happy, by-gone times invaded my thoughts: Tet at my grandfather's house and the family beautifully dressed up in their special clothes. While waiting for the festivities to commence, I would take a red silk cloth to wipe the orchid leaves. When my grandfather appeared at the threshold of the house, each of us, in turn, would kowtow to wish him good health and long life, after which he would throw us coins that were wrapped in red silk paper. A brick-paved courtyard separated the house from the garden with wild flowers that pushed up in-between the bricks. When I picked up the money, I saw a violet corolla in front of my eyes. Several years later, for the *Tet* festivities, my grandmother gave me a gold necklace and a silk *ao dai*.

Among the villages that we tried to enter, I recognized my friend Nan's birthplace—the one that he had mentioned so often to me. His family had a big house there, big enough to be able to lodge all of us. But when I thought about the band of vagabonds that we were, dressed in rags and exhausted, I preferred not to let him see me in that state. For sleeping, we had to be satisfied with the railroad tracks and there was no risk of being awaken by a train. In the end, the stones turned out to be less uncomfortable than cold, wet grass. Head on the rails, curled up in the theatrical streamers, falling asleep, I knew that I couldn't go on like that for much longer. I had to find a way to change my condition.

Without the musicians, we had much more difficulty in attracting people when we arrived in the villages. At our leader's request, each of us was to try to play an instrument. I chose the banjo. When we played together, it was a true cacophony.

In Vinh Thanh, close to the seaside, as we were busy preparing the show, we heard cries and the sound of gunshots. The French soldiers were landing. Everyone fled and we hid out in the forest until dark. The next day, we camped out in temple next to a hospital in Bach Ngoc. For some time, my comrades had noticed my discouragement and criticized me for not trying even harder to keep up the morale. As one of my friends, Hao Thu, felt the same about the situation as I did, we decided to go and see the head of the hospital. Thanks to the few months of experience that I had had interning as a mid-wife, I could perhaps continue to study or work as a nurse.

There was another doctor in his office, short, stocky, slightly bald and with protruding eyes. Both of them observed us as we were talking and then nodded without saying anything: "Go back to your unit. We'll let you know later on." We returned to the pagoda and during the evening the hospital director came and spoke to our leader: "Phuong and Thu have already worked in a hospital and would like to stay here to work with us. Since we lack personnel, we would be glad to be able to have them." Sung's answer was not long in coming: "No! It is out of the question. This troupe has already had too many losses and these two are my principal actresses. How would we make out without them?" "I can't take it any longer!" Almost in spite of myself, I got up to speak. All eyes were glaring at me.

"Ah, Phuong, you're clearly losing your morale. It is obvious that you come from a bourgeois family. You don't have the attitude of a true communist." This time, it was the last straw and I couldn't stop myself: "That is true. I am not a communist, I am weak, and I lack courage. It is also true that I am not worthy of all that you have done for me. But I am sure if you give me the chance to study in this hospital, I'll be able to make it up to you." My comrades looked at me in total astonishment, but I had nothing left to lose. It was the first time that I showed any kind of revolt and it was impossible for Sung not to take that into account. "You really want to leave? You do not have confidence in us any longer?" "I can't go on like this; that's all there is to it." Seeing my determination, the hospital director insisted: "Comrade Phuong doesn't want to stay on with you. She has already studied in Hanoi. Why refuse her this work?" "Let me think it over," Sung answered. The next morning, he came up to me: "Leave, both of you, if you like. Leave immediately."

It didn't take long for us to roll up our clothes and say good-bye to the group. Our farewells were brief, for we had the impression that our comrades considered that we had betrayed them.

The hospital was set up in a straw hut, with bamboo beds lined up one after the other on the clay ground and matting that served as mattresses. That makeshift ward, which obviously was lacking even the bare essentials, was the first stop for the wounded from the front.

The doctor who was in command of military health in the Fourth Zone—the bald one with frog eyes and very thick glasses—welcomed us with *"Bonjour, Mesdemoiselles,"* a greeting that we were no longer accustomed to hearing. "From now on, you are part of the administration of the department of military medicine in the Fourth Zone." What that meant was that we were not to help care for the injured, as I had hoped, but would have to keep the list of patients up-to-date, take stock of the medicine, and distribute it. It was purely administrative work, but for what it was worth, it was still better than the roving life that I could no longer stand.

We stayed with villagers, and every morning we left to work at the hospital. The entire hospital compound was comprised of four straw huts, each for a different service. One of them was reserved for offices, and there I was allotted a huge bamboo table. I kept a log in which I entered in ink the name of the injured, his identity number, the place where he had been picked up, and the state in which he was found, symbolized by a number from 1 to 8, according to the degree of his injury. A red line was drawn across the name when one of them died. Lately, due to the lack of sanitary conditions, the pages were covered with red lines. When the family was too far away, they were not even notified of the death, and the body of the unfortunate soldier was buried in the village cemetery. Otherwise, arrangements were made so that the family could come and pick up the body. When the injured was considered out of danger, he was placed in a peasant's home to make room for someone else. Friendship sometimes grew out of this house sharing, but, alas, it was not always the case.

On occasion, we would go to other hospitals in the Fourth Zone to do the same work. The relationship with the medical students of our age was a cordial one. Some of them had just begun their studies when they had been drafted. During those years, many would learn their trade on the job, like myself. Seeing me so often in the hospital, certain patients ended up calling me "doctor."

One day, Thu and I went to list the wounded in another hospital beyond the river. We worked until late and found ourselves in pitch darkness on the road back. In a straw hut that was used as an inn during the day, we took turns sleeping on a bamboo bench that served as a bed. When one of us was sleeping, the other stood guard. As Thu was dozing off, I remembered being a child, demanding that my amah make my bed without the least wrinkle in the sheets, and being incapable of falling asleep without having two pillows—one for my head and the other for my feet.

It was not unusual for us to find the gate to the village closed when we got home late from our expeditions. In that case, we had to spend the night outside. At eight o'clock, the guards went home until the next morning and if we called out for them to come open the door we risked surely getting fired upon. Besides, I was also scared out of my wits of the dogs barking at the slightest noise.

Another day, Thu and I had to accompany the head doctor to another military hospital, which was quite far away. He had a skiff for his trips, something which made this kind of mission more agreeable than others, with assured meals and less fatigue. Of course, there was as usual the counting of the casualties, the assessment of their condition, and all the rest. I noted once again that the red lines were more numerous. At four o'clock in the afternoon of the second day, the doctor was getting ready to leave the hospital. "It is already late," I told him. "We'll never arrive at the village before eight o'clock and we won't be able to get in." The oarsman who was in charge of taking us back was not happy about that either. But there was nothing to do about it: we had to get back in the boat again. The craft was narrow and, as in the trip over, there were the peasant couple that steered the boat, their children, plus the three of us. We were crowded against each other and when we arrived, it was pitch black out. There was nothing else we could do but sleep in the boat. Suddenly, I was jilted awake—a hand was caressing my breasts.

"Be nice, let me continue," the doctor whispered. His breath was reeking of alcohol. "No!" I pushed away his hand and got free as best as I could. My friend was also awakened. "Shhh, don't scream. You're going make him lose face." He seemed to calm down but a few minutes later, I felt that he was getting closer to me again. "I prefer to die rather than continue taking this." Then I jumped into the water, followed quickly by my friend. Fortunately, the current wasn't too strong. When the peasant held out the oar, I laid down my conditions before climbing aboard: the doctor had to move to the other end of the skiff.

After that misadventure, I had a bout with malaria, which was due, perhaps, to my being in the water. I ached all over and suffered from hot and cold spells. Doctor's orders: from now on, I had to get up at five, instead of six o'clock in the morning. I was in such a state of fatigue that sometimes I couldn't even get up at all, which allowed me to be present at the wedding ceremony of the daughter of the villager in whose house I was living. She was twenty years old and the groom, thirteen. In that village, the daughters were married off for money. They, in exchange, were to become the husband's family servant.

One evening, I heard horrible yelling in the courtyard. Four people were tying up the young girl to a bamboo stalk, binding together her hands and her feet with her hair trailing on the ground. The fiancé, a young boy who had come to take possession of his bride, and her parents looked on in silence from the entranceway of the house. Once the young girl had been secured, the four men took the bamboo on their shoulders and walked away, the body of the unfortunate girl swaying with the rhythm of their steps. How could it be that the Vietnamese were capable of such atrocities?

Sometime later, a meeting of the Youth of the Fourth Zone was to take place in Hau Hien, about forty kilometers from where we were living. Notifications in hand, Thu and I went to obtain authorization to go from the doctor: "Thu, yes, but not Phuong," he decreed. "She is too undisciplined." Ever since the episode on the skiff, he didn't miss a chance to get back at me. "Since I received an invitation, I'll be going anyhow. It is a rare occasion for me to see how others run the youth movement."

In truth, I had learned that my friend Nam was coming to the meeting. I hadn't seen him for a year. This time around, I wasn't ashamed of myself, with my silk shirt and my army pants. "If you go to that meeting, I'll throw you in solitary confinement at your return." "Never mind that, I'm leaving."

In Hau Hien, we were lodged at people's homes. There were two hundred or so of us, all bedding down on straw matting on the ground, the girls separated from the boys. In the streets of the villages, old friends found each other again and lively groups formed. My heart leapt when I saw Nam again.

He was still as handsome as before, with a strong, intelligent look, but there was something in his attitude that told me he had changed.

The first day we didn't have a chance to speak to one another. With the others, however, there were excitingly rich discussions, each of us telling about our experiences and our hopes. That allowed us to better understand the general situation in the country, the difficulties encountered, and the progress made by the Resistance. But, in spite of that, it was extremely hard to concentrate because I was anticipating the reunion with Nam. On the second day, between two meetings, he edged in to me: "Phuong, if it's all right with you, we can see each other tonight. We have to talk."

When we got together on a jetty near the village, we sat down on the ground not too close to one another, as if we were shy. "You know that I am an only son," he began. If I join the Resistance, you will have to take care of my parents. I can't abandon them. You know, as well, that I don't really want to stay on in the village. If you agree, I am going to tell my mother to ask for your hand. When we are married, you will go and live with my parents."

I had always thought that I would someday marry Nam after we were victorious, but certainly not under these conditions. "No, I'm sorry, that is out of the question. I don't want to lead the life of a housewife." "In that case," he answered, "I must marry another girl that my mother will have chosen." His words fell on me like a bolt of thunder. "Nam, we love each other. Why are you reacting in this way?" "I must do my duty as a son."

We went on talking all night long, each trying to persuade the other. But it was to no avail—he kept on asking me the same question: "Where can this vagabond life lead you?"

The story of the doctor made him blow his top. "With such disgusting people, how can you continue to work in the Resistance? You would be better off if you came back to us. You would found a family and lead a respectful life: well housed, well fed and, especially, well loved by a devoted husband." At the first glow of morning light, I realized that I could never get him to change his mind. That day, I understood what love-sickness meant. Over-ridden with grief, I couldn't even get myself to stand up.

When I told Thu about our conversation, her reaction was immediate: "You'll find another man." She was a very practical girl who would not let such a situation get in her way.

I did not even see Nam again. If I felt like I had wings going over, coming back I had lead feet. On top of it all, I was thinking about the punishment that the head doctor was keeping in store for me. On arriving at the hospital, my comrades looked at me strangely. As soon as the doctor saw me, he cried out: "Solitary confinement!" He seized me by the arm and dragged me to a stable in the middle of the village. The dirty stall was empty, filthy and it stank. I started to pull backwards: "There! That's what happens to someone who disobeys!" he yelled. "I had given you orders not to leave!" He pushed me violently inside and slammed the door. I could hear the sound of the padlock.

There was no longer any way to escape. In a corner, I could make out straw matting on the ground and a jug of water. Flies were swarming about and, exhausted, I collapsed onto the matting and fell into a deep sleep. During the night, I heard whispering: "Courage, Phuong, we're going to try to get the doctor to free you." "No, it's not worth it. I prefer to die here." From here on in, I no longer had any reason to live. I didn't even touch the sweet potatoes and the little rice that my friends had slipped under the door. After three days of that diet, without being able to wash and having to use a corner of the stable for a toilet, I must have resembled more an animal than a human being. Nevertheless, my determination remained intact when the head doctor came to see me. "Are you ready to repent, now?" "I haven't committed a fault, so I don't have to repent." "You maintain that you didn't commit a fault, whereas I had forbidden you to leave?" "You forbade me without any reason. I was summoned to that meeting as member of the Youth Association. Why did you give authorization to Thu and not to me? That was unjust." "Beg forgiveness and I will let you out." "I would rather cut off my tongue!" This time around, it was the true ending of the sweet, innocent girl. "Poor fool!" As soon as he had closed the door, I began to cry. His pity affected me even more than his anger. The following day, he came back: "Ask me for pardon and I'll free you." "I'd rather die." From that moment on, I think he began to be afraid of me. I saw him again, in military dress, ill at ease in the stench, a colonel invested with total power under the pretext of being a communist and heading the service of military medicine of the Fourth Zone. That evening, when my friends brought me food, I refused to swallow the least grain of rice. I really wanted to die and I kept on falling asleep. At dawn, on the fourth day, I saw Luong enter. He was one of my schoolmates whom I had met again at the hospital: "Phuong, there is no purpose in continuing like this. Take a hold of yourself." "Leave me alone, please." "The head doctor gave the order to free you."

After leaving the shack, I went bathing in the river for a long time. But even weeks later, my hair still stank of urine. The village tailor agreed to me his scissors and I went down to the riverside to cut off the head of hair that had been my pride and joy. The long strands floated away with the current. It was as if I had changed skins. All of a sudden, I felt freer.

On the way back to return the scissors, I couldn't resist the temptation to look at myself in the mirror. An unknown person looked hard at me: a funny round head, sharp eyes amidst a lean face, and a determined air. I began to laugh all by myself. It was true—I was another person. All I needed now was to change jobs once more. Then, it was a chance meeting that one more time would play an important role.

Shortly afterwards, Huu, a friend of Nam's, stopped over at the hospital for a night. We talked to each other all evening. At one moment during the conversation, he asked me: "You aren't really happy here, are you?" "No, I hate this place. But I don't know where to go." "At present, students from our school, intellectuals like us, are being recruited to make explosives. Why not come along?" "I don't know anything about it." "I don't either. You'll be instructed." He went on to list the twenty or so names of those who had accepted enlistment in this new adventure. They were all serious students from Hue, a few years older than me, mostly from bourgeois backgrounds, and all having left their families and a career to join up. I quickly made up my mind. "Very well, I'll leave with you." "Tomorrow?" "Tomorrow." He had brought along already-signed, blank applications from the Defense Ministry. My friend filled in my name, then Thu's, and that of two other boys who also wanted to leave. The next day, we went to see the doctor with our papers. He was furious: "How on earth do you know those people so that you can come here with their mobilization orders signed?" he asked my friend. "We have known each other since middle school. The Ministry knows that these people would be more useful in the army than here." "Let me think it over."

My friend left the office and I remained alone with the doctor. What was he going to come up with now? As soon as the door was shut, what do you know but there he was in tears, down on his knees in front of me.

"Don't leave. I want to marry you. You will have an assured life. I tortured you because I was jealous. I knew that your fiancé was at the meeting." I refused his out-held hand. No and no again. I found him revolting. Suddenly, he got up and leaped at me. Not wanting to cry out for help, I picked up a rattan chair and gave him a hard blow on the head. He fell down and I ran away.

Two grams of fulminate = one life

In August 1947 I arrived at Yen Son, fifteen kilometers or so from the hospital, in a Fourth Zone annex of the Institute for Technical Studies and Research on Explosives, known in Vietnam under the initials N.C.K.T. As is usual for that kind of site, the buildings stood near a river, so that, in case of an alert, it would be possible to escape in a skiff. There were seven straw huts enclosed within a bamboo stake wall. There was one for the girls' dormitory—in fact, there were only two of us—one for the boys, another for the directors and the engineers. The other ones contained the laboratories. Nothing singled them out from the other huts in the village, in case of aerial surveillance. The laboratory installations were rudimentary: there was a big table with test tubes. Our leader, Thieu Lieu, a doctor in physics, took great pains to explain our tasks, relying on a French chemistry book entitled *Chemistry and Explosives*.

There were about forty of us, divided into several groups, and we were supposed to manufacture fulminate, an explosive that is used in percussion caps. The instructions were simple: As in a cookbook, I was to follow the recipe. A chapter heading read: "Two grams of fulminate = one life." In other words, two grams of fulminate that explode cause a sure death.

Inside the hut, each of us had a small platform on which to work, with a shelter underneath. At the least spark, we were to turn the table over so the explosion would go off outside, and then dash for the shelter.

Once the fulminate acid had been obtained by adding saltpeter and other various chemical products, white smoke evaporated from the boiling mixture. A gray powder collected at the bottom of the receptacle that had to be dried by fanning very, very carefully with a goose feather. Otherwise, it might go off. Those were very intense moments when we could not let our minds stray. It was dangerous all the time, what with the risk of explosion and the French reconnaissance planes that regularly surveyed the Zone. It happened on occasion that the French army got quite close to the area where we were hiding. From our hillside, we could hear the report of guns and see huts on fire. In the beginning, I was frightened all the time but, little by little, routine took over.

The days then passed with an unchanging rhythm. The gong sounded at six o'clock: a quick wash with water drawn from the river, then collective calisthenics in the field that separated the huts. In the meantime, someone got busy with cooking—that is to say, cooked the rice with salt and sesame seeds, which was our regular fare. We ate quickly and then got to work.

Our methods were purely amateurish and there were frequent accidents, in which case the casualty was taken to the hospital in Madame Lich's skiff. This craft served as a home for her husband, who was a fisherman, for herself and for their daughter. When they had fish to sell, Monsieur Lich would put up a pole with a piece of cloth attached to the top. The evenings of full moon, all my comrades went down to the river to be around the young girl with whom many were in love.

In that region, the summers were very hot, even stiflingly so, and the winters very cold. Around December, it would begin to rain and the good weather did not return until April. We had no idea of the general status of things, but life at the Institute was quite lively, and that was enough for me. The work there and friendly relationships ended up chasing away my sadness. Three times a week, in the evenings, we would teach the alphabet to the children in the surrounding villages. Their parents, who often were illiterate, appreciated our efforts. We set up shop in the largest house and, by bamboo torchlight, gave our lessons to the children seated on the floor. It was quite moving to see them so sharp-eyed and attentive, while their parents, standing at the door, did not let the slightest detail of the lesson escape them.

Not far from the Institute, there was a center for pharmaceutical studies with which we collaborated. It was headed by a rich pharmacist from Hue who had joined the Resistance with his two daughters. Outside of work, we often got together for fun. Some evenings, we would put on plays that we had written ourselves. It was always the same recurrent theme of the Revolution, which today, would seem so incredibly naïve. Due to the airplanes, performances were held by the dim light of oil-lamps. On occasion, we heard the audience protest: "We can't even make out who is who!" Then, we would bring the light close to the actor's face. The villagers loved those kinds of plays and applauded enthusiastically.

Other evenings, we would play soccer or have swimming meets in the river. It was necessary to have relaxing activities after a day of dangerous work and the incessant menace of the planes. So, despite it all, we remained in good condition and, since we were fed by the State, we were assured of at least a bowl of rice a day.

In spite of our destitution, we always found a way to give presents to one another when we visited other centers for arms research in the Fourth Zone. In fact, we shared all we had and it was really a very exhilarating period. True, we toyed with death at every hour of the day, but we had close ties with one another and we were as happy as could be. That is, until 1948, when we received a visit from Monsieur Huany Dinh Phu, an important character from the Resistance center in Viet Bac. He was the Director of the Institute for Technical Research on Explosives in North Vietnam or, in other words, the Head of all the arms manufacturing in the Third and Fourth Zones. He had come to fetch his young wife in her native village, about a hundred kilometers from our Institute. Twenty years old, she stayed close to his side and looked quite energetic.

I knew he was carefully observing us, one at a time. When he asked our leader to point out the best of the lot who would be the most likely to want to leave, he did so immediately, selecting five people, four boys and myself. Although leaving was a high price to pay, it was out of the question to shy away from an order. How was it possible not to be proud of being selected to join the headquarters of Ho Chi Minh and his government in the jungle of North Vietnam?

We did not even have time to say good-bye to our comrades and barely managed to pack up our scant possessions. "We're leaving," Monsieur Phu declared. "You," he said to me, "are to stay with my wife. We have to cover a thousand kilometers, all by boat."

In order to travel up the Lo River, we got on board an army ammunition boat. It was a large, ocean-going skiff with an awning slung high enough to stand up under, and was rowed by four soldiers who were dressed as we were, in peasant clothing. Whenever the current was too strong, we went ashore and walked along the bank; and whenever we heard an airplane, we fell to the ground and hid under bamboo foliage. Sometimes we had to stay hidden a whole day long waiting for the night, to be able to resume our trek.

The trip took about one month. In March 1948, we got close to Mount Khe Khao, one thousand meters high in the middle of the region of Bac Can, near the Sino-Vietnamese border. The French had a tin mine concession there. After leaving the boat, we still had another forty kilometers to walk in order to get to Dam Hong. There, we found a steam locomotive and wagons that used to transport the tin loads. Hopping into one, we cried out for joy when the dusty engine finally began to move. We felt as though we had returned to childhood: well dressed, we would take the train with our parents. Whenever the locomotive ran out of fuel, we had to go into the forest and cut down dry bamboo stalks to refill the boiler in order to continue the last few kilometers. All along the tracks, wandering merchants offered their goods and, to our delight, Monsieur Phu got us a few pieces of sugar cane.

Ban Thi was the end of the line and from there on in we had to walk along the cables on which small cars transported the tin ore from the mines. The slope was steep and we tried to avoid the grasses that were very tall and sharp-edged, so as not to re-open wounds that had healed on our feet. Soon, we got onto a clearing where the grass blades had been flattened to the ground, making our progression easier. But all of a sudden an unbearable stench developed and we came upon animal carcasses strewn all over the place.

"Let's get out of here, this is a lair of tigers!" one of my friends cried out. A part of our group had taken a different route and when we told them of our misadventure they really had a good laugh at our expense.

Khe Khao had the first national research center on weaponry and we discovered its slate- or tile-roofed brick buildings in which the French used to store the ores: three main ones close to one another and several others, smaller and scattered around.

It was the first time in quite a while that I was sleeping in a real house, and I was all the more happy about it as the French had left behind a lot of items that reminded me of my past. There were a coffee maker, a sugar pot with sugar lumps still in it, and pewter lampshades that no one except me recognized for what they were. Although it had brick flooring, we decided it was too cold to sleep on mats and we set upon making bamboo beds.

There were about fifty of us in that Institute—thirty were "intellectuals," experienced physicists, or former students like me; the rest were workmen or volunteers. On the day we arrived, the director was away on a mission and we were welcomed by Hoan, a comrade from Hue whose brother used to be in my class. He told us: "Here, you are going to be able to do your research under the best of conditions."

At the Institute, besides the production of fulminate, they also worked on delayed-action mines, the fine-tuning of bazookas, and production of chemicals needed by the Ho-Chi-Minh banknote printing shop that was at the foot of the mountain. I was to continue my work on fulminate started in the Fourth Zone and teach it to my fellow-workers. The difference was that we had now far more extensive means and equipment for our experiments, and we were at long last using precise dosages, no longer gambling away our lives with haphazard mixtures, as we had done so far.

That first evening, the sky turned stormy. Thunder rumbled all night long and I huddled under my blanket. I had never been in such a violent storm, with flashes of lightning illuminating the room, and I would have liked to go out to admire the sight, but I did not dare.

Alas, from the very next morning on, everyday life was going to prove even more difficult than everything we had known until then. In the mountains, there was a dire lack of supplies. In order for us to get them, they had to be carried up seven kilometers of steep slopes, under the permanent threat of tigers. Occasionally, peasants from down in the valley would give us rape-cabbage seeds that we would plant; otherwise, we ate wild herbs, of which we had found a variety, the *co tranh,* which grew rather fast and proved edible. We prepared it in every possible way: as soup, as stew, and so on. Because of the speed with which it grew, we used to call it the "airplane-vegetable." We also lacked salt, because trying to get it meant sacrificing lives. All along the tracks that led into the villages there were small French outposts with soldiers that were ever ready to shoot at anything that moved.

Explosives and raw material were our priority, not salt. We found out that when the "airplane-vegetable" was burned it turned into ashes that had a slightly salty taste, which sort of improved our soup. We had rice, turned half-rotten from having been lugged about too long through the forests. When it was soaked in water for cooking, it gave off a horrible stench, but we would have eaten anything. What was of utmost importance to us was the gripping research in which we were participating and, again, the exhilarating feeling of being useful to the Resistance.

At the Institute, I was also lucky enough to be reunited with my uncle Phan Tay, the one who used to house me in Hue and who had given me illegal leaflets and flags to pass through Japanese checkpoints. My uncle was the political commissar of the Institute, as he had been among the earliest communists in the country, and he was extremely strict.

He seemed happy to see me there; yet helping me in any way was out of the question: I was on equal footing with everyone else. I preferred that, anyway, since everybody knew he was my uncle, but I felt reassured by the idea that someone from my family was close by. I was flabbergasted when he asked me whether I would enroll in the Communist Party. "What for?" I asked. "Are you an imbecile, or what? In the Party, you would have a lot of advantages. First of all they would trust you much more. Then you would ascend the hierarchy. Your future would be all arranged," he replied. But to me, things were clear: there was no question of belonging to the Party and I definitely did not want to be ranked any higher. I simply wanted to be able and continue to speak freely as I had always done, nothing more. My uncle just shrugged his shoulders, finding it hard to believe. He had a hard time understanding my refusing to take advantage of the opportunity he was offering me. And so had my comrades. Even though I was contributing to the development of weapons, I did not have the feeling I was betraying my ideas. Short of foreign aid, we had no means of fighting back and we had, therefore, to make our own armaments with which to stand up to the enemy.

Cuc, the other woman at the Institute, had been there before me but did not work with us. Instead, she took care of supplies and, when we met in the evening, we reminisced about the past: "What if, suddenly, we had a white calico blouse, as we used to?" The clothes we had been wearing since we came were made by mountain people out of wild pineapple fibers. They were rough and, even worse, did not absorb sweat. When it was a hundred degrees in the shade, with constant humidity, they gave you the feeling of being shut up in a bag. When we washed at the river, or at the well, we used to dream of *Cadum* brand soap.[1] I remembered its fragrance as if I had

---

[1] *Cadum*: another popular old pure soap, used for babies.

just smelled it the day before. We were convinced that those days would sometime return.

Alas, Cuc died of tuberculosis a few years later. Some of our comrades, unlike us, had a hard time adapting to this way of living. They worked because there was no way out of it, but they were tense, nervous, and incapable of communicating. Because of the cold, we did not sleep very much. The small community of mountain dwellers had taught us how to use the bark of a tree named *xui*. It was put to soak in the water of the spring, and after three or four months, it would rot away with the current, leaving fibers that were then put to dry and braided to make blankets. They were rather stiff at first, but after a while, they got to be more pliable and almost comfortable. Many miners had stayed behind when the French left, but survival was rather difficult. They had beehives and collected honey that they would sell, along with dried bamboo shoots, down in the plain. They also went fishing in a lake that was rather far away, but nothing discouraged them. For our part, we tried to teach their children how to read and had also set up an advanced class for the older ones. This is how several eventually became liaison agents and then rose from the ranks to become officers helping to run the Institute.

Discipline there was extremely strict. Within five minutes of getting up every morning, our beds had to be perfectly made. Every one had to answer for his or her work. I had a small wooden case that I kept with me at all times to store my documents. We were trained to gather up quickly all our belongings at the slightest alarm and to follow the given instructions. A large part of our material was kept permanently hidden in a cave that could only be reached by a secret path that we had cleared and which was unknown even to the miners. Several times a week we had mock warnings and we all had to be at our stations, with all signs of any activity erased, within five minutes. It was a matter of life and death. The documents we used, mostly French chemistry books, were systematically copied by hand for fear an explosion might deprive us of any means of pursuing our work. We used only the handwritten copies.

By the end of the day, we used to gather around the galena wireless[2] to try and listen to the news. But there was a lot of static because of the mountains and we could only get fragments of the news. We did not really care, however, as the progress of our work in almost total isolation meant much more to us than the general situation.

No one ever discussed politics. Evenings, we all preferred to get deeper into chemistry books, and I took advantage of it to brush up on my French. In an abandoned house I found a tattered *Larousse* dictionary and every evening I would dutifully read one page of it, repeating the words to myself until I knew them by heart. For light, we whittled a bamboo shoot until its end was sharp enough to be able to skewer grapefruit seeds, or any other wild fruit. All we had to do was set them aflame and, thanks to the oil contained in the seeds, we would have enough light to read for as long as we wished. I really enjoyed my *Larousse*, especially its pink pages[3] and the names of all the famous people: Napoleon, Victor Hugo. I knew all their dates and the titles of their works by heart.

It was at that time also that the heads of the Institute launched a small newspaper entitled *Dong*, which means

---

[2] galena wireless: an AM radio made with a galena ore tuning crystal.

[3] pink pages: The French Larousse dictionary is divided into two different parts, separated by the so-called "pink pages." The first part is, strictly speaking, a regular dictionary, and the second, a kind of encyclopaedia with names of famous people. The pink pages give the meaning of foreign language phrases or sayings that can be found in French literature, with an emphasis on dead languages like Latin and ancient Greek.

"detonation." Along with two of my comrades, we were given the responsibility of gathering and editing articles and, if need be, even writing some. We found it a lot of fun. The paper's only goal was to report on life at the Institute, often rather run-of-the-mill stuff like: "This morning, comrade Khai killed a stag" or the performances of this or that workshop or even a detailed account of the wanderings of those who went to town to get supplies.

Nho, a comrade who was older than me and a former medical student in Hanoi consistently refused to collaborate on the paper. I pestered him so much that, at long last, he gave me an article: "When I lived down in the plain, I had a master who was very harsh and, like Phuong, he always used to force me to tell stories. Here, then, is what I have chosen to write: Where I live, on a wall, there can be seen a large poster on which the following words are printed: "Either smoke Job^4 or do not smoke at all." Over the next fifty lines Nho had repeated again and again the same line: "Either smoke Job or do not smoke at all."

Neither my comrades nor I ever used to go to town. Maybe because we were not trusted enough to be allowed to. Those who did go were forbidden from having any contact with the townspeople—they had to buy whatever was needed and come back as fast as possible. They were not very keen on lingering about since they knew the French gave rewards for denunciations.

Usually they went in groups of three, one of whom usually carried only a knife because we did not have enough ammunition to let him take a gun.

Sundays, nobody worked. It was the day the big laundry was to be done at the river. Our clothes were filthy

---

[4] *Job*: a French brand of cigarettes made in Algeria.

from black gunpowder and saltpeter. Afternoons, we used to perform plays, which in the Resistance were the main form of entertainment. Above our heads, airplanes kept passing without interruption, but we were so accustomed to danger that eventually we would no longer heed them.

Another great Sunday pleasure was to go down to Dan Hong, about seven kilometers from the Institute, for a bowl of slightly sour Pekinese soup made by a Chinese man. That was the period when they had started giving us a small salary that allowed us such fancies.

Ever since my separation from Nam, there had been something broken in me and I felt incapable of starting up any relationship with another man. However, the assistant director of the Institute, Hoang, seemed to me a serious man, well deserving of trust. I particularly appreciated the little attentions he had for me and his understanding when I did not manage to deal with a given task. He was seven years older than me and had been in his third year of physics at the University of Sciences in Hanoi when he had to leave for the war. As he was a Colonel in the army, he was the only one to wear a uniform—olive green shirt and pants. As a specialist in explosives, he often had to walk to different areas in North Vietnam to watch over the manufacturing at the other plants and workshops spread out everywhere in the forests. Our work being highly appreciated at the Defense Ministry, we were visited by great physicians or writers who, despite the extreme hardships involved, considered it a matter of honor to come and encourage us. Also came numerous high-ranking officials from the Ministry or the Arms Department. One morning we even saw soldiers arrive with a load of clothing. The Defense Minister at the time was one of our former teachers at Hue, a great mathematician who had studied at the Sorbonne and at Oxford. He had had us sought out by Army Services in order to send each of us two quilted coats, "coats to protect the soldiers on the borders," as they used to be called, as well as khaki sleeveless waistcoats, equally padded. On top of that, there were also two complete soldiers outfits for each of us. On the other hand, there were no shoes, which would have been highly welcome since our feet were deeply chapped and became extremely painful with the cold. We were not given time even to rejoice, however. The assistant director did not want us to accept the presents. We had to thank *Monsieur le Ministre*, but we could only accept one waistcoat and one outfit. The others were to be presented to our comrades on the front who were far more miserable than we were. I was not surprised at this, coming from him. In fact, I was even quite proud of it. From the way he looked at, or spoke to me I sensed that he was in love with me. It was not yet reciprocal, but I bore him some sort of admiration and trust that made me feel close to him. With him I could speak open-heartedly, reminisce about my family without feeling shame or the need to hide the slightest regret, since we had come from the same social background. On too rare occasions, we would be joined by Viet, our friend from Hue, and the three of us would spend hours in conversation.

The visit of the Director of the Arms Department and his assistant, under whose control we were, was a considerable event. As high-ranking officials, they had been entitled to three horses for the trip—the third one being used to carry their loads. As soon as they arrived, they secured the animals at the entrance of the cave and then went on to tour all the workshops, greeting everyone and congratulating all on their work. It seemed they liked it at our Institute since they decided to stay over.

That night, we lit a bonfire in a cave and we sang and told stories. Afterwards, our visitors went into one of the houses to sleep.

The next morning we found out that two of their horses had been half-devoured by tigers and the third was spread out on the ground and shaking all over with terror. After much effort, we managed to put it back on its legs and make it move around. We brought it grass to eat. It was all in vain—the next day it, too, had died. Ordinarily, bullets were far too precious to be used against animals, but this time under those exceptional circumstances the incident awakened an old, buried hunter's instinct in one of our comrades. "I am going to place a horse's leg as bait in front of the entrance of the cave to lure the tiger, and I am going to kill it," upon which two men left for the kill with a rifle and six bullets. We heard shots during the night and, come morning, they were back empty handed. The tiger had swiped the horse's leg while they were asleep. Fortunately, there was still a lot of horse meat left and someone—I do not remember who—turned to me then and said: "A fine cook like you, Phuong, I am sure you are going to prepare this good horse meat." However, the unfortunate animals had reached quite a ripe old age and their flesh was particularly tough. Without fat or salt, it was not easy to turn it into edible meat except by letting it boil away in water for a long time. After several hours of such a treatment it was still just as stringy. I then hit upon the idea of cutting it into slices, covering it with *co tranh* ashes for a slightly salty taste before hammering it flat on a big stone, as I had seen peasants do, and then putting it up to dry. The result being rather satisfactory, we decided to keep the dried meat for our guests and, given the frequency of visitors, our stock was quickly used up.

When he came to visit with his wife, Madame Ha, and his four bodyguards, General Vo Nguyen Giap seemed shocked at our living conditions. A short time later we got a letter from him informing us that we were soon to leave the mountains because we were too isolated from the rest of the movement, and our conditions were too harsh. "Wait and see" was our reaction since we were so taken by our work that it made us forget everything else. This was also when the Ho-Chi-Minh government had started printing its own currency. Its value was based on the *paddy*[5] in as much as peasants were already paying their taxes with rice in the free zones. One *timbre* was worth one hundred grams of *paddy*. Fifty *dong* amounted to fifty kilos of it.

To print the banknotes, some chemicals were needed that could only be found in Hanoi. Trying to get them amounted to sacrificing lives since taking road Number One to get out of our Zone meant sure death. The Ministry of Finances thus asked the Ministry of Defense to solve the problem and the latter, in turn, called on us to try and find new processes that dispensed with the said chemicals. I would be hard put to explain how we did it, but I remember our first banknote being of a pale ochre color that was rather uneven and certainly far removed from the evenly colored, beautifully bright ochre we had been commissioned to produce. Nevertheless, it looked like a banknote. On one side there was a map of Vietnam with Ho-Chi-Minh's portrait and on the reverse the face value of the note. The note had been designed by Nguyen Sang, a highly renowned artist from South Vietnam who had come to study at the Hanoi School of Fine Arts but had joined the Resistance at the beginning of the war. This currency came to be called "trust money" or "Resistance money." Often, we would be out of certain chemicals and would only print one side of the note—the kind of thing that collectors eagerly seek today. Actually, the printing was not controlled in any way since the

---

[5] paddy: rice that has not been hulled.

one, ten, and twenty *dong* notes were not numbered. After printing, they were sent to the State Finance's Central Service, which would then pay us one or two ten-*dong* notes each as salary.

Access to the printing shop was highly protected because this activity proved to be at least as strategic as the making of explosives. The place where it was set up was called Ban Thi, five hundred kilometers away from the Capital city and seven from our Institute. But the contrast was striking: Ban Thi was in a primeval forest where the leaves of its plane trees were as large as those of lotuses or giant ferns. They were like huge umbrellas.

To set up the press, a tunnel was dug out first, and then railroad tracks, salvaged from somewhere else, were laid to move the equipment underground. Everything was brought from Hanoi in parts and pieces, first shipped by boat, then carried on men's backs down to Ban Thi. Once all the elements were in place, the tracks were dismantled and creepers planted on top of the shed to simulate the forest. After a few days it had become impossible to distinguish the site from its surroundings. On several occasions French paratroopers were dropped in the area after intelligence was obtained on the existence of this print shop, but they never managed to discover its location. Later on, when I wanted to return to the site, I had a hard time, myself, finding my way back. One had to know at what precise point the vegetation had to be pushed aside to uncover the passage leading to its entrance.

The currency was used to buy rice and sugar from the peasants in the free zones, but not in the occupied ones. Fortunately, it so happened that city people would come to the countryside and pay with the official currency, which allowed us to procure medicine. What was most difficult was to cross back to the free zones, because there were lots of checkpoints.

Identity cards and travel permits were controlled, and such questions were asked as: "Where are you going? What for?" It was absolutely essential to hide the medicine because the French soldiers knew they were for the Vietminh.

At least a hundred people used to work and live in the caves around the Institute. Pham Quang Chuc, the director's wife, was originally from Hanoi, where her family owned an ice-cream parlor, "Les Glaces Zephyr," selling sherbet and cream at the price of gold. Her second sister had married Pham Van Dong who already belonged to the Ho Chi Minh government. Mr. Chuc and his wife had first lived in one of the caves in the vicinity before settling in a small house in Khe Khao. Thanks to her sister, Mrs Chuc was privileged as far as food supplies went, and she entertained every Sunday, as was the tradition in Hanoi. Her house was well furnished and she had flowers everywhere. She would customarily be attired in a silk blouse and black pants, and her beautiful long hair would be gathered up in a bun, all of which contrasted with our own austere outfits. Usually, she prepared rice cakes that reminded me of my mother's and, displaying utmost refinement, served tea. Far from being revolted at such privilege, we were happy to see that such an artful way of living still existed; we had survived so long on rotten rice and ashes that sometimes we had the feeling of having been turned into savages. On those Sundays, when we came back from Mr Chuc's, we felt a little bit more human, again.

I remember the winter of 1948 as being extremely cold. In the mountains, the average temperature was 59° and we were always cold. Mornings, we woke up surrounded by clouds of a whitish color hard to describe. My comrades appeared to me wrapped in an aura of magical mist and, to get warmer, we would run several laps around the buildings before setting down to work on an empty stomach. When finally the sun managed to pierce through, we felt better. The only solution we had to fool our hungry bodies was to drink. The mountain people had taught us to recognize the edible herbs and we brewed rather acceptable hot beverages, the main merit of which was to fill our stomachs. When eventually the gong sounded to call us to lunch, nobody lingered. The lampshades abandoned by the French, their center holes stopped with bamboo, served as plates for the rice. Another piece of bamboo, split in two, was used for a bowl. Further from bamboo, we made chopsticks as hard as ivory. Sometimes, besides the rice, we had cabbage brought back from the plain; but, despite the gnawing hunger, rushing at the food was out of the question. It had to be divided first into equal parts. And whenever the children we were teaching brought us potatoes or cassava, we made a soup with *co tranh* ashes for salt.

Around half-past five, the sun disappeared, the clouds returned and, once again, a cold, biting dampness set in. At night the mosquitoes were attracted into the house by the warmth and, no matter what fires we made to smoke them out, we were all horribly bitten. As if all this were not enough, it was torture to wake up in the morning and have to put our chapped feet down on the ground.

The only thing that enabled us to withstand such sufferings was the friendly atmosphere that prevailed at the Institute. Never again would I find such good companionship. All the Vietnamese know the story of *Thien Thai*, otherwise called the Story of Paradise. A thousand years ago, two poets, Luu and Nguyen had repaired to a cave. Suddenly, as if by magic, the far end of the cave wall opened onto a road that led them to a garden full of peach trees—a paradise where everyone was happy. There, Luu and Nguyen met two beautiful fairies and no longer wished to leave this idyllic place. But being the only mortals among immortals, in spite of their happiness at being there, they eventually began to feel nostalgic about their birthplace. So, Luu and Nguyen asked their two beloved fairies: "Let us return just once and see our parents. We will come back immediately afterwards." The fairies, in tears, let them leave. At their place of birth, however, two centuries had gone by—as one day in paradise was equivalent to several years on earth—and no one recognized them. In an old inn, they heard the story being told of the two who had disappeared, an event that was supposed to have taken place a very long time before. So, Luu and Nguyen understood that they did not belong in that world and had forever crossed the line to the other side. When they returned to the cave to go back to their fairies, however, they could not see anything. The road had disappeared, and so had their paradise. The moral of the story is that when you choose to leave paradise, you can never go back again. The unique experience of our passage at Khe Khao—with professors, students, and workers all together in the same community—could never be renewed by any one of us. Whenever I think of that period, I am gripped by the same feeling that Luu and Nguyen must have experienced when they remembered their paradise lost.

Some time after Giap's visit in September 1948, and without our being given any reason for it, the Khe Khao Research Institute had to be quickly abandoned and we had to resettle in the jungle, two hundred kilometers from Hanoi, in Tuyen Quang Province. We were so used to the alarm procedures that it took us but a few hours to be ready. The miners watched us go with great sadness; their feeling was that we were abandoning them.

Carrying our burdens, we first went down to Ban Thi and then got on the train to Dan Hong. There, boats were waiting that took us to Dong Chiem, a village on the river Claire settled by the Cao Lang, who lived like the Thais in houses built on piles.[6] The change was a radical one. We had been totally isolated in Khe Khao, whereas here we lived in the midst of the population, dwelling in houses like theirs, though we also occupied straw huts that were scattered in the bamboo groves.

We, ourselves, continued to work in the same field, research on explosives, but around Dong Chiem there were several arms production plants. We were the researchers; the factory workers put our ideas into practice.

Living conditions were far easier than in the mountains. Everybody here cultivated manioc and potatoes, but the rest of the food supplies came by river. The population was happy to help out, despite what French historians have written. Working conditions had a lso changed a lot. There were about a hundred of us by now, of which many were skilled workers who, earlier on, had been scattered over all the other zones. There were also many volunteers, among whom were some of our former school comrades from Hue. The work was much better organized than it had been in Khe Khao, where the director or his assistant had only to say: "Do this!" and it would be done. We were divided into several sections: the ballistics department for research on firing, the gas production department, and our chemistry department, still specializing in explosives. Also, not to be overlooked, there was electricity here, furnished here by a coal-burning generator. So we finally began to feel alive again.

Having us live in houses similar to those of the population was a way of helping us avoid attacks by French planes. In other villages, however, it happened on occasion that traitors used mirrors to signal the pilots and certain dwellings would be bombed. Our security thus depended in a large part on the villagers, as did theirs on us.

---

[6] Cao Langs and Thais: names of ethnic minorities.

Under normal conditions, mornings began when the men let the women get washed first. But we had to be on the watch and run as soon as an aerial attack alarm sounded. The gong would strike out in halting blows. We then had to run for shelter. Besides the underground ones, there were shelters known as toad holes in the sides of the hills. Each one of us had to dig one out upon arrival at the Institute. One morning, my friend Thuan had been surprised by a gong as she was washing herself. Naked, she had to run for a shelter carrying her clothes and was the object of great laughter by the others. After we had washed, the day's work began.

Every week we reviewed the situation. When I had to make a kilogram of fulminate, it was my responsibility to organize the work of the seven people in my group in order to have it finished by the end of the week. When it was ready, it had to be carried off to another hill and divided up for the making of percussion caps. It was compulsory for deliveries to be made by people of our organization because the mountain people were to be kept in the dark. There were frequent lethal accidents during the transportation, and that deeply affected our morale. When there was time to spare, we would go fishing in the river to improve our meals and, sometimes, villagers agreed to sell us some cassava flour as well. Copying the mountaineers, I would make giant pineapple fibers more pliable by soaking them in water. I could then manage to knit small waistcoats for children and traded them for eggs and sugarcane. Using a cast iron pot with a lid for an oven, I even succeeded in baking cakes. We used to cook by night, as far from the house as possible, so the smoke could be channeled out through the bamboo to prevent aerial detection. Bamboo was used for just about everything, even providing water: if the trunk was full, it produced a dull sound when tapped with a knife.

But what was most insufferable, as I already mentioned, was the lack of salt. When we woke up, we could not open our eyes and during the day we constantly fought off lethargy. Salt was a precious commodity that was reserved for soldiers. As a research establishment we were not entitled to the privilege. Every month, each one of us was given thirty grains—one a day, that is, to be put on the tongue one second in the morning, just for the taste. Then it was carefully stored. Too bad if the allowance was swallowed all at once. I became so deprived of salt that I developed hypocalcemia.

We were kept informed of the general situation by our messengers sent to the plain to find supplies. As a bonus they often brought back lumps of sugar wrapped in white paper. I long kept some of those wrappers with me, as well as the memory of that sugar melting in my mouth.

At eleven we all sat together for lunch. Each of us had a ball of rice with bamboo shoots in vinegar and, if lucky, some fish. Then we napped till two in the afternoon. Afterwards, we set out to work again. That was the toughest moment. At that hour of the day in the tropics, the sun shines hard through the trees. Our heads ached; there was no air. In the huts, the heat was stifling. Half asleep still, we had to get back to work, measure carefully each of our movements, and remain watchful all the way to five o'clock. Often, we played volleyball to relax, using a liana for a net and a pineapple wrapped in string for a ball.

Little by little, we got better organized in our everyday lives. For a toilet, each one of us had from the start dug out a hole in the ground and was responsible for its maintenance. Cao Lang people taught us about the disinfectant properties of ashes from a certain plant. One had just to pour some into the hole to eliminate odors. After three months, we filled the hole up with soil and dug out another next to it. Six months later we would obtain rather clean fertilizer. To brush our teeth, we used a dried out plant root, with some salt on it, when available.

On every hill, the huts easiest to access were those in which no secret operations were hidden. They were notably called "houses of happiness." Whenever women who lived in the occupied zones defied danger to come and see their husbands who were working in the Resistance, they spent the night with them there, which guaranteed greater security.

Other than that, we lived among ourselves twenty-four hours a day. On our little radio set we could only get the Vietminh broadcasts and so we hardly had any international news. But that was not something we really missed.

In the house on piles where I lived, there were four other women with me. I was the only one to work in research; the others cooked and served meals. The men were separated from us by a bamboo partition, but at night we carried out conversations across it, which was a lot of fun.

My relationship with Hoang had strongly evolved and even though we never spoke about it to anyone the comrades knew our feelings for each other.

To do our work, we occupied three big houses on a hillock overlooking the river. Fifty years later one could see there a small plaque inscribed: "In 1948, the scientists of the Institute for Research on Explosives (NCKT) for the Resistance resided here." At that time, there was no longer a unique front against the French, but many combat zones. The army needed everything: hand grenades, bazookas, and recoilless cannon. Soon, the making of hand grenades fell upon our group.

On February 4th, 1949—I remember the date precisely—I was busy working at my station with two other comrades, Tri and Luong—brother to Doctor Tran Duy Hung, former mayor of Hanoi, who was then Ho Chi Minh's personal physician. While they were filling the grenades, I left the room for a short time. A terrible explosion was heard and, rushing back inside, I saw through the smoke that Tri had had one hand torn off and Luong's face was covered with blood. Very quickly, they were taken to a hospital in the free zone, near our former quarters in Chiem Hoa. Hanoi's Medical School had been transferred there and it had highly competent practitioners. That evening, I was quite sad, sitting by the playground and staring out at nothing, when Hoang came up to me: "I have come to tell you that I will soon be leaving for the front." After what I had been going through that day, that was too much and I burst into sobs. "Why are you crying?" I was ashamed to confess that I was feeling totally depressed and without the strength to go on living. Up to that point I had always considered I was invincible, but seeing my friends wounded for the first time, I had realized this could very well happen to me, one day or another. "Let's get married, Phuong. This way there will always be two of us to face it all." I had always been honest with Hoang and he knew that I had never quite forgotten my first love. But, suddenly, this proposal seemed to me to be the only solution for not being alone any more, and especially, for not betraying the Resistance by leaving its ranks. He repeated: "Let's get married. We will be living under the same roof and you will no longer be afraid." Hardly had I said "yes" when Hoang was off to see the director to convey our decision. By the next afternoon, after work, our friends had started building us a small house next to the playground, a nest for our children, as they jokingly called it.

The house was completed on February 28th, 1949, the very day of the wedding, which was the first we had ever celebrated in the jungle. It was declared a day of festivities and in the morning about a hundred people gathered in the main square. For the occasion, Madame Le, the wife of the Director, Phu, lent me a pale blue *ao dai* and a pair of white pants, which were a welcome change from my usual rags. My hair had grown somewhat and I felt softer and more feminine again. The groom wore his officer's khaki uniform, the only one he had. "Today, we have the pleasure of announcing Hoang and Phuong's wedding," declared Phu. We climbed onto the platform that was usually reserved for official speeches. Everybody applauded. Hoang was shyly holding my hand, as if he could not believe what was happening. Phu then gave us the presents sent by the Minister of Armies and the high officials who knew my husband. All in all, it amounted to forty-five *dong*. It is impossible to reckon what that might represent now, but I had not been in possession of so much money since I had left my family.

"On this day of happy celebrations," Phu continued, "we shall sacrifice a buffalo." No matter how happy and moved I was at such demonstrations of friendship, I could not help being nervous about my first night as a married woman. The day went like a dream and, come night, I headed towards our brand new house. Inside, there was a large bamboo bed and a chest for clothes. I sat on the bed to wait for Hoang. About nine o'clock, when I was on the brink of sleep, he came in carrying a bundle on his back, similar to the one I had already stored in the chest.

That first night, we slept side by side, intimidated, not daring to make the slightest movement. The next morning, my comrades teased me, asking: "Tell us, Phuong, how many times?" I was terribly embarrassed. In the evening, Hoang confessed that he was ashamed, too, because of all the questions that had been bombarded on him. The following days, I felt already different for I was no longer alone—there was someone else in my life who occupied my thoughts.

We no longer ate our meals with the others. With the rations given us, I would cook our meals. When our friends came, they brought along their own rice. In the beginning, we would sit on the ground. But very shortly later, and without letting us know, our colleagues had set up a wide bamboo table in front of the house and we then spent many a very friendly and warm evening there. Being a couple changed the relationships we had with others—with Phu and his wife, in particular. She was an excellent cook and, very often, she would prepare our dinner. Although she was about the same age as my husband, she quickly became my very good friend.

The Research Institute for Vietnamese Aviation was eight kilometers away from ours. From there, my husband received an order to welcome a military man of German origin who was to live in a house close to ours. He was a former engineer in the German Air Force, had joined the Foreign Legion, and had been taken prisoner by our troops. The Vietnamese Headquarters had quickly understood from his background just how useful this man could be to us. Tall and slim, he spoke German, which nobody among us understood, and, fortunately, some French.

Schultz, who had been re-named Nguyen Duc Viet, very quickly demonstrated incredible knowledge. Not only did he know how to make shells, but he had excellent teaching skills. He was married to a Vietnamese from the forest. The intellectual gap between them was almost shocking, as he was an engineer and she just stayed home and seemed to be quite ignorant. Still, it was easy to imagine that, being alone in the jungle, he had not been able to resist this beautiful woman.

For a long time, Duc Viet was to work with our friend Ha Dong. Through some mind-boggling miracle, the two of them had managed to lay hands on Bao Dai's three planes, left in Hue, and they used them to teach flying and train pilots. Ha

Dong was in charge of Vietnam's Air Force and Duc Viet served him as his secret advisor.

After victory in 1954, the Vietnamese government decided to repatriate him and he came and told us: "I have to return to Germany; I will come back soon for my family." But he had to wait fifteen years before he would be in a position to come back. In 1969, all the formalities for his return to Vietnam were complete and we were very happily expecting him. But a few days before his departure, he was killed in an airplane accident.

One month after my wedding I didn't get my period. I did not tell anybody about it, not even Hoang. However, when I started feeling nauseous and was sure of my condition, I did tell him and he was overjoyed with the news. He was twenty-eight and had been longing for a child.

I had been pregnant three months when an incredible event occurred. I was at home, studying English—some people from the plain had come to buy ammunition and brought us a few books among which there was an English textbook—when someone knocked at the door. A tune I knew very well was being whistled and my heart started beating madly in my chest: it was the tune that Nam kept whistling whenever he came to see me in Hue. Nam came in, dressed like a minority peasant with black pants and a hand-woven shirt. He looked more wire-thin than ever.

I was struck dumb and could not get up. "Phuong, why did you get married?" he asked directly. "You were no longer willing to wait for me? I thought I would die when I heard of your decision." He watched me with eyes full of tears. "If you only knew how much remorse I felt. I thought so much of you that I could not sleep anymore. Then, I looked for you everywhere." From one of our friends he had eventually learned that I was still working with the same research institute on explosives, but in North Vietnam now, and that I was living in Dong Chiem with Hoang, my husband. Nam had then immediately headed toward the town and it had taken him a month's walk through plains and mountains at the peril of his life to come and find me. "I have brought you a present," he said handing me a can of honey. He had remembered that we used to have beehives on the plantation and that I liked honey very much. This is when I fainted.

When I came to, I was lying on the bed and Nam was sitting at my side. "I have never forgotten you, but nothing is possible between us any more now. I am pregnant and I love my husband." Although he was extremely unhappy with Nam's visit, Hoang let us spend the evening together without interfering.

There was a tree at the edge of the forest that bore white flowers which were gleaming in the moonlight like butterflies. We sat under its branches, held hands and talked all night about ourselves, our families, our projects. He told me again how much he had suffered after I had left. I confessed the extent of my despair at the time. Nam had first been a militant in the youth organization in his village, and then had been promoted. He had just graduated from the *école normale.*[7] When morning came, it was time for us to part. I asked permission from my laboratory head to escort back my "brother" Nam. I also sought the agreement of my husband, who had waited in our house for me the whole night through.

I walked Nam to the Institute's boundaries, which I was not authorized to cross. There we kissed for the first time and I slowly went home where my husband was sitting on the bed waiting for me. "I thank you from the bottom of my heart," I said, "Thanks to you, we have been able to sort the situation out." "It's all a matter of fate," was his reply.

---

[7] *école normale*: training school for teachers.

A few days afterwards, when I opened my door, I saw a young boy huddled there on the ground. His forehead was burning. When I took him in my arms to carry him inside and lay him on a mat, he was light as a feather. I managed to make him swallow some water with sugar-cane syrup. By evening he was still drowsy.

He remained thus prostrate three full days and when he recovered some of his strength he told me his story. Tham was a so-called "child-trooper," that is to say an orphan who had been brought up by the state to become a soldier. His unit had been crossing the area when he had started feeling ill. It soon worsened and he could no longer keep up with the rest of the unit and he had collapsed in front of my door without any one noticing his disappearance. After a couple of weeks, Tham was back on his feet and wanted to return to his companions. I gave him some supplies for the road. "I could never thank you enough," he said before leaving.

At the end of 1955, we had returned to Hanoi and it was bitterly cold. We still lacked everything. One day I received a note from the post office asking me to come fetch a present from the Soviet Union. It had to be a mistake, as I did not know a soul there and in the building where I lived there were a thousand residents with at least a hundred Phuongs. I sent the note back but there came a second one that I also sent back. My girlfriends told me I had to be crazy; I could not refuse a gift. I ended up going to the post office where a bulky package was waiting for me, bearing the name of an unknown sender. Inside, there was a fan with rubber blades, what we called an elephant-eared fan. It was an incredibly luxurious item, the kind for which I would never have dared to hope. As soon as I had it set up, our neighbors crowded around us to take advantage of the coolness it offered. A few months after I had already totally forgotten the name of the sender, I received a letter. "Dear sister," it said, "I have been looking for you everywhere for years. I am the small boy you saved." Tham had returned safe and sound to his unit. At the Russian military school where he had been sent after the war was over, he met another Vietnamese who was none other than one of Hoang's nephews. "This is how I was able to send you the fan to thank you," his letter went on, "I think it might prove useful. I know that right now in Vietnam, just after the peace, life is not very easy."

Ever since I became pregnant, I had been spared some tasks, especially those at which I might be exposed to sulfuric acid vapors. Now I was in charge of drying Cheddite, a type of flaky explosive. It was to be heated in a pot set within a larger one filled with water to make a kind of double boiler, and watched over until it stiffened enough to be worked. I had to check the water level constantly; otherwise, the whole thing could explode.

Mine was a difficult pregnancy; I was very thin and vomited all the time. One morning I was so exhausted that I fell asleep, head back against the trunk of a bamboo stalk. Someone came just in time to add some water to the pot and this produced a terrible noise. A few more seconds and everything would have blown up. I continued at the same work, however, because, all things considered, it was the least dangerous.

As expected, Hoang soon received his orders to leave the Institute and prepare to go to China. That year, 1949, Mao's victory and the opening of the Sino-Vietnamese border were expected. Hoang was first sent to Cao Dang, not far from where his friend Dang Van Viet lived, and when he left I felt lonely. The house seemed to me so dreary that I often preferred to go spend the night with girlfriends. The birth of my child was expected on December 14th.

On the 13th, the eve of his departure for China, my husband had permission to come and see me. When he arrived, it was pouring torrents and he had had to ford an overflowing spring. He kept shivering close to the fire we had lit to help him dry out and I could not help complaining, "How am I to raise our child when you are away?" In the middle of the night, I felt the early pains of childbirth and my husband, who obviously had no experience whatsoever of such a situation, kept repeating, "Please, make an effort, wait till daylight."

Towards two in the morning the pain was excruciating: "I have to go to the hospital." Hoang was to leave soon, but before going he helped put me on the Institute's boat. The oarsman and his wife would take me to the hospital, five hours away downriver. The woman told me, "Try and wait some more. Don't be afraid to scream, it will help." That was hard to do for someone like me who had always been taught to bottle up everything! Soon I felt liquid wetting my legs. "I can't take it, I'm going to die." The woman held my hand and I heard her husband praying to Buddha. How I wished my mother had been with me to help out.

It was not yet daylight when the actual birth began. The woman encouraged me: "The head is right there, make an effort." I started pushing as they had taught me to do it at the hospital and suddenly I heard crying. The woman had completed the delivery of the child who was still attached to the cord. It was a boy. When I heard my son's first cries I was overwhelmed by an intense feeling of love and I held him against my heart, imploring him, "Don't die, please, don't die." The woman then separated a piece of bamboo from the awning of the boat, took off the bark to make it sharper and handed it to me to cut the cord. At that very moment I heard a rooster crowing; we were arriving at the village where the hospital was located. The oarsman kept crying and repeating, "A young lady like you, in such terrible conditions."

In broad daylight now, I saw that there was blood everywhere. The baby was asleep; I was exhausted. As soon as we had reached the bank, the man called out and a woman came to give me some tea and a ball of rice. Then someone else came with a hammock on a long bamboo pole. I managed somehow to lift myself out of the boat, holding the child, and I lay down in the hammock with a sigh of relief. Two men lifted the pole onto their shoulders and I let myself be swung along. After a short time we reached the hospital.

It was a week before Christmas. I was alone there. I had been given a sheet in which I had wrapped the child. I was exhausted.

The hospital was set up in huts similar to those of the villagers. The surgeon, Doctor Ton That Tung—son of a mandarin in Hue—was one of my husband's cousins. Although he was enjoying a brilliant career in Hanoi, he had chosen to join the Resistance, thus setting an example to numerous students. His wife worked with him as an anesthetist.

My bed was separated from the other patients' by a bamboo partition. I slept all the time. Whenever I did awake, I swallowed a little soup that they had placed by my bedside while I was asleep, and I nursed Phuoc—a name meaning "happiness" that Huong and myself had chosen even before knowing whether it would be a boy or a girl. Rather scrawny but strong, he slept all the time, too. Very young adolescent girls training as nurses took care of him with great kindness and I wondered where on earth they still managed to find all those clean diapers. Days flew by.

On the evening before I was to leave, Doctor Tung and his wife invited me to spend that last night with them. They lived in a hut that had a flowerbed in front like a true country house. In my bedroom there was a real bed, with sheets, and Madame Tung had brought out all the baby clothes of her son, Bach, who was already five years old.

When I fell asleep that night, Phuoc in my arms, I felt I did not ever want to wake up again. The next morning, it was as if I were leaving my family once again. A short time later, the hospital had to be moved because it had been spotted by the French and Doctor Tung, who was hiding in our Zone at Chiem Hoa, was being actively sought. One day, in his hideout, he heard a voice shouting in a megaphone: "Doctor Tung, we know you are here. Come with us, you'll be much better off in town." After Dien Bien Phu, he would go back to Hanoi and become again the eminent professor he was—liver specialist and member of numerous surgical academies the world over.

The boat had come back for me, and when we arrived at the Institute everybody wanted to have a celebration for us. In those times of war, children were few and far between for the minority peoples who suffered from a deficiency of iodine. Sometimes, when I opened my door in the morning, I would find a potato on the threshold, or bananas. These gifts, in fact, came from the same minority peasants who, knowing I had a baby, wanted to help out.

In the early weeks after my return, I stayed with my son. Then I started resuming evening classes for children. In exchange, their parents would give me a little food. Once, I even received four live chicks and my friends built a coop to protect them from wild animals. Soon my son would have an egg or two every week.

When I had to go back to work, it was out of the question that I take him with me; it would have been too dangerous. With the help of my friends, I built a "child coop" out of bamboo. It was sort of like a dog kennel with a gate that could be locked. When I left, I would lay my son in it on a mat. I came back two hours later and had to wake him up to change and nurse him. In the evening, after work, I still had to put him back in his "cage" to go wash his diapers at the spring. Lacking soap, I used saponin, a wild plant whose dried fruit foams nicely in hot water but not so well in cold. Often, a diaper would slip from my numbed fingers and I had to run to retrieve it from the current. Repeatedly soaking my hands in the ice-cold water eventually gave me very painful swollen joints.

Whereas at the hospital I had been well fed and could provide Phuoc with plenty of milk, here, our daily hundred grams of rice ration was now quite inadequate. I tried to plant corn using seedlings given to me by peasants. After work, off I went—my child in a backpack—carrying a pickax and four bamboo torch lights, with a rag end dipped in oil that could be set aflame to keep tigers away.

Once my little patch of land was cleared and my seedlings planted, I started growing tobacco from plants the peasants had also given me. Every evening I had to go water my future crops, returning very late, my son asleep on my back. At times I got to be so tired I could not muster up enough strength to go home. I sat against a tree trunk, my son next to me, and woke up in the middle of the night chilled to the bone. When the tobacco matured, I cut the leaves and, like the minority group peasant women did, went to sell it on the road. With my chapped hands, swollen by rheumatism, my tattered clothes and my feet all black and dried out, no one could imagine that I was Vietnamese. I even pretended to be deaf to avoid speaking. Passers-by took pity on me and willingly bought my tobacco. I also managed to plant some cassava. I grated the tuber on a piece of metal pierced with holes; then, after decanting it in water, got a sort of flour that I covered with sugar cane juice. To my son, this concoction was a feast. I could not get over what I was capable of inventing to feed him. This still left me with a problem that was difficult to solve, that of water. Despite all the sand-made filter-systems that we had devised, it was never really drinkable. Phuoc had worms; his belly was all swollen. Several kilometers from the Institute, on another hill, a minority group peasant had a reputation for being knowledgeable in remedies. Carrying my son on my back, I went to consult him. In front of a tiny cabin on piles, about twenty women were waiting along with children whose feet were swollen and who looked depressingly forlorn. They were wearing the indigo colored clothes of the mountain people, thick and stiff in order to fend off the cold.

When my turn came, I saw an ageless man wearing an indigo turban on his head, a little dog by his side. He gave me a plant that had seeds in it which had to be mashed and given to the child. A few days later, Phuoc's belly had deflated and he seemed to be perfectly healthy. According to that man, toads were full of vitamins and the child had to be fed toad legs. No matter, I was ready to do anything. With a bamboo hoop net that I'd made, I caught more in one night than was necessary. A soldier agreed to prepare them for me and I had only to grill and turn them into powdery stuff that I sprinkled on my son's food.

Alas, the French bombings soon became more frequent and with every alarm we had to pick up and leave. With my child on my back and continually exhausted since giving birth, I could not help feeling that I was going to have a breakdown. I spoke to my son as I walked: "For the moment, ours is a very difficult life. But don't worry, one day everything will be all right. Try to withstand all this as best you can." One would have thought he understood me. Most of the time he did not even cry, but slept.

In 1951 I learned that my husband had been ordered to join the Vietnamese artillery. The Chinese border had just opened. Dang Van Viet had been victorious on Colonial Road No. 4[8] and the French had retreated to Nationalist China. Arms and ammunition were finally getting through to us. Hoang wanted me to join him with our son and, at the Institute, my colleagues agreed that explosives were far too risky a business for us to stay on anymore.

I had no more choice in the matter. Despite ill forebodings about leaving, I knew I had to go. What was to become of me now? Ever since my son was born, I had lost my saucy recklessness.

This time, my husband came to fetch me. He had been designated as director for research and development on artillery and was currently working on 175 mm cannon. To celebrate the departure, our friends organized a big dinner party using whatever was available. The evening extended into late night and my heart bled at the thought of abandoning them, of leaving a place where so many important events in my life had taken place. We had to go twelve kilometers to a place named Deo Vai. The path led through extremely sharp-edged rocks shaped like cat's ears, so we progressed very slowly, taking turns carrying the child. The evening before, using rice flour, and eggs from my hens, I had managed to prepare a few cakes to have something to eat on the road.

At Deo Vai we were lodged by peasants. In those families, men and women were not allowed to sleep in the same room. So, once again, I found myself alone with my child. The bamboo flooring of the room barely isolated us from the buffalo, cows, hogs, and other animals that were kept under

---

[8] Former Colonial Route No. 4, which became National Route No. 4, ran along the Sino-Vietnamese border. It was a strategic stake for the North Vietnamese Resistance.

the house. They produced a pestilential stench and the noise they made when they moved about was unbearable. Moreover, it was impossible to go relieve ourselves outside during the night because of the tigers: we had to use a split piece of bamboo as a chamber pot. It was a real nightmare. Mosquitoes kept my son from sleeping. I was afraid his screaming would awake the entire household, so I took him in my arms and, half asleep, fanned away the insects. During the day, I left him in his dog-kennel and did my best to come and see him as often as possible. I still worked in shell manufacturing, but now I was entrusted with ballistic calculations, an activity which was not exactly exciting. I barely saw my husband, so my son remained my main preoccupation. Fortunately, by then, he was in perfect health. In the houses of the minority peasants, the fire was kept going continuously under terra-cotta pots which everybody used indiscriminately. Every morning I put my ration of rice on the fire to cook and, having planted a few hot pepper plants I had been given, used their leaves to concoct some kind of soup to vary the menu a little bit.

How long would we have to continue leading such a life? I had never been so wire-thin. One evening my husband came to tell me that he had to go take a training course for commissioned officers in China. He would be away for a long time. Consequently, he thought that I might go to Tuyen Quang and stay with his sister, whose husband was the Finance Representative for Central Vietnam. That looked to me like an ideal solution—why had we not thought of it earlier? I immediately endeavored to ask Headquarters for the necessary authorizations to go stay with my sister-in-law. The warnings came from my friends: "You'd better watch it, Phuong. Ever since you joined the Resistance, you have been living a community life. With your kind of uncompromising temperament, how are you going to put up with the pettiness of regular social life?" Their reservations seemed excessive to me. After all, I was going to live with an in-law, not a stranger. For my husband, everything was simple: given he had found a solution, there was nothing left to discuss. But he certainly had not thought out how I was to travel the hundred and twenty kilometers to Tuyen Quang.

In May 1951, I left with my son on my back along with a yoke bearing the basket that contained my chickens, pots, and a bundle of clothes. Our friends had offered me a pair of rubber Ho Chi Minh sandals[9] for the trip. Tay, a young boy of the ethnic minorities, escorted me as guide. The forest was thick and we had to take side paths. Tay walked ahead to open the way. On sunny days, after rain, things got even worse. Thousands of leeches came to the surface, so when we crossed a bamboo forest we could feel the leaves moving under our feet. At night I climbed up a tree to sleep more safely with my child. Sometimes we found an abandoned inn, but I was especially happy when we saw a light in the darkness of the night, an inhabited house. Often then, I would be given food, hot water to wash, and provisions for the road. People were intrigued to see us travel in this way, but I could not explain anything. Actually I felt quite forsaken and had already bitterly regretted my decision.

It took me about a month to reach Tuyen Quang. At daybreak, when I asked where my sister-in-law's house was, I was directed to a big straw hut at the back end of a large, flowered courtyard.

"Hue, Hue, here I am." No one answered. I stepped in and called out again. A stern voice replied: "Oh! That's you?" In another room, my sister-in-law was seated with her daughter, who seemed to be about my son's age. She was

---

[9] Ho Chi Minh sandals were made of soles and bands cut out of rubber tire treads.

wearing silk pants and a white calico blouse. Next to her I must have looked like a beggar with my tanned mountain woman complexion. She did not even bother to get up and greet us. With a flick of her hand she indicated a room by the kitchen: "There is your room." I was floored. She was treating me like a servant. "Put your stuff there," she added without even offering me something to drink or eat. And as soon as we left the room, she closed the door behind us. For Tay, there was no hesitating: "You have to come back with me. You can't stay here with that woman." But I could not muster up the strength to start out again, especially with the child. When we parted, Tay burst out crying.

I did not know what to do, for my son was hungry and I did not dare move about. Around noon, hearing dishes clatter in the next room, I finally emerged. My brother-in-law, his wife and the girl were quietly having lunch. When she saw me, my sister-in-law, startled, cried out: "You were not expected. You were not expected. You were only to come this evening!"

As for her husband, he did not say anything. He just looked me over contemptuously, as if I were some animal that had inadvertently come into the room. "Give me at least some rice for my son to eat." She then took a chipped plate that probably served for the cat and, with a spoon, scraped some rice from the bottom of the serving dish, put it on the plate, poured some *nuoc mam* on it and, handing it to me, said: "Gobble that down."

I went back to my room and gave it to my son. It had been a long time since he had eaten such white and fragrant rice. For that reason alone, I had to stay, even if I was to be submitted to the worst humiliations. Phuoc fell asleep immediately.

At five, as planned, we had our dinner with the two servants in the kitchen, next to the chicken coop. When I told the two young girls of our misadventures, they burst into tears, but refrained from commenting on the behavior of their mistress.

The next morning we were hardly awake when my sister-in-law burst into the room and threw a bag on the bed. "Look in there. You should be able to find something your size. Tomorrow you are going to work." The worn clothes seemed magnificent to me, even if they were much too large. My sister-in-law was at least five foot six inches tall. However, with the sewing kit provided by the servants, I quickly adjusted them to my size and also made a couple of outfits for my son.

The next day my brother-in-law came for me. "I am taking you to the Finance Service. You are going to get a job." The Finance Service in question was in the village, spread out over a series of huts on piles, with tables that once more served as office desks. Despite its shabby appearance, that was where the entire financial organization of the Vietminh government was concentrated.

Hardly had the introductions been made than I felt the irony of the situation—the official who ran the department was showing me respect because of my position as elder sister to the boss.

"What is your specialization?" he asked me.

"I have studied chemicals, explosives and ballistics."

"We don't need any of that here. What else can you do?"

"I also took care of the Journal at the Institute."

"Well then, in that case, you're going to take care of the Ministry's journal."

Entitled *Le travail sur le riz*,[10] the journal covered several provinces and, thanks to a staff of about twenty, gave accounts of everything that had to do with rice: how many types of crops there were, how the stocks were guarded, what the rice quality was, etc. I immediately had a feeling I was going to like this work. At least it was a drastic change. Every day I went to the office with my son and, like the other mothers, I attached him to my chair with a creeper, which served as a leash. There were six of us in the same situation and our children seemed perfectly happy to be able to stay with us like that. As for myself, I found it comforting in this milieu where nobody knew anything about my family life. In their eyes, I was merely the highly honored sister-in-law of the director's wife.

On the other hand, at my own sister-in-law's house, the situation became more and more intolerable. She could not go out of her way to humiliate me more. In the evenings, for example, it was my job to boil water in a huge caldron without handles so that she could wash herself. In order to do that, I had to pick up leaves and put them to dry before going to work. But the leaves didn't burn well and they let out pungent smoke that made me cough. Further yet, I would burn my fingers holding the pot. It was nine o'clock before I could join my son in our little bamboo bed. Another one of my tasks consisted of hoeing my brother-in-law's manioc fields behind the house when I got home from work. There was nothing I could do for my son when he was hungry. My brother-in-law would decree: "Ho Chi Minh said, 'If you don't work, you don't eat.'" My poor son was not even allowed to play with his cousin. I was living a real nightmare. Fortunately, though, we did not suffer from bombing raids in this Zone. The planes sometimes flew over the region to get to the theatre of operations, but that was

---

[10] *Le travail sur le riz*: The Study of Rice

all. One evening I felt light-headed in the field and lost consciousness. Then someone shook me and I saw my brother-in law's furious face: "Don't pretend," he yelled, "if you don't work, you don't eat!"

I consoled myself from this miserable life through my work. It was even more of a consolation because I would travel about in the surrounding provinces. For these trips, I had the privilege of being given a Chinese bicycle. It was almost taller than me and not so easy to pedal because of the crossbar. I was to visit the neighboring zones to note the status of the rice deposits—the quantity that the population had contributed. In the free zones, after the monsoon, it was the population that provided rice for the fighters in the form of a tax. If the results were satisfactory, they would be published in the journal to inspire others to do the same. On every one of my expeditions I was given a long list of things to buy: food items, toothpaste, or a few meters of calico fabric. Several of my childless colleagues offered to look after my son when I was away and he was only too happy to escape the atmosphere at my sister-at-law's house.

Every twenty days I would go to the printing shop by way of camouflaged tracks over which netting had been spread and plants allowed to grow in order to make them invisible to planes. On the way out it was all downhill going, but as my bicycle did not have brakes I would drag a thick branch behind me to slow down. To cross the bridges—two bamboo trunks across the spring—I had to get off and carry it. Today, I would certainly not be able to do so.

The printing shops were always hidden in caves or in perfectly dissimulated tunnels. Just as with the tracks, enormous nets were cast over them, on which vegetation flourished. In the caves, it was very hot and humid during the summer; freezing cold and windy during the winter. Most of the workers— usually about thirty—had worked at a printer's shop in Hanoi. They were not allowed to move about and lived under ghastly conditions. Almost all of them had malaria stamped on their faces. They could only go out to grow rice or vegetables. When I arrived I would give them the articles that they then set in lead type. When there was ink, it took them two days to print the journal. Otherwise, someone had to go into town in the Occupied Zone, putting his life at risk because, if he were caught, it would not take long for the enemy to understand that he was running errands for a printing shop. It was the same with paper. In the meantime, I lived like the workers and helped them cultivate their fields.

At first, the journal had four pages; then it was expanded to six; then twelve. It was printed on yellow paper made out of straw. The run amounted to a hundred copies. Five went to each of the Provinces, where they were hand-copied and reprinted to be distributed to the population. For security reasons, not a single copy was allowed to remain in the shop. All the original documents were burned and the fonts destroyed.

Sometimes on the way back, what had been a tiny spring when I had crossed over it had become a tumultuous river. In that event, I would have to wait several days until the level receded, meanwhile trying to find something to eat.

Along the way I deposited the journal at the various post offices that, in turn, were to get it to the places where the rice was stocked. Back at my office, there were about twenty copies left. We kept two of them, one for archive and the other for the Minister of Finances. In the Museum of the Resistance in Hanoi, a few of them have been preserved, although the paper, with bits of straw in it, has darkened and the printing is hard to read. But for us, that journal represented something extraordinary. In the years 1952-1953, all the problems related to rice were essential. That rice was what would feed the fighters at Dien Bien Phu in 1954.

One evening, as I was working in my brother-in-law's field, I heard my name called out. "Phuong, Phuong." It was Zoanh, one of my husband's friends, back from China. Hoang had asked him to come and check on how I was faring. I was ashamed to let him see how undernourished and exhausted I looked, but hardly did I open my mouth when he cried out, "What's happened to you, Phuong? You don't look well at all. I am not going to let you stay on here."

My two in-laws had come out into the yard when they had heard him call out, "Why have you been treating your sister-in-law so abusively? She gave up everything to come here, believing she would find a family. You are criminals," he said to them.

Within the hour, and despite the couple's protestations, I had written to my husband telling him what had happened, gathered up my belongings and took off with my son. For a long time my girlfriends had been inciting me to go stay with them in the large straw hut where they were living, not far from the Ministry. The time was ripe to go.

There were large dormitories, with women on one side and men on the other. As soon as we arrived, someone put up a partition to allow us separate quarters. There was a common kitchen where we would have our meals together very early in the morning before going to work, and then at about eleven thirty, and again at six. The monthly salary amounted to around a dollar—about five francs—but it was not distributed since it went directly to pay for our housing and food. We only had one obligation: once a month, usually on Sundays, we had to go get our ten-kilo rice allotment from a depot in the plain.

On that day, with only a yoke on our shoulders and without any weapons, a group of about twenty of us would leave dressed like Cao Lang. As soon as we reached a village, we would split into groups of two or three and, most importantly, would avoid speaking to anyone. For the locals, we were just another group, among many, of minority peasants. We went to the depot as fast as possible and came back burdened like mules. Whenever we passed by an inn and we smelled soup, we were terribly tempted to stop and get a good hot bowl of meat broth. Generally those expeditions were quite gay, even if French airplanes happened to make lightning raids in the area. Fortunately, they could be heard well before they were overhead and we had time to hide in the forest.

Rice rotted rather fast in those depots, where the temperature could exceed 110 degrees. Once it was washed, we often found that the grains were hollow. In any case, it was out of the question to start eating the new rice before we had finished off the old. Only on my trips to the printing shop could I eat peasant rice and I somehow always managed to bring back some to my son.

Our only real festive moments were the evenings when there was a movie. After 1951 and the opening of the Chinese border, groups of projectionists started to roam the country. For security reasons they used to stop quite a distance from secret organizations—about fifteen kilometers in general. But the news of their arrival spread quickly. They remained in the same place for three or four days and showed a different film every night. Once our work completed, we quickly gathered up a few bamboo sticks to make torchlights with rags dipped in oil. I tied my son onto my back with a scarf and set out in semidarkness. We were so excited that distance at that time did not really matter, nor did even the crossing of springs. The place where the films were projected was hidden deep in the middle of a heavily sheltered bamboo forest because there were nearly one hundred people who would come for the entertainment: soldiers, people from all the different organizations, and inhabitants of the neighboring villages. The team of projectionists would hang a huge sheet up between two tree-trunks and, since the films were in Chinese, there always had to be a Vietnamese translator present, one who could also speak loudly enough to be heard by everyone in the audience.

The subject was always the same: for poor girls abused by rich landowners, the arrival of Mao Tse Tung's Chinese Liberation Army and agrarian reform would return them to their loved ones and a better destiny. A classic example was a film entitled *The White-Haired Girl*. Although we knew the story inside out, we sobbed all the same every time we watched it. And when the landowner abused the peasants, some soldiers would fire at the screen. But when, suddenly, the lookouts cried "*mai bai*," meaning airplanes, lights went off and we all rushed to the shelters to wait out the alert. After the movie, the audience dispersed quickly and we went home, happy as could be, with the children asleep on our backs. The return trip seemed shorter because we were so busy discussing the show and talking about meeting people from the other groups again.

There was real change in our lives now. Meetings were held every month aimed at helping us understand the meaning of our struggle. The point was to demonstrate how cruel capitalism was, how much it exploited the proletarian class, and how we had to fight against it. From then on, the working class was the only thing that counted. Every month, therefore, stern and tough looking Political Commissars, who were obviously of peasant origin, cropped up from I do not know where. The meetings lasted several hours. After listening to the speeches, we had to take a piece of paper and write the story of our lives, ending with a personal comment: what did we think of our pasts? The aim was to criticize ourselves, and our social class as well. We had finally come aware of our faults. Before, we were ignorant. They insisted: "Are you sure you really understand now?" "Yes I am sure I do understand now." Hours could be spent just repeating the same thing. That was the time we first saw Ho Chi Minh. He lived in a house on piles in the heart of a bamboo forest on the other side of the spring, not very far from us. In that hut he led a very quiet, highly organized sort of life, surrounded by bodyguards. In the morning, he washed at the spring. Then he did calisthenics for an hour or played volleyball with his attendants. Later, he held political meetings and saw visitors. Every Sunday, small groups of people like us came to pay their respects. When I saw him, I had the impression I was seeing an uncle, or a family man. Nothing we had heard about him corresponded to this man in his fifties who was nothing but skin and bones. With piercing eyes and a small beard, he dressed in the way of ethnic minorities, with brown shirt and pants, and his famous sandals. He smoked cigarette after cigarette. Out of a very heavy terra-cotta bowl, one of his guards served each one of us a delicious, sweet soup made with ginger-flavored sticky rice. Ho Chi Minh was full of solicitude towards us, more concerned with giving practical advice than with conveying a message. "With the kind of life you lead, it is always of utmost importance to keep a clean bed, be attentive to cleanliness, and never get sloppy. To avoid malaria, you must burn dead leaves in the evening to keep the mosquitoes away." And when, about twenty minutes later, we were about to leave, he added, "Be careful not to slip into the spring while crossing it. And you, young ladies, beware of not putting your feet in cold water when you have your period—that is very bad for your health." I was really very moved by such affectionate advice, especially coming from the master of each one of our destinies. One day, later on, he came on an unexpected visit.

"Uncle Ho is here! Uncle Ho is here!" we heard someone cry out in the courtyard. Everybody ran home, as we knew he would not fail to inspect the premises. Since I had no closet, nor any time to tidy things up, our little cubicle was usually a mess. As for the boys, they never bothered to make their beds. I heard one of my friends cry, "Phuong, hurry up! Run and tidy up your room. He is coming." I had hardly made it to my room when I turned around and he was hard on my heels. "I simply cannot imagine you being so negligent." He then launched into a systematic criticism of our conduct. He was no longer the affectionate uncle I had met. A bit later, we were all gathered in the dining room—a straw hut with a long table of woven bamboo with bamboo poles on either side on which to sit. Ho Chi Minh saw that we only had rice to eat, with a few bitter papaya leaves for vegetables. I heard him put a question to my neighbor: "Is it any good?" The man was struck with terror and kept repeating: "Oh, it's extremely good. Extremely good." "No, my child, it is not good at all. When I see you eat that," he said, "it makes me very sad. But to be able to eat better, this is where you have to start. We have reconquered our country empty-handed. Now we have to worry about eating better. You have no right to think that is any good, and still less of a right to say it."

Everyone to Dien Bien Phu

From 1953 on, a change in the situation was in the air. The printing shops were taken out of the caves and functioned at full capacity, producing leaflets and posters. We were at long last surfacing from the underground. There was no longer any need to dress like minorities and although we still were just as careful when we moved about we were met with less and less hostility from the population, with people sometimes saying to us, "You are with the Resistance." In the area, all the bombed out houses had now been replaced by huts. In fact, things looked almost normal, so used had we become to hearing the airplanes overhead. But thanks to the information being circulated, we knew that victory was near. The French were finally backing down. We started sending supplies into Dien Bien Phu. All the rice depots had to be fully stocked and their conservation was secured with the use of rattraps and poison that we now had the means to procure.

Every day at the office we got news of what was happening on the various fronts. The Political Commissar of our organization gathered us together every evening to take stock of the situation. On a large map, pins with red flags marked the combat areas, and small labels had the number of French casualties. The atmosphere was electric. Night and day, volunteers kept passing by, their bicycles loaded with rice for the front. Every area was to provide a certain quantity of rice and any peasant between eighteen and forty who did not go to the front to fight had to be registered as a laborer. I kept wondering to what extent they had really volunteered. In any case, they greeted us as they went by and looked enthusiastic enough.

Hundreds of people carrying baskets crowded together at each of the rice depots. On foot, or riding bicycles, they all took different routes for security reasons. Women carried the rice on their backs for twenty kilometers, left it for someone else to take over, and so on, like ants. A hundred kilos of rice, plus the weight of salt and ammunitions, as well: a load of up to two hundred and fifty kilos for those who had bicycles—which, by the way, were often made in France. They came from the *Manufacture de Saint-Etienne*, but their frames were reinforced with two sturdy sticks, and the tires wrapped up in rags or straw to make sure that they would survive the several hundred kilometers through the mountains.

Within a few months, the atmosphere had changed. We were no longer in constant fear of bombings or of traitors. There was excitement in the air, everywhere. Musicians, writers, journalists, all wanted to go to the front to support our troops. At night, floating bridges were launched. Come daylight, they were taken apart so as not to be spotted by the airplanes. Roads were banked up to allow trucks to carry weapons and ammunitions from China. One morning, I was riding my bicycle and was overtaken by a truck. It was the first in nine years. I filled up my lungs with the scent of gas as if it were real perfume.

Volunteers came from every corner of the country, wearing different clothing. Along the way, people sang, talked to one another, and exchanged poems. There were moving encounters like that of a father who, having joined the

Resistance in the early days, met up with his eighteen-year-old son who had become a soldier. Another, who had left his wife three days after their wedding, recognized her at a crossroad where she was working as a laborer. Friends who had not seen each other since school suddenly came face to face. All those who had not had news from their kin in a long time continually kept up hope that they would recognize someone. Back from China, my husband had come to spend an evening and night with me. The next day he had to leave again to lead an artillery battalion there at Dien Bien Phu. In spite of his usual self-control, he hardly managed to hide his excitement. It was a new life that was beginning for him too—an awakening after a long sleep.

Deep down, I was extremely frightened of his going there. It was all the more so as I realized I was pregnant with my second child. Every night I went to sleep repeating to myself, "Let's hope we'll soon be the three of us together, let's hope we'll soon be the three of us together."

On the one hand there was general enthusiasm, on the other the personal anxieties of each one of us. All my colleagues whose husbands were soldiers shared my fright. Even though we were sure we would eventually win, the forces seemed to us to be so unequal—like locust attacking an elephant. We did not really understand why, but the names of our casualties were never revealed immediately. Thus, people kept up their hopes. Some of the women even remained without any news for nine years straight, until one day in the tenth year they saw their husbands turn up out of the blue. Once during the battle Hoang came back, on foot, with his two bodyguards. That evening, everybody gathered around him to hear news from the front about how General Giap had ordered cannon hoisted up still higher in order better to sweep the valley below. My son was very happy to be with his father.

The following day, Hoang went back to Dien Bien Phu, still horribly tired, but with mixed feelings—happy with the prospect of having another child and furious about my misadventures at the hands of my sister-in-law. Much as I had been angry with him at that time, I understood upon his return from Dien Bien Phu how trapped he was in his rigid way of thinking, and how incapable of conceiving any life other than that of the military. I could no longer bear him any grudge.

"We work one and all for Dien Bien Phu"—such was the slogan that was being repeated as the battle grew more imminent. In the Institutes, it was the sole subject of conversation. Our monthly ration had gone down from thirteen kilos of rice to only eight. The other five kilos were channeled to Dien Bien Phu. All day long, the galena wireless broadcast information. I knew that my husband was in command of an artillery unit on the *Geneviève* Hill, and I was very worried. Our leaders claimed that if we were victorious in that battle, the country would finally be liberated after nine years of war.

I remember the precise moment when I learned of our victory of May 7th, 1954. I was at a printing shop talking with a worker and there was static from the wireless in the background. Suddenly, I heard yelling; the broadcaster was shouting. It had happened; we had won! We rushed outside. "We've been victorious at Dien Bien Phu," people kept repeating, crying all the while.[1] We saw laborers who were heading towards the front suddenly drop their rice burdens and rush directly home. People on bicycles dropped whatever they had been carrying and turned around to head in the opposite direction. It was an incredible sight. In fact, one of the first tasks we would have to accomplish later would be to organize an inventory of bicycles and to retrieve the rice.

---

[1] The 55-day siege of Dien Bien Phu resulted in the bloodiest and most humiliating defeat for the French since Hitler's *Blitzkrieg* 14 years earlier.

But for the time being, I had to put the final touch on the journal. I cast the headline in block letters: "Victory at Dien Bien Phu. Peace has returned. Long live the Vietnamese Army." We published two special issues with, in each one, an editorial written by an official from the ministry on the following subject: "Be vigilant." We would have much preferred to dispense with these texts and throw them in the fire because we had become tired of being vigilant all those years and did not feel at all like reading or hearing such speeches anymore.

No one was fooled by them. People kept saying: "Always the same song." It was such a relief finally to have peace, and particularly not to be afraid of bombing any more, that we suddenly could not bear any hindrance to the joy we felt. At the end of 1954, my son was playing with other children when a plane flew overhead. They all put their arms around their heads in a protective reflex. They could not yet imagine the existence of an inoffensive plane.

After Dien Bien Phu, it was decided that our organization had to move back to Hanoi. The Finance Ministry set up a list directing who was to go and when. First, the men who did not have families, last the women with children. Almost three months after the victory, on July 28th, 1954, I gave birth to my second son, Phuong—meaning "orientation" or "direction."[2] I would have liked a daughter, but then again he was an adorable boy. My pregnancy had been much easier to bear than the first one and I had felt in perfect shape all the way up to delivery. That time, I gave birth in a real hospital, under almost normal conditions, not far from Tuyen Quang.

---

[2] Mother and son do not carry the same name, despite appearances. Xuan Phuong writes her name with a dot over the letter o, which changes it completely from the point of view of pronunciation and meaning: the phoenix of spring versus the flamboyance of spring.

Afterwards, I retrieved my elder son who had been in the care of a minority group woman. All that remained was to wait for my husband. Most people had already left; the houses were abandoned; the place had become sinister. It was now everyone for himself.

Back from Dien Bien Phu, my husband and his division were reassembled at Phu Tho, by the river Claire. When he arrived with his bodyguards in a Chinese Jeep to fetch us, I barely had time enough to put my children on board and pile up a few kitchen utensils, our clothing, and a basket containing a few chickens.

In Phu Tho I was able to rest up for a few weeks. The village, called Go Gai, was on a hill covered with tea fields. At that time of the year, the tea blossoms gave off a delicious fragrance. My husband and I spent entire evenings outdoors, talking about the future. Now that there was peace, I would be able to continue working for the Finance Ministry. Hoang would still remain an officer, but he would be able to return home more often, or even maybe live with us. I imagined a rather easy sort of life that would allow me to raise my children properly. However, we both preferred to remain rather vague about it all. How could we imagine what was to happen after those nine years of living in the jungle with the Resistance? What was most important was that we were still alive and peace had returned.

Hoang was a serious man. I have to confess that he had believed in our struggle far more than I had. And in spite of his aristocratic origins, he remained a soldier, deep down, repeating to any one who listened, "I want to be a soldier to my last day."

After a few weeks, unfortunately, his division had to be redeployed. Left to my own devices once again, my decision was quickly made. Without waiting for anybody's help, I was

Before departure on
Operation Ho Chi Minh
(Hanoi 1975).

My parents in Dalat at the end of the
1930s.

My sons in Hanoi, 1958. Left to
right: Phuoc (1949), Phong (1957),
Phuong (1954).

My husband, 1954.

Colonel Dang Van Viet, "the grey tiger of Colonial Route No. 4," in 1956.

Photo (above) taken in Hanoi in 1954 on occasion of the visit of my South Vietnamese mother-in-law. Left to right, seated: the daughter of my sister-in-law, my mother-in-law with the 2nd daughter of my sister-in-law, my elder son Phuoc; standing: me carrying my 2nd son, my husband Hoang, my sister-in-law.

My husband, colonel during the entry into Hanoi in 1954, after Dien Bien Phu.

With Joris Ivens, 1964.

Serving food in a little courtyard. Hanoi in the 1960s.

After a bombardment of B-52s at Vinh Linh (17th parallel), 1964. The group survived safe and sound.

At the residence of Ho Chi Minh (1965). Seated, 5th from left: me; in the middle row, 3rd from left: Ho Chi Minh.

Me, the doctor! (1965)

With the Polish writer Monika Warneska before leaving for the 17th parallel. Hanoi, 1967.

With Marceline Loridan during the filming of *17th Parallel.* At an underground shelter in Hanoi, 1967.

After a bombardment at Dong Loc (in Ha Tinh, center of Vietnam).

South Vietnam in 1973. Left to right: me, cameraman Trung Viet, Madame Nguyen Tri Binh, Minister of Foreign Affairs of the Revolutionary Government of South Vietnam, Hong the group's guide, cameraman Van, and a guide from South Vietnam.

Before departure for the South to film the great battles of
Operation Ho Chi Minh. At my room in Hanoi, March 26, 1975.

Portrait to the left: my 2nd brother Nguyen Xuan Phat, South
Vietnamese Air Force Colonel, now living in California.

Filming of *Vietnam and the Bicycle* on the Ho Chi Minh Trail, 1984.

Paris, August 20, 1989.

going to go back to Hanoi by my own means: two hundred kilometers on foot, with a six-year-old boy and a three-month-old baby did not even faze me any more.

It did not take long to pack—some trousers and tattered shirts, necessities for the children, and one kitchen pot. Before going to bed, I baked three cakes with what manioc flour I had left and eggs from my hens. My sons were already long asleep and I finally followed suit, to the sound of noises in the night.

In the wee hours of the morning, we were ready to go. A basket with the three hens and the pot was attached to one side of the yoke; on the other, my elder son and our clothes. My three-month old baby was on my hip. We had barely started out when my elder son turned around and said, "We're never coming back to our house?"

"No, darling," I said, "We're going to a place where there's a lot of light."

"But I want to stay here."

"It's no longer possible. Can't you see there's no one left?" He started to cry.

To get to the road to Hanoi, we first had to follow the tracks leading to the printing shop. I knew the way by heart, but with the burden I was carrying it was impossible to advance quickly. When I felt my head start to get light, I stopped and rested. Phuoc ate a little piece of cake, while I nursed the baby. The stream was never too far away and we could always get enough water. But I could not swallow anything before I was sure of procuring some more food.

In the forest, I found tubers that I cooked together with bamboo shoots in my pot, and I threaded it all on a creeper around my neck for reserves.

After a full day's walk, we were still deep in the forest and we found shelter for the night on the wide branches of a tree. I roped my children to the trunk to prevent a possible fall and I also secured the basket with the hens. We were safe. Despite my exhaustion, I could not sleep. Between the trees, I stared at an area of star-studded sky. Soon, all this would be over. At dawn, it was freezing and I was still exhausted.

A few kilometers further, we came across a narrow path lined with huts where there was sure to be an inn. To go faster, I asked my elder son to wait with the basket and the hens by the side of the path, and I hurried along with the baby. Seeing how tired I was, a couple of innkeepers agreed to accommodate me for the night. I left the baby to their care and hurried back to fetch my other son and the hens. The next day I did the same thing and again all the other days of the trip. The innkeepers gave us rice, the means to wash, and a place to sleep. What more could we ask for? When they saw me, they immediately understood that I was with the Resistance, but there was no need to be scared at the sight of an overly thin, penniless, weaponless peasant in rags, carrying two children. To help me, a tearful old lady even offered to adopt my baby, Phuong.

When I eventually reached the main road to Hanoi, my feet were bleeding. There was a temple nearby so I went up to the doors and knelt down: "Please, help me," I said, "I am dead tired and can't go on." The baby was asleep on my shoulder; my elder son was also very tired. Half asleep, I took my baby in my arms, lay him down on the ground and fell soundly asleep. Suddenly, as if in a dream, I heard voices speaking with a pure Hanoi lilting accent: "Have you seen this poor girl with her two children?" I opened my eyes and saw several very elegant women, dressed in *ao dais* and bejewelled turbans, bending over towards me. One of them, who wore the scent of a deliciously sweet perfume, got closer and asked, "Why did you fall asleep right here?" I was struck dumb for an answer and started sobbing. Another, who had splendid hair, wanted to give me some money. I got up: "No, thank you. I cannot accept that. I belong to the Resistance and am on my way to Hanoi." There they stood, then, gathered all around me, and ready to listen to my story. They were fabric dealers from Hanoi who had taken advantage of the new peace to rent a large car and come thank Buddha by presenting their offerings: fruit, pastry made with sticky rice, and plenty of other sweets. Phuoc could not stop eating, and I enjoyed the food, too. We had Buddha to thank for it, I guess. Upon learning that I worked for the Finance Ministry, the woman who had wanted to give me some money invited me to share their car. But when I told her I came from Dalat, she took a closer look at me. "I used to know Mr. Can, the school director at Dalat." "He is my father." The next we knew, she had decided we would come and live with her. In the car we were crowded in tight, but my sons and I immediately fell asleep despite the noise of the Gasogène.[3]

Somebody was shaking me and I woke up. We had arrived. We found ourselves in a spacious room flooded with light, with a real bed, sheets, and a bathroom just next to it. Without delay, I put my children on the bed and started to fill up the tub for a bath.

I took a long bath with fragrant soap and when I came out of the bathroom I felt lighter and younger again. At dinner, Mrs Tung Hien told me that she used to get her fabric from France, and that all of Indochina came to her shop. There were at least ten different dishes on the table and the servants stood behind our chairs ready to help us to more food, just as in the old days. My elder son who had never tasted such delicacies cried out: "Hurray for pork meat!"

---

[3] To relieve the gasoline shortage during World War II, private vehicles in France were equipped with a *Gasogène* system, a noisy contraption made with a large tank and burner that generated methane fuel from coal.

The next morning our benefactress brought us a pile of clothes and I even had to stop her from calling in a seamstress. The first few days, I just stayed and enjoyed idling away my time: "I can put you up as long as you wish to stay," she said to me, "All we have to do is add two bowls and two pairs of chopsticks, and that's it." Her employees, ten people at least, had their meals with the family. She had an ailing husband whom we never met and four children, two boys and two girls, one of whom had Down's syndrome. We spoke open-heartedly and she confessed that, while she had simply followed her instinct when she had first taken us in, she also hoped her good deeds would eventually sway the Goddess to induce a cure for her daughter. She was not a cultivated woman and she could not speak French properly, but she was generous. With her several strands of gold pearls around her neck, she looked like my mother. "Do you think the communists are going to nationalize my shop?" she would ask me very often. Her question seemed incongruous to me. Most of her friends had already left. The very next morning after the victory, the government had given those who wanted it permission to leave and go south. They had three hundred days to make their choice.[4] She preferred to stay because of her daughter, mostly. "Phuong, get me information," she insisted. "Is my shop to be taken away from me? Am I to become a servant to high officials?" "No! Never, ever." How could I have guessed at what was to happen?

In Hanoi everything was new to me. After nine years of living in the mountains, after all my adventures, I felt quite disoriented on that first evening when I wandered around with my two sons. Electricity was magic to me and the stores were overflowing with food. I thought about how difficult it probably was for people who had never lived in a city to adjust

---

[4] This was stipulated in the Geneva Accords of 1954 (see page xi).

to it, especially after all the warnings we had been given about the dangers of the capitalist classes: "Beware of evil iced with sugar." Evil iced with sugar referred to the appeal that a city's sweeter aspects might hold for us. Given such an attitude, no wonder there was no solidarity between those who had been in the Resistance and the city-dwellers. They could not even understand each other. City people were scared of the savages who had come down from the mountains, ready to take away their belongings. As for mountain people, they were paralysed at the idea of absorbing that "evil iced with sugar."

Thus, in the early years of peacetime, we lived separately. The people like us, who came from the Resistance, wore short shirts and pants, "Ho Chi Minh sandals," or our old-fashioned wooden clogs that clunked noisily on the sidewalks; whereas Hanoi ladies still wore their silk or velvet *ao dais*.

I finally decided to go to the Finance Ministry, which had installed itself in huge buildings next to what is today the Museum of the Revolution. The staff had already come back and a lodging had even been reserved for me. The office rooms were spacious and had kept the type of furniture used in the old days. Mine had a walnut table and a 1930-style *armoire* to store documents. On the other hand, when I went to see the lodging that had been allotted me in a former opium depot close to the ministry—an area divided up into rooms—I was horrified. It was 140 square feet, with a tiny window that made it hard to breathe. I was polite about it and assured them that I would be back. The atmosphere in the ministry was tense. There were by then two different types of officials: those like us who were back from the jungle and the others, the financial experts who had preferred to stay in the North, trusting in the Vietminh administration. They were called *luu zungs*, meaning "to be kept." They were treated in a very different way altogether: they were mistreated, rather, and received smaller salaries. In fact, many of them would choose to leave the ministry very shortly thereafter.

Under the control of a department head, I was responsible for the files relating to missing people—in other words, those who had left the Vietminh to return to Saigon, or those whose history was not "clear." We had to research their origins and their whereabouts. I had five people working in my department, whose mission was to check all the documents that were in our possession and, if necessary, to find others. The idea was to determine for certain whether the "missing" had really left for good or not and, in the latter case, to muster them back to work. Officially, this department was called the Personnel Census Bureau.

In 1955, when the soldiers started coming back from the war, Hanoi was all in celebration. People stayed out on the street, men wearing suits, girls in white, and women in multi-colored dresses. There were flowers everywhere, very loud music and tears in people's eyes to welcome the heroes back. There is a photograph of my husband standing in his jeep, being acclaimed by the population. My son had maneuvered his way to the front row that day, but Hoang had gone past him standing straight and without giving him the slightest sign of recognition. It was only at the end of the day that we were able to meet again. He was lodged in the barracks and refused to come stay at Madame Tung Hien's. "Why are you living at a bourgeois woman's house? You must not stay here. You have to go to the place you have been allotted by the Ministry." I argued vainly, " In that room, there's no air; it's very gloomy and unhealthy for the children." He remained inflexible: "Phuong, why don't you behave like everybody else? Don't go on in this way!" In his opinion, not only was I trying to appear to be conspicuously different but I was being influenced by the bourgeois class, which was even more serious. It was to no avail that I kept repeating, "It is not what you think; they are simply people who remind me of my parents. I would like you to meet them at least once before forming an opinion." There was nothing doing—I couldn't get through to him.

It had been hinted to me several times at the Ministry that I would be better off if I left the Tung Hien's household. The message got more and more insistent, so I eventually decided to comply before they actually forced me to leave and I would harm my benefactress. Finally, I told her that we were leaving. Before deciding to move, I had gone back to check again on the room provided by the Finance Ministry of the Free Zones. It was so gloomy that an oil-lamp had to be lit all day long. When I gathered up our clothing, my heart was in my throat and the children cried. Madame Tung Hien refused to understand that I had no choice in the matter. One of the servants carried our luggage to our new dwelling and quickly left. I remained alone with my two children in that stifling room. Soon, curious faces showed up at our door: the women who lived next door had come to meet us. When I opened my suitcases, all the clothes I had packed seemed suddenly superfluous and I decided to give them away. The word spread quickly, whereupon a real fashion show began in my room, everyone helping herself until I had only two outfits left, which under the circumstances were more than enough.

From then on, all our family life, including the cooking, took place in that hole, or on the stoop next to the ditch that drained used water. We had no furniture, just two jute sacks spread out on the floor for bedding. When my three-year-old son wetted his, it took ages before it dried.

As coal gave off a rather toxic smoke, I eventually managed to set up a sort of little kitchen on the stoop with tarpaper spread between two bamboo poles. But even with the burner outdoors, I was still compelled to keep the children a safe distance away.

The day began at five in the morning with loud speakers blaring the latest news. There was just one tap for three hundred people. One had to hurry with a water bucket, but the pipes were clogged and water only dripped out slowly. From a population of twenty thousand under the French, Hanoi had now swollen to five hundred thousand and the infrastructure was failing all over the city. The line up for the toilet was endless and some men were seen running around in their underwear while the women were already busy at the ovens. When the children woke up there was shouting and yelling everywhere. As there were only bamboo partitions, it was as though we were living together—no one had a private life anymore. To keep up an appearance of some kind of order, a council had been created to administer the building. It consisted of a woman—a retiree from the Foreign Affairs Ministry—and four men, two of whom were more especially in charge of repairs. The woman spent all her time watching people. The building was U-shaped and had about fifty other rooms like mine. Every day she inspected a few of them. "What are you eating today?" she asked when she came to mine. Without waiting for an answer, she lifted the lid that protected the dish from the flies. On the day I had managed to buy meat without my ration ticket, she noticed immediately that the quantity was superior to the regulation one hundred grams, and just as quickly reported it to the administration council.

"Today, Phuong ate more meat than the other days." Nothing escaped her attention. But fortunately, as compensation for all that spying, there were marvelous child-care providers in our building. One of them was my neighbor, and she freed me from a lot of worries about my sons. As I was still nursing the youngest, I was entitled to a fifteen-minute break every three hours. My office was close by and such breaks provided real moments of relaxation with other women who had also come to nurse their babies. Once in a while, my husband would agree to leave his barracks and stay with us, but it never lasted very long. He could not breathe in that room, what with the children crying and the laundry hung up to dry all over the place. So he would go hurriedly back to the barracks, leaving me alone with my sons. From time to time I went to see Madame Tung Hien, but always on the sly. If it was ever discovered that I had an on-going relationship with someone of the bourgeois class, it would have meant a lot of trouble for me.

Besides my census work, I was in charge of the people's health in my building. Although I had never completed my medical studies, I had learned a lot during my years in the jungle. Thus, between the office and the building, I was never at rest. Thanks to French translations I was given to do, I made a little extra money and our life was ever so slightly easier. I had managed to find some of my classroom friends who had become artists or were working in other Ministries. But our little group refused to get involved in politics. It happened though that some of these friends had important positions, although they were not communists. This of course meant they had given up all hope of promotion. Nobody was forced to become a member of the Party, but they never gave up trying to get you to sign up, either. There was always one communist who had no qualms about openly surveying us: "I have been asked to approach you. Try to behave well in order to become a communist." We always answered politely, "But of course."

Every week, the Party held a meeting at the Ministry from which we—lost souls—were naturally excluded. Among ourselves, we mainly talked about art. One of our friends, a painter, invited us to come discreetly over and visit him. When the door was shut tight, he took several canvases out from behind a curtain. They were nudes, which were strictly forbidden. If he were caught, he would be accused of being decadent and taken for judgment. Most of the time, we met on Sundays by the banks of a little lake where we brought the children to play. We had ice cream. During one of those outings, I was told that an encyclopedia of the world's classical works was being translated from the French and I managed soon after to be put in charge of the section for letter D: "Damsel of the Lake," "Dance of the Swans," and so forth. A brief encyclopedic summary was needed for each entry. The man who had introduced me into the team got 65% of the official salary. I received only 45% and there was nothing I could do about it. Evenings, after cooking, washing up, and visiting the ill in my building, I translated. Writing in purple ink with a penholder and a nib on bad quality paper, my younger son would fall asleep in my lap. In the meantime, my elder boy, who was seven by then, assembled pre-cut envelopes for the post office. All he had to do was fold the flaps and glue them together using a brush with some kind of flour-based mixture. He earned one *dong* for every thousand envelopes. I used to wake up quite often in the middle of the night, head down on my paper, my two sons quietly asleep, one on my lap, the other with his nose on the envelopes.

All the people I knew lived under similar conditions. A couple of artist friends hit upon the idea of using old film negatives found in a French studio. They tinted them in different colors, framed and sold them on the street—pictures of small animals or cocoanut trees. When you went to their flat, you would always find them with multi-colored hands. Other friends who were stronger would work as rickshaw carriers, but this had to be done in secret, as it was frowned upon. Others still, who had some fashion notions, suddenly became tailors, made buttonholes, or knitted for retail stores. Hanoi turned into a sad city. There were no longer any colors to liven up the streets for all the women were dressed in black pants. Actually, it was just as well we did not have much of a choice since ration cards had made their appearance. Everyone was entitled to one ticket for fabric and one for food, and that included the children. For my family, I was allowed five meters of material a year, to which was added two extra meters of black calico for the making of pants, which was a special privilege for having been with the Resistance. With just one salary for three people, I did not even have enough money to buy the fabric I was entitled to. I preferred to sell my ticket to someone who was wealthier, so as to have a little more money for our basic needs.

I had been decorated many times for my Resistance work. Although I received the Resistance Medal, the Medal for Distinguished Work, etc., nothing changed the situation of my daily life. I was still only allotted twelve kilograms of rice, three hundred grams of meat, some vegetables, and half a kilogram of sugar per month. My children were always hungry and my husband was absent most of the time. When he came home, what remained of his officer's salary was not enough for him to eat correctly, either. Twice a week there were political meetings at the Ministry where the prime topic of conversation was the struggle of the classes. Little by little I realized that those of us who did not adhere to the Party formed a separate class. In the Resistance, everyone used to share everything—the same joys and the same pains. But now, all the important positions and all the jobs holding responsibility were reserved for Party members. Consequently, many people who sought high-ranking posts went after membership at any price, which was in total opposition to what Ho Chi Minh had advocated: Party membership is not for personal advancement, but for the general interest. This was not at all what was actually taking place, particularly in the organization where I was working. There, all the key posts were not only occupied by Party members, but *they*, furthermore, had got it into their heads to re-educate *us*—us, the non-communists. The whole thing revolted me. From then on, a kind of tutor was imposed on each one of us who, at every instant, was to detect and correct our bourgeois ideas. At the office, there was always someone who would suddenly interrupt a conversation with a suspicious question: "What did you just say, Phuong?" Even in the course of daily routine, anything became a pretext for criticism: was my son wearing a shirt that had been tailored out of fabric given by Madame Tung Hien? Immediately, I was questioned: "Where did you get that fabric?" Every day, similar scenes took place. Even at night, it would sometimes happen that I suddenly spring up out of sleep with the impression of experiencing a bad dream. This atmosphere of suspicion became unbearable—not to mention all the deprivations we had to endure. My children had fallen ill two years in a row and I wasn't even able to feed them correctly. I got to the point where I had to sell my own hair. When I looked at myself in the shop mirror where it was sold, I found that my face had changed and that I looked older. My elder son began to cry when he saw me. "Don't worry," I told him, "it is more practical for me this way."

I never could have imagined that this time of peace would be so hard to bear. In the past, we went about in rags and it didn't faze us. Today, in the streets of Hanoi, one's appearance was a delicate matter. My sons, who went to school, needed clothes, sandals, and notebooks—all of which cost money.

As in the jungle, movies were our great pleasure on Saturday nights. There were cartoons for the children and, for us, a Chinese or Russian film that was given a simultaneous translation. Every week, it was the same ritual. I would buy tickets ahead of time in order to be sure of getting seats. We would get dressed up in our finest clothes and off we would go! There, no one thought of hardships. There was always a dealer who sold drinks in front of the theatre and one glass of orangeade for the three of us was all I could afford. The children marked their share on the frosted glass: "You can drink down to here; you, to here. The rest is for me." When my younger began, he always drank a little more than the other. But we were all so glad to go to the movies that no one wanted to pick a fight.

In Bat Trang, twelve kilometers from Hanoi, pottery making had been a tradition since the 16th century. In 1954 the Vietnamese government decreed that bowls and other kitchen utensils were instruments of the bourgeois class and that it would be more useful for the nation to manufacture industrial products. Overnight, only electrical wiring insulation or industrial parts were turned out. It became almost impossible to find bowls for eating. The translation of an article for the Ministry of Foreign Affairs had paid enough for me to buy a dozen of them, so I stepped happily into a shop with my husband and my children. The salesgirl handed me a set of bowls wrapped up in rattan. Four out of the twelve were chipped. "May I open other packs to find ones in good condition?" I asked. "That's right, why don't you start choosing while you're at it?" she yelled back at me as we were chased out of the shop. "Next!" My husband said nothing because he didn't want it to seem as though he were criticizing the government. As for me, I refused to let it go by. But before I could utter a word, the salesgirl screamed at me: "Don't

bother coming back 'cause I won't sell you anything. Next!"
Seeing that it was of no avail to insist, we went off and spent
the money for the bowls in an old French restaurant called the
Bodega.

How had the country come to that?

1955 marked the year of the beginning of Agrarian
Reform. At the Finance Ministry we were told we were no
longer to have city dweller ideas but that we should consider
ourselves country people. For that, there was no better training
than actually working with the villagers, an idea that came to
be known as the "Three Togethers"—work together, eat
together, live together. However, work was not always outside
of the city. For example, it was decided to create a park—to be
known as "Reunification Park"—to take the place of the huge
lake south of Hanoi. Every week, in the company of the seven
other people who made up my group at the Finance Ministry,
we would devote two days of work building it.

When we arrived at the lake, the organization that
distributed the tasks would give us two picks, two shovels and
several buckets. One at a time, we would dig, fill up the
buckets with the soil, and dump it into the lake. The
loudspeaker cried out: "Team A has dug up such and such
square meters. Everyone else should follow their example!" Or
again: "Unit C has not been working well today. It hasn't even
filled half the daily requirements." In this case, Unit C would
be told to accelerate its rhythm in order to attain the established
goal of one square meter per person per day. As if the vocal
rantings from the loudspeakers were not enough, we were also
entitled to listen to songs exalting the glory of manual work.
On those days, the offices remained closed.

After having transformed this lake into a park, another
lake was to be created on the west side of Hanoi. Those who
were in charge sent their reports every day to the Finance

Ministry in order to signal that this or that team had not achieved the daily average—in other words had not respected manual work. To be accused of such an underachievement was extremely serious. Thus, fear motivated us all to reach the norm.

So things went on for years to come: two huge lakes transformed into parks, followed by the excavation of another lake. Whether one was a doctor, an engineer, a manual laborer, or a student, trying to get out of what had begun, more and more, to resemble forced labor was out of the question. Our days were regimented like in the army. I took my place in line in front of the Ministry at six in the morning, after having left my children with my neighbors. We worked from seven o'clock until eleven. The same invariable lunch was provided for us on site: rice with sesame, a few pieces of meat or fish, and tea to wash it all down. Afterwards, we were allowed a half-hour to nap, lying down wherever we could find a bit of ground to sprawl out on. Then back to work until five o'clock, and return home.

At that point, however, we were far from having completed the Three Togethers. After our work in the city, the country version of the motto meant working with the villagers, eating with them and also sleeping in the same house. So, once again, I left my children with friends and went to harvest the crops in a village in Tonkin. This was a first for me, but most of my group had never even lived in the country.

When I first penetrated into the house that I was assigned to, I had the impression that I was walking into a tunnel. It was dark, stuffy and lit with only one single oil lamp. The rooms were small enough, but the ones for women were minuscule, with a narrow skylight and mats on the floor.

Our arrival was a blessing for the peasants because we served as cheap labor. They also took advantage of our two hundred-gram-a-day rice rations, which we gave them so that they would have enough to feed us.

Wake-up call was at four o'clock. After a bowl of rice, we took off with the peasants for the fields. As soon as the sun began to rise, the temperature quickly reached ninety-five to ninety-nine degrees, sending a kind of steam off the surface of the water in the rice paddies, making the work even more difficult. Although the peasants tried hard to show me how to cut the rice, I continued to be particularly awkward at the job.

Each one of us was to harvest one thousand square feet in a morning's work. I noticed that many of my comrades moved very quickly. At my rhythm, though, I would have needed three days to accomplish my task. I treaded water with my badly cut straw while my astonished hostess observed me. "You have never done such work?" No, I have never done such work, but if she had any clothes that needed adjustments, she could give them to me. Furthermore, I proposed sewing pants and shirts for her whole family. So, between the two of us, it wasn't hard to finish off my parcel. But after all that, we still had to put the harvest onto a small boat and drag it along to the house. Back at the house, I was covered with leeches and began better to understand the work the peasants endured. We stopped at five o'clock and then each one of us went fishing in the swamps. Here again, I wasn't very gifted for that sort of activity, so I took over the preparation of the fish, the crayfish and even the snails that the others brought in from the catch. Once cleaned, the peasant would throw the lot into an earthen pot, to which she added a little salt, and bury the receptacle in wood shavings or straw, which would then cook over a slow fire. Three hours later, the result was a kind of caramel-coated fish, which was eaten with rice. It was so delicious that the taste is still on my tongue. After dinner, despite the fatigue, we had to conjure up enough energy to wash ourselves in the swamp. Indeed, that cesspool had many functions—it was where we washed out our mats, our clothes, and the rice, not forgetting that the water buffalo also bathed there. The first day I couldn't get myself to wade in. The second day, with the accumulation of grit, my skin started to itch, so on the third day I dove in like the others. It is easy to understand why there was so much dysentery and conjunctivitis in the country.

The evenings, however, were a sigh of relief. We dined by moonlight on a huge mat that was spread out in the courtyard. Some families brought out their oil lamps in order to see better, but most preferred to economize on the fuel.

After a few days, the villagers started to talk about their lives, wondering how they could better their situation. Through the discussions, we realized even more just how our presence was of utmost importance to them and, in particular, the addition of our rice rations to their allotment. The period that preceded the harvest was extremely critical for them because "the young rice had not yet arrived and there was none left of the previous crop." Although it didn't have the same nutritive value, we compensated by giving extra portions of dried manioc to the children when there was a lack of rice.

Our relationship with the peasants quickly progressed to the point that it became almost friendly. But all this didn't prevent me from missing my own children. Despite the reassurance I had in knowing that they were well looked after, there was no means of communication possible—whether by mail or by phone. My heart sank every time I saw a mother stretch out her arms to her baby. I counted the days.

Although we tried to give lessons to the peasants, they were much too tired after a day's work and fell asleep during the classes. Therefore, we had to satisfy ourselves by simply teaching the children to sing. Ho Chi Minh had said that three wars had to be won: the war against famine, the war against invasion, and the war against illiteracy. Between 1954 and 1955, there was an important movement against the third. In order to remedy it in the country, certain humiliating methods were developed. For example, at the entrance of a market, poles were erected with a very low cross bar. Whenever a peasant woman turned up, she was given a few lines to read. If she couldn't, she was to crawl, like a dog, under the bar to get into the market place.

Upon my return to Hanoi, I was very quickly confronted with the problems of every day life. It was even more difficult for me to stand the propaganda that kept harping our ears, particularly when at the office. The radio never stopped repeating: "The peasants are content. The rice has arrived." The citizenry had no idea of the superhuman labor behind the production of rice and to what extent such a slogan was totally indecent. But their own situation was hardly more enviable. They were rationed to twelve kilograms of rice per month per family and half a liter of a briny sauce, which had an unpleasant taste and was an awful substitute for *nuoc mam*. We were also allotted a kilogram of salt-water fish, brought into the city from Haiphong in one frozen block, and then hacked into pieces by the fishmonger—and in which there were remains without heads and heads without bodies. But who was to be choosy? It was better than nothing. Finally, there were the two hundred grams of meat and two pieces of soy cheese. Try and figure out how to make that last for an entire month, particularly when there was no way to refrigerate the supplies! The only solution was not to buy everything at the same time. If the meat merchant was nice enough, she gave you two hundred grams covered with fat and a small chop, as well. Once home, we would strip the fat away and melt it for later use. The rest of the meat was chopped and then sautéed over the fire with salt and citronnella so that it could be preserved for two weeks. We bought our vegetables fresh every day for the soup, which was tasteful enough because of the addition of a spoonful of that very salty meat. Two weeks later, when we were out of meat, I would buy the kilogram of fish. I would melt the ice block in water and pick out the heads, which I then chopped into the smallest bits possible with a knife, simply because I didn't have a grinder. Then I would shape out fish paddies to be fried. With the different types of flesh, I cooked a very salty, caramel dish, which could also be eaten for a number of days. Finally, if I still had enough fat, I would take care of the soybean cheese, which I fried to obtain food that would not turn bad for a few days. By then, the month was soon over.

There was often a line up to get the rice. Most of the times, we were still given rice that had been produced during the war and stocked in the depots. My brother-in-law from Tuyen Quang, who had just been appointed Vice Minister of Agriculture and Rice Supplies, decided that people would waste less time if basic foodstuffs, like rice, were distributed directly in their buildings. From ten on, women came to sell it directly at our doorstep, along with sweet potatoes, manioc, and special, bitter-tasting, yellow noodles that were imported from other socialist countries.

Even if we were attending an important meeting on the subject of major domestic projects, whenever there was a delivery of rice or noodles in our building—as soon as someone cried out: "myve, myve," that is, "the noodles have arrived"—we all jumped up from the table and ran in the direction of the supplies. Once in front of the merchant, depending on her mood or how you spoke to her, you were given either good, white noodles, or ones that had gone sour. The children remained outside in order to sweep up any bits that might have fallen to the ground.

Life at work in the different organizations took on a particular nature because of all these problems of supplies. When we arrived at the office at eight o'clock in the morning, we would form groups to read and comment on the Party newspaper, *Nan Zan* or *The People*. But most of the workers like myself did not listen. Rather, our thoughts were oriented towards how we were going to obtain meat and vegetables. The only advantage in these readings was to learn in advance what the Party had in store for us.

At exactly ten thirty, we deserted the office to go and buy vegetables. If we had waited any longer, there would have been nothing left. Following the market, we all went home to prepare the noon meal for our families. Then back to work until five o'clock, after which I would pick up my children, respectively, at the day care center and at kindergarten, clean them up, and prepare the evening meal as early as possible in order to save on electricity. They were in bed by eight thirty and I was able to turn my attention to doing the translations.

During the period when we were supposed to be learning the value of manual labor, the movement for the nationalization of private properties took force. One morning, the people who were targeted received a letter inviting them to present themselves to the neighborhood committee. There, they were met by workers, hand-laborers, and bicycle repairmen who were often illiterate, and were very worked up over the decision. They were told that their property was to be nationalized: "You have already well taken advantage of the situation; it is time the rest of the population can do as much. It is we who have participated in the Resistance and not you. So, do you see our point?" Those who opposed it had no other choice than to leave for South Vietnam, in accord with the famous three-hundred-day truce.

Three quarters of the entire population of Hanoi preferred to give up everything and leave. Overnight, the shops, factories, and printing presses were run by executives who did not have the least experience, but who were considered worthy of trust only because of their belonging to the proletariat. Madame Tung Hien was confined to only one room in her house, the others given over to the neighborhood poor. It is easy to imagine how trying it must have been for her to see her beautiful home thus transformed into a hovel. As far as her shop was concerned, once she had taken inventory, she was retrograded to a simple employee under the direction of civil servants working for government trade services. I tried to pass by the shop as often as possible. I would ask the price of fabric as if I had the intention of purchasing it so that I could furtively take a hold of her hand and show that my thoughts went out to her. Dressed in a simple shirt and pale pants, and pale, herself, she had lost weight and was no longer the woman I had had the pleasure of knowing.

It was during that same period that my mother-in-law, my husband's mother, took advantage of the "three hundred days" in her own way by coming to see us in Hanoi. Considering her aristocratic background, it was all the more incredible that Dang Thi Ngoc Do had obtained the right from authorities to travel by train and see her family again. One morning my niece, who was now seven years old, brought me a brief letter from her mother: "Elder sister, our mother is arriving tomorrow. You must prepare your house in the eventuality of a visit from her." How on earth could I be in a suitable position to receive my husband's mother—someone whom I had never even met? Too bad, but I was not going to change my ways. Besides, according to tradition, she should have warned her elder son before her daughter.

Upon her arrival in Hanoi, my mother-in-law went to stay in her son-in-law and daughter's big house, which was not far from mine. One evening, a woman in a silk velvet *ao dai* and gold earrings showed up at my door. She came in like a queen, escorted by my sister-in-law, and eyed the room with contempt: "Oh, my, what a pig sty! Why don't you live in a house like my daughter? Where is your husband? Why aren't you living with him?" I did not even have a second to protest when my sister-in-law gave me orders: " You must go get your husband." Hoang was then at the military school in Son Tay, forty kilometers from Hanoi, where he was teaching. But I had no choice, and at daybreak the following day, after having left my children with the neighbor, I set out on my bicycle for Son Tay. There, I still had to wait until evening for my husband to return from maneuvers. "Your mother has arrived and you must come home." Perhaps it was because of his mother's feudal ancestry, but the orders needed from his superior could not be obtained in less than forty-eight hours. When he arrived in Hanoi two days later, I saw my husband distant and awkward in the presence of his mother. I couldn't understand his attitude. Had I been reunited with mine, I would have taken her in my arms, overcome with joy. Was this still another case of class conflict? After ten years of separation, he hardly dared speak to the aristocratically mannered stranger his mother had become to him. That visit was another occasion for me to prove to my sister-in-law that I was no longer the same submissive woman. She had decided that I should leave my children every evening in order to come over to her house to take care of her mother and give her massages. As the daughter-in-law, such a task apparently befell me. I staunchly protested I had no one to look after my children and, strangely enough, she didn't pursue the matter. Several days later, there was a new visit from my mother-in-law: "I have decided to take my grand-son to live with me in Hue," she blurted out. "He will have a more decent life there." I jumped at her: "You haven't the right to do that!" "Why not?" "You can do anything you like with your daughter's children, but certainly not with mine!"

"You are a communist!" she exclaimed.

"No, I'm not a communist, and in any case that has nothing to do with my son."

On that note she left, looking totally offended. Hence, I never had to bother myself with her. Sunday, we went to eat in a restaurant. My mother-in-law had invited us to lunch in a luxurious French establishment near the *Petit Lac*, of the kind that it was still possible to find just after the victory, during the period that had come to be known as "the time of the *petite bourgeoisie*." For the occasion, I donned a violet shirt-dress, which had been bought overseas by a friend of the Writer's Union. After having worn pants for so many years, wearing a skirt felt very funny. My children were very handsome in clothes that had been kindly tailored by Madame Hien. They gaped, eyes wide open, at the table covered with food. In particular, at Chinese dishes that they had never seen, like Peking pigeon or sautéed noodles with seafood. After the meal, we went to a portrait studio to immortalize the meeting. Then my husband let me know that it was time for me and the children to go home because he had to discuss their future with his mother and his sister in her home. He remained silent when he came home a little later in the afternoon. Realizing that she would not get what she wanted, my mother-in-law attempted to give me some money and two gold bands to help feed my children. But the humiliation of such a furtive gesture, seeing that it was made behind my sister-in-law's back, made it impossible for me to accept. As soon as I had calmed down, my husband proposed inviting his mother to have dinner at our flat a few days later.

To honor her presence, I went to the market to trade my violet dress for some fish and shallots. On the other hand, it was out of the question that the whole family be received in our one hundred and forty square foot room, furnished with one table and wooden crates for makeshift stools. My mother-in-law seemed displeased when she arrived. My husband said nothing. I felt him torn between his duty as a son and that of a husband and father. "Why haven't the others come?" my mother-in-law asked me. "You were invited to their house, weren't you?" She picked up the bowl that her son had filled as if she were saying: I'm going to eat only because I pity you. After which, she got up and left, followed at close heels by her son. Rid of her presence, my children made a dash for the leftover food, thrilled at that sudden godsend. I never set eyes on my mother-in-law again. I learned later that the Ministry of Home Affairs had invited her to visit North Vietnam by train, escorted by two others. Then she came back to Hanoi before definitively returning to Hue. During her stay, I could never manage to obtain news of my kin in Hue. My husband's family did not keep up a relationship with my father who was a high-ranking civil servant, but much too "European" for their taste.

The "three hundred days," during which the border between North and South Vietnam remained open, marked an exceptional period. Among all my comrades from the Resistance, very few chose to leave. Those who did left discretely, so that the police would not notice. There were poignant farewell evenings with distribution of souvenirs. The majority of those who left were Catholics, who exiled *en masse*, abandoning all their possessions after selling what they could. It looked as if it were a grand flea market. There were piles of precious objects in front of some houses, which was, indeed, a sad sight. As we had no money to buy anything, we could merely look at all those beautiful things. Between Hanoi and Haiphong, the port of departure for those who were exiling, there was a continual caravan of overloaded cars and rickshaws. The roadsides were strewn with objects of all sorts, left behind because they were too heavy or cumbersome.

In the city, as soon as houses were abandoned, they were taken over by the government. In theory, two years after reunification, the owners should have been able to return to their homes. In fact, they were quickly divided among several families, with the high-ranking civil servants reserving the more attractive ones for themselves.

At the end of the "three hundred days," it was still possible to buy post cards with twenty or so lines to send to one's family in the South. But most people preferred not to write in order to avoid the risk of being taken for spies. These cards were quickly suppressed, however, and very soon the total cut-off between North and South had come about. As a result I had to wait until after 1958 to obtain news of my family in the South. My sister-in-law, My Dung, another of my husband's sisters, had married a Frenchman who was an advisor to King Sihanouk of Cambodia. Letters could thus be relayed from Saigon to Phnom-Penh and from Phnom-Penh to Hanoi. But in a ten-year period, that only happened two or three times at most. My brother-in-law had to be content with writing: "I have news." It was of utmost importance that no one know that I had been keeping alive an ongoing correspondence with my family in Saigon. Had the Americans known that my parents had a daughter in the North, they would have encountered enormous problems. Conversely, had one learned that I had family in South Vietnam the situation might have been extremely dangerous for me.

The agrarian reform

The new movement of land reform, whose declared aim was to return the soil to the peasants, began in 1955.

After having nationalized the cities, the next step was directed towards the property owners. Because I belonged to the "undesirable class," in other words, the undesirable intellectuals, I was assigned to the first teams designated to participate in the reform. I was transferred to a village one hundred and twenty kilometers away from Hanoi with five physicians, two of whom had lived, like me, in the jungle; the other three were military doctors during the French occupation. Each one of us left separately—I can't remember any longer if we walked or rode bicycles—and we were to meet up at the village. My first impression of the area upon arrival was that it was dead. There was neither a dog barking, nor a rooster crowing, and the villagers dared not even look at us. We were to assemble in a pagoda and, by nightfall, everyone had turned up.

The head of the group was an ophthalmologist, one of the two doctors who had belonged to the Resistance. After spending the night in the pagoda, we presented ourselves to the *doi*[1]—the person who was in charge of enforcing the land reform. What was going to happen? We didn't even dare discuss it amongst ourselves any more. In a peasant's house, a stately woman lay imposingly on a magnificent teakwood bed that had probably come from a rich family. She was difficult to understand because she spoke with an accent that was typical of the Vietnamese minority.

When she smiled, one could see her gold teeth. "I am from Cao Bang, and belong to the Tay ethnic minority," she explained. "I have been designated as group leader to apply the land reform here. In every village," she continued, "there are land owners who have been exploiting the peasants for much too long. That situation can no longer endure." Her mission was to find three or four of them in the village, which was not an easy task for a stranger to the area. But the technique was simple: single out the most destitute houses; find the poorest peasants —those who were called "the roots"—and you could count on them to tell you who the rich ones were, unless, as in a very poor village such as that one, there weren't any. It was apparent that our *doi* was afraid of not being able to accomplish her task. "You people, you are intellectuals," she said to us, "you have benefited from good living in the past, whereas us, we have always been exploited. We are going to make you understand what land reform really is and why it is necessary to wipe out all landowners without the slightest pity." Little by little she began to yell a sermon at us as if we were her servants. Terrified, we huddled together into a corner

---

[1] The word means "group or team" in Vietnamese. During land reform, the entire name was *doi cai cach ruong dat* or "group of officials in charge of agrarian reform." But in the villages, the peasants were so terrified by their presence that they did not dare pronounce the entire title and opted for the simpler one: "Ladies and gentlemen of the *Doi*."

of the room, convinced that one single word of protest would suffice to have us thrown in prison, or even executed.

At the end of that harangue, we were taken to one of the more shabby houses in the village, inhabited by a drunken peasant, and in an unspeakably filthy state. After having made enough room to sleep in the hovel, we turned our attention to how we were going to eat. But as the peasant had nothing at all we didn't, either. One of us made a sacrifice to go and see the *doi*, who consented to giving us two hundred grams of rice per person. The peasant watched us as we cooked our feast. With a full bowl, himself, he sat down with us and we all ate together in silence.

At daybreak on the second day, the *doi* endeavored to take the roll call. There were twenty-two of us who were divided into several groups. According to the instructions, each group was to find a rich family. As luck had it, our drunkard was quite incapable of indicating anybody at all. The other groups, however, had one house or another pointed out to them, and then all they had to do was write up a report: "We have found the house of Mr. X, who has so-and so many acres of land. There is equally that of Mr. Y and of Mr. Z," after which the head of the group would account for it to his superior. It was the land reform council in the district that judged whether or not to attack such or such property owner. Meanwhile, we eventually began to understand what was really brewing.

The night of the third day, I was unable to sleep. Come morning, I was in a terrible physical and mental state. On the one hand, there was the squalor and, on the other, things had reached the limit of my sense of morality—I was ashamed at having to back such an absurd situation, and well aware that the worst was yet to come. As soon as the sun was up, the population of the village was assembled in the pagoda's central courtyard. The *doi* stood erect with us at her side. The peasants all sat down on the edges of the courtyard. Suddenly, two very young boys with rifles appeared, holding the end of a rope, which tied the two supposed property owners' hands. Immediately, the *doi* cried out "Down with the exploiters!" and the peasants echoed "Down with them! Down with them!" She made a gesture for us to cry out as well, for we were being watched. Each one cried out louder, "Down! Down!" The two unfortunate ones, whose families had come with them, had to turn and face the crowd. They were middle-aged men who, neither in their way of being, nor in their clothes, looked any different from the other villagers. I witnessed that kind of trial several times and I shall never forget the terrified expressions on the faces of the accused. "You!" the *doi* cried out at one of them, tell us about all the horrible things you did during the period that you were a land owner!" "But I am not a land owner," the man protested. "Down with you! Down with you!" the woman yelled back with even fiercer conviction, accompanied by the crowd. "He resists, he is reactionary, he doesn't want to tell the truth about how he exploited the people. Because it is so, he is going to be tied up outside in the heat of the day."

At that moment, the pressure mounted to the point of being unbearable. The poor man began to utter whatever came into his head. "Yes, I have led a comfortable life. I hired laborers and exploited them by paying badly." And, lo and behold, a young woman rose from among the peasants: "Do you remember me? One day, you came home and raped me." The man didn't have a second to protest before the yelling started all over again: "Reactionary! Reactionary!" He ended up in tears and confessed: "It is true, I raped her." Immediately, another young girl stood up: "You! You raped me, too!" I couldn't take it any longer and I closed my eyes. "Look!"

yelled the woman who hadn't stopped eyeing us to catch the least reaction. The peasants looked hard at our faces with great hostility. They hated us almost as much as the others because we were the intellectuals. By making us participate in the land reform, the real aim was to reform us, too. The woman went on: "Thus, we have in front of us, Mr. X who has raped twelve women." She was joined by another peasant who was weeping: "Do you remember the day that you pretended that I hadn't harvested enough rice? You made me lie down on the floor and you put a stick on my neck so that I couldn't breathe. You remember that, don't you?" The accused answered that he couldn't really recall. "Ah, then, that's what it is: you just don't remember. That's too easy. Down with you! Down with you!" At this point the other man got his memory back. It was true, he had done it, he said. The two unfortunate men ended up recognizing all the wrongdoings that the peasants held against them.

By evening, the emotions of the crowd had reached their peak. A moment arrived when the woman asked for silence: "Death sentence," she decreed and the people began to yell at the top of their voices: "Bravo! Bravo!"

That horrible show lasted the whole day long. Not one person even thought of leaving the scene, which revealed just how deeply rooted their hatred was. I thought of all those secret organizations that had worked day and night during the war in these very same zones so that the people would rise up against the French, and without which there would never have been such a huge mobilization at the front. Since the start of land reform, these very organizations had been considered reactionary and systematically dismantled. Some members of the communist party, who had formerly belonged to these organizations, were even accused of hiding reactionary beliefs behind the communist label.

That night, not one of us was able to sleep, but we did not dare utter a single word for fear of being accused by our host of some conspiracy. The next day, in front of the entire population, the young boys executed the two men.

Some time later, in another village that was also placed under the leadership of a woman, we had to be present at the execution of a man whose mistake had been trying to find out about certain goings on in his village. He was an alleged landowner who had sought refuge in Hanoi and had returned to check on his property. But, as truth has it, as far back as the French rule, he had been the owner of five taxis that shuttled between Bac Ninh and Hanoi. He was well off, but that was all, hardly a landowner. To hear the crowd, not only was he rich but he had also raped who knows how many women: "Reactionary! Reactionary!" the people yelled. There was no way to escape the sentence. At the moment of the execution, the young boys of the firing squad wanted to blindfold him. But he refused: "No, I want to look at this slaughter up to the end. I know that you will regret it one day." Then, adding at the last second: "It's shameful. Down with communism." The adolescents fired quite awkwardly and only succeeded in wounding him: "Bastards, bastards, you don't even know how to kill! You have to aim here!" He placed his hand on his heart and the crowd calmed down into a strange and sudden silence. The boys fired again, but the man was still alive with his blood spurting everywhere. His nails scraped the soil and I looked away. Someone cried out: "Let this rotten dog die!" and the crowd waited for him to die as if it were a show. For a long time afterwards, I kept dreaming of that man suffering a long agony of death.

What had all those long years in the Resistance been sacrificed for—our years of deprivation—for that? What had happened to our lofty ideals?

The next morning at eight o'clock, we were to return to the temple for the burial. Family members were ordered to bring a coffin, and old men had to go fetch the body from where the execution had taken place. They placed him in the coffin with a piece of cloth over his face in order to cover up his devastating smirk. Once closed, they took turns carrying it, changing shoulders when they were completely exhausted. We followed behind them and for a moment, I could hear one of them say a prayer for the soul of the deceased to rest in peace. Then, one of the boys with rifles cried out: "Comrade, that man there just said a prayer. He said 'Down with the government!'" "Did you say something?" the *doi* asked the unfortunate man. "No, comrade, I was praying for his soul ..." "You still have pity for him?" The procession was called to a halt. The woman began to bark like a mad dog: "You have pity for him! Pity for him!" The old man prostrated himself before her: "Pardon me. We always say a prayer when we carry the dead." "The next time you do so, I'll cut your tongue off." The procession was then allowed to continue, but this time in silence. Having arrived at the site of the burial, a field that had belonged to the deceased, the old men had to dig out the grave using pickaxes. The soil kept falling back in and they could not even manage to get the coffin completely covered.

Every day in Hanoi, the loud speakers would announce the progress of the land reform. Very soon, nobody could escape it any longer. My brother-in-law was Vice-Minister and originally, like Ho Chi Minh, from Nghe An. It was a very patriotic region where the reform was applied with even more vigor than anywhere else. His belonging to the government did not prevent his parents from being sentenced to death. As for my friend Nam's father, under the accusation of being a landowner and having a more attractive house than the others in his village with several acres of land as well, he was forced to cede his house and all his belongings to the peasants. Moreover, as if that weren't enough, he was left to starve to death, locked up in a shack. At that moment, Nam had been in Hanoi, but he wouldn't have been able to intervene without being killed as well. Viet's father, who had owned five hundred acres of rice paddies, was condemned to death. It is thought that he was shot, unless he, too, was left to starve to death. Denunciations multiplied in the villages. Every day we learned of new executions. We felt as though we were witnessing an enterprise of total destruction. Even the former patriots of the Resistance, those who had been leading the country, were considered reactionaries. A new team had taken power: ignorant people who were ready to execute orders that came from out of the blue.

This madness lasted for two years, until the parents of one of the present high officials of the National Assembly were sentenced to death. At that moment, the movement had gone so out of control that the Central Committee finally got wind of it. I could not believe that they had not had knowledge of it before. In any case, nobody had wanted to pay any attention to it previously. But the losses were already irreparable. The morale of the population was at its nadir.

Since the nationalizations, the standard of living had been plummeting. The nicest shops closed and in those that were then managed by the State the quality of the products became appalling. The supply service even prohibited restaurants from making real *pho*[2] under the pretext that it wasted rice.

The soup that was presented to replace it was made of rotten rice noodles, a little bit of tough meat, and a tasteless

---

[2] Pho (pronounced "fhuh"), a beef or chicken soup made with noodles, was popular in Hanoi. It was a meal in itself, and was eaten in the street at any time of day. It still is. (See *The New York Times*, August 13, 2003, p. F1.)

broth. Even so, it was necessary to line up in order to get any. Oftentimes, the woman who served you would just dump the soup ladle into your bowl and shower your clothes. To avoid people stealing spoons, someone even came up with the idea of piercing a hole in the middle of them: the soup had to be gulped down very quickly for, if not, it all dribbled out before it got into your mouth. The chopsticks were never washed and tables were never cleaned. From there on in, to designate something that was dirty, one would say "It's disgusting, like the State *pho,*" although, to tell the truth, we considered ourselves already fortunate enough to have the means to buy any. As for the small street peddlers, they no longer had the right to sell *pho,* but instead, a vile soup in which there were noodles made of potato flour. Fortunately, the people of Hanoi were too bent on trade to endure this for long.

Little by little, the rules were overlooked. To deceive controllers, the street merchants placed a small basket of those shriveled up noodles on display. But the *pho*, the real stuff, was underneath. It was almost as good as it had used to be and hardly more expensive than the substitute. We all passed on our lists of secret addresses. "I would like a bowl of soup with potato flour noodles," we would say out loud, just in case any State officials were hanging around. The merchant would understand immediately. But then the *pho* had to be downed very quickly to keep the unfortunate man or woman from having his or her equipment seized, as well as a fine to pay. The customer, on the contrary, didn't have much to fear and, if he left, always had time enough to finish off the bowl.

The streets were lined with Volgas, the cars used by the important members of the Party, as well as Russian, Chinese, or Romanian Jeeps, which had been sent by our fraternal countries. The presence of bicycles was still rare. Military colors dominated clothing: officials wore black pants and white jackets, soldiers their khaki fatigues, and most civilians dressed in black pants and brown shirts. Foreigners were scarce—only a few Russians or Chinese—but talking with them was prohibited under law.

On the local level, everything had to be cleared by the administrative committee that, by then, had become all-powerful. For whatever needed to be sold, one had to go to the committee and explain the reasons for selling this or that thing. It was the committee's role to certify that one actually did live in the neighborhood and that one was really owner of the object. If the terms were not met, no transaction was possible. Marriages and deaths were also under the committee's auspices, as were authorizations to leave Hanoi, even if only for a day. Each time, it was a rather uncomfortable experience, for these new lords dealt with the people like the old nobility had treated their subjects. They couldn't care less if we had participated in the Resistance. Having been a Resistance fighter was now only really useful when time came to enroll one's child in a school and a *curriculum vitae* had to be drawn up. The children of the rich bourgeoisie were not allowed to go to college, not even to the people's college that was established after the war. As far as the children of the civil servants who had first worked for the French and then for the Vietnamese were concerned, they were not even given the right to complete high school by taking the *baccalaureate* exams. Like the children of the bourgeoisie, they were entitled to be enrolled only in people's schools where they were limited to technical studies. Neither French nor English was taught any longer. Russian was, and Chinese, too, which few students opted to take. My own son took Chinese as his first foreign language and Russian as his second. But all the young students, particularly the children of high-level civil servants whose parents wanted to see them sent to Russia, took Russian at evening courses.

Little by little a new class was seen to emerge—that of the regime's privileged rulers. More than from the difficulties of daily living, it was from this new order that people like myself suffered the most. The largest villas, the most beautiful homes were set aside for members of the Party. The higher one ascended in the hierarchy, the better one was housed. Those gentlemen had official cars, and their chauffeurs drove their children to school. It was true that their salaries were quite low, but, on the other hand, they had so many privileges—like obtaining their supplies in special shops—that money wasn't even an issue. One evening, I received an invitation for dinner from a high official who was in charge of surveying the work of the writers and intelligentsia. The table was splendidly set, the meat tender and the rice delicately flavored. He felt obligated to make a point: "Everything that you have eaten did not cost more than two hundred *dong*." On the black market—because being able to find such good quality food anywhere else would have been out of the question—it would have cost at least two thousand *dong*.

In cities, the loud speakers hooked up to the national radio center set our daily pace. The first yelling of the day erupted at five in the morning for gymnastics. To the sound of the radio, people assembled and sung while doing their movements. That lasted for half an hour, after which the national anthem was played. My elder son would get dressed in blue pants and a white shirt that I had tailored for him, but he walked barefoot, like most of the other children. At seven-thirty, after having left Phuong with my neighbor, I would accompany him to his school, six hundred meters from the house, before going to work. Then I would fetch him at eleven for lunch, return him at two, and pick him up again at five.

The schoolteacher taught him the alphabet and how to read. As there was not enough paper, the children first wrote in their notebook in pencil. When the notebook was all filled in, it was turned over and this time violet ink was used to make it easier to read. When finished, if the pages were not too pierced with holes, it was turned over yet again and this time red ink was used. As there was an insufficiency of books as well, parents would copy them by hand. They did not have to be reminded of the importance of schooling.

On Sundays, the children were in charge of cleaning the streets. They had to sweep and pick up papers and empty bottles. Each school child was to collect one kilogram of rubbish and shame on the one who did not fill the quota.

My sons were the ones who suffered most from our living conditions. It was always dark, hot, and humid inside our lodging and, when it rained, water seeped in everywhere. The state refused to make repairs so all we could do was suffer in silence. I had succeeded in finding some tarpaper and I climbed up on the roof to try and tie it in place with bamboo string anyway I could. There was always a long line in the middle of the courtyard to use the only tap of drinking water. The toilets were public, too, and one had to wait there, as well, just like in the shops. In the mornings, I couldn't get used to seeing all those people, half-asleep, shivering from the cold.

Just across from the front of the house, there was a shed with three loud speakers, one of which was directed straight at my flat. The shrieking began at five o'clock and I soon found the noise intolerable. One morning, by using a pole, I succeeded in disconnecting the wire from the loud speaker. Silence returned. A woman approached me to ask who the reactionary was who had dared stop the voice of the Party. Fortunately, nobody had seen me and everyone else was happy to be able to take advantage of the quiet. But when I returned from work in the evening three days later, the loud speaker was discharging its screams all over again—someone had come to repair it.

At the end of 1956, the communist party had the courage to recognize its errors. It undertook work entitled "rectification of the torts" to redress the exaggerations of the agrarian reform. I was to return to Bac Ninh with the same group in order to repair the horrible misdoings that had been committed the year before.

One could easily imagine the hatred that the peasants had for us when we returned to the village. "What have you come back for? Don't you think enough blood has been spilled?" But this time, the *doi* was a poised and reasonable elementary school teacher from Bac Ninh. The People's Committee had been newly elected and was made up of honest and reputable members.

As before, the *doi* called the people to a huge meeting. The feudal class was still condemned and the rice paddies were shared among the peasants, just as were the big houses that had been divided up into lodgings for the poor families. But almost all the citizens that had mistakenly been accused of being "property owners" were rehabilitated. Those unfortunate ones who had been "deprived of class" had now the right to return and live in a part of their own homes and to recuperate a few parcels of their rice paddies. Still more important, though, they were allowed to have the endorsement "middle class peasant" figure on their *curriculum vitae,* which would give their children better prospects for the future. All these changes, however, didn't take place without certain difficulties. Most of the living quarters that were occupied by several families had been completely ransacked and it was quite a task to find a room in which the former owner could settle. Henceforth, and as final settlement, a small patch of three hundred square meters was returned to former property owners. The horrible gold-toothed creature that had directed the land reform had disappeared, as had her bloodthirsty acolytes. But the tombs of those who had been unjustly executed remained, witnesses to that shameful episode of our history. The times when everyone in Vietnamese villages had lived together in harmony were over. At present, the people were divided and hated each other. I would return from those country missions totally drained. My children, alone, gave me courage to go on.

Almost immediately afterwards, a great cleansing movement began within the ranks of the officers. First there had been the period of nationalization, then the land reform, and now it was the army that was targeted. This latter was all the more difficult to accept because it was those same officers who had allowed us to win the war. My husband, as well as his friends, Viet and Du Duc, could not escape the actions. Zu Duc, whose parents were laborers, was very quickly spared. My husband, however, without any warning, was summoned to headquarters: "You have done your work as a patriot in the army," someone declared, "and now you are to return to civilian life." For the good of the people, all the officers who had feudal origins were forced to leave the army.

Viet accepted the news better than my husband did, although he had just lost his father in the land reform. It was as though he were expecting it. He was assigned to the Ministry of Marine Products where he would soon make a name for himself by installing refrigeration units along the Vietnamese coasts.

When Hoang returned home from his visit to headquarters, he said nothing. He looked like a sleepwalker. At noon, he refused to eat and went to bed. When I came home in the evening he was still lying down on the bed, now in the dark. The children were worried and it was only later on, in the evening, when I insisted on knowing the reason for his mental state, that he finally confessed: "I have been demobilized and transferred to the *Institut polytechnique* in Hanoi." I felt relieved. After so many years, we were finally going to be able to live together. "It's good news, isn't it?" "Why good? I can't accept a return to civilian life. In the military, everything is so easy. I felt really good with my comrades." Seated on the edge of the bed, I looked at him without saying anything. I, too, had suffered from the return to civilian life and from the meanness of people. With time, I had found a way of adapting to it. He had only to do the same, which was exactly what happened. At the *Institut polytechnique* he succeeded in finding his own place, making friends with other professors, writing books and receiving rewards. But the early period, just after having left the army, was a terrible one for him. He was no longer the same man. I was sure that he had more than once thought of committing suicide, although he never actually told me anything about it.

In any case, there was no purpose in lamenting, for he was not the only one in that situation. Therefore, we avoided going on about the past and our principal subject of conversation was about how we were going to survive during that period. Lacking everything, our major problem, principally, was finding a way to feed the children. Try as they might to harp on about the ills of imperialism as the source of all our ills, the war was over; and yet we still had to keep our belts tight: there remained the South to liberate.

At the end of 1956, realizing that I had once worked in a hospital, the Ministry of Finance offered me a chance to go back to my studies. There was a special school for officials who had already studied medicine during the war years. But first I had to earn my baccalaureate in Vietnamese, for which I had to take evening courses held in schools after classes were out. In that way, the people who had returned from the front could make up for lost time. So, like a schoolgirl all over again, I started studying mathematics, history, and geography. What was most difficult for me was to translate into Vietnamese what I had learned in French. In the end, I passed my baccalaureate without too much hassle, but it was when I was preparing for the competitive entrance exams to medical school that I discovered I was pregnant again. With three children, continuing my studies was out of the question. After a long discussion with my husband, we decided to send our eldest son, now age eight, to the school for South Vietnamese children in Chong My, forty or so kilometers north of Hanoi. The government had set up that particular boarding school so that the officials who were working secretly in South Vietnam could make sure their children would be sheltered in the North. Since my husband and I were originally from the South, we obtained the privilege of being able to send our son there. When we announced to him that he was going to leave home, I was not sure that he really understood what that meant. "Very well, I will go," he agreed immediately and it brought tears to my eyes.

Very early in the morning of the first day of classes, we set out together on our bicycles. Upon arrival, the director showed us the huts, which served as classrooms, and the dormitories with their bamboo beds. Very quickly, the other children came over to greet my son. There were about fifty of them, all dressed in blue pants and white shirts and obviously very close to one another. In the beginning, his absence was very hard for me to bear, but going to visit him once a month, I realized just how good it was for him to be there. He was working hard at his studies, was learning to play the violin, and seemed perfectly happy.

My third son was born at military hospital number 108 under conditions that were totally modern compared to my previous deliveries. I would have preferred a girl, but seeing that big baby, weighing in at 4.8 kilograms, I was greatly moved. We called him Phong, meaning "the Wind." I left the Ministry of Finance immediately afterwards and because of my seniority they did not take my room from me. I could at long last begin my studies at medical school.

There was a day care center there, which made my life much easier, and with a grant and free meals I could even keep all the ration tickets for my children. I was twenty-eight years old and it had been a long time since I had experienced such a worry-free life. We had excellent professors who were former teachers from the *Institut de médecine français* and a Russian professor, Doctor Mazorine, who had a very good reputation in the Soviet Union and whose classes were translated into Vietnamese. I had been hoping to learn Russian well enough in order to read Tolstoy and Dostoyevski in the original texts, but without much success due to my lack of time. I finished my studies in 1961 with a *brevet rouge* (red diploma), which meant that I had obtained excellent marks.

From then on I was in charge of consultations that were under the auspices of the Ministry of Health and I was also continuing my translation work for the Ministry of Foreign Affairs.

The Ba Dinh neighborhood where the health clinic was situated was very diverse. It was where the ambassadors lived, but also workers, laborers, and very poor rickshaw drivers. My consultation room was set up in a former Carmelite Convent, one that reminded me of the *Couvent des Oiseaux*. The French nuns had left after 1954. When I arrived, the huge garden was still full of white rose bushes in bloom with magnificent flowers. Somewhat later, it would be transformed into a manioc field. What is there to say?

There were three doctors and seven nurses for the five examination rooms at the clinic. Visits began at seven o'clock in the morning, but there was already a line-up by five. One ill child meant the father, the mother, the uncle, the aunt, and the grandmother—at least five people to accompany it, and whatever food that was needed, all of which explained the hundreds of people who were waiting. It looked like an unimaginably rowdy funfair. With the nurses, we had perfected quick examination methods. Listening to more than seven points on the patient's chest was out of the question because the others would have to wait too long. Three diagnostics were thus possible: bronchopneumonia, tonsillitis, or a sore throat. The nurse would take notes with a pen that she had hardly the time to dip into the ink.

Worst of all was the lack of medication. Each patient had the right to a minimum dosage. If ever they had any money, they could get a complementary dosage at the pharmacy. When I arrived in the cold of winter, I found small, terribly pale children, wrapped in meager jute sacking, whose coughing was enough to break one's heart. I tried to give them priority care, but I knew that only one injection would not be enough to cure them. The following day, they would be back contributing to the inflation of the number of sick people to be treated.

The major health problems were bronchopneumonia and dysentery. But chicken pox, German measles, and other contagious diseases spread at alarming speed.

For the children of the rich, I would give the allowed ration, but for the poor, I would double it. This was the reason why the stock of medication that was intended for three months disappeared in one. I was thus confronted with interrogations from the commission in charge of surveying the consumption of medications.

"Have you been selling medicines?"

"Of course not. The medicines are supplied by the pharmacy. They deliver what I prescribe, that's all."

"So why do the other neighborhoods in Hanoi have enough for three months, whereas you ask for more at the end of one month?"

"Because I have too many poor families."

With that answer no one dared say anything more. Beside the work at the clinic, I had many other tasks to perform: make house visits for the tuberculosis patients and the elderly, make sure that the public garbage containers were emptied, and give rudimentary first-aid lessons to the population. All day long, I would run from one place to another and nights I would sleep badly. I always had the impression that I had forgotten something or made a prescription error.

At that rhythm I lost weight so quickly that I was down again to my 40 kilos, clothes and all, as I had been when in the Resistance.

In 1963, the government launched a huge campaign in favor of the equality of men and women. In certain cases, women might even be chosen over men so that they could have access to important positions.

The new Minister of Health was the uncle of one of my friends from Hue, Aline, a Vietnamese despite her French name. Knowing that I wouldn't be able to continue working long under such difficult conditions, I went to see him to discuss my situation. Shortly afterwards, I was summoned: "It is true, Phuong, you have done good work. We have received numerous letters complimenting you. I have spoken with my friends on the council of the Ministry of Health. They want to name you Assistant Director of Hospital E. If all goes well for the next three years, we will be able to name you Assistant Minister of Health." It was difficult not to feel honored by such a proposition. However, judging from the size of the clinic and the present state of the country, such a mission seemed to me condemned to fail from the start. I thanked him wholeheartedly and we took leave of one another without the slightest decision being made.

Therefore, I pursued my work at the clinic—until, that is, fate entered the picture. In the street near my house, I came across a man who was a member of the Cultural Committee in charge of relations abroad, and whose children had been my patients. He asked about my situation and I told him about my difficulties. "Why don't you come and work with us?" he asked me. "In fact, we need someone like you to survey the health of heads of state and other important personages on visit to Hanoi."

Thus, in 1963, I began working at the Committee of Cultural Relations with Foreign Countries, which was a department of the Ministry of Foreign Affairs. The change was enormous for me, mainly because I found myself in an office with nothing to do. The heads of state were all in good health and in the department no one was ever ill. As part of planning for the forthcoming visit of VIPs, I was given several *ao dais*. In the bathroom at the end of the corridor, there was a mirror split down the middle, but that was enough for me to see myself. I had the impression of discovering a stranger: a face tanned by so many bicycle trips and the unflinching eyes of someone astonishingly self-determined.

Thanks to my new work, I came into close contact with foreigners, ministers, and secretaries of state. My French came back to me little by little. The instructions were very strict: only speak about their health. That was fine with me since, short of other data, I would have only been able to talk about my personal impressions of the country and, had I actually thought of doing it, would have been much too afraid of having my words repeated or, even worse, deformed by others, elsewhere. Over the past few years, being careful had helped me avoid many problems.

My husband was quite content with my new position, which allowed me to get home on a more regular basis, and spared me from night duty at the clinic.

At the Metropole Hotel, I was given room number 28 where, on fixed days, foreigners could come for a consultation. The special luxury for me was using the room's bathroom, which my children did not hesitate to do when they came to visit me. It changed our lives to be able to take a bath in a tub. My sons were often invited by the foreigners to share their meals, after which they would go on at length, excited by the quantities of food and the varieties of the dishes. They had difficulty in understanding that everyone could not enjoy as much.

In that hotel, we would come across people from every walk of life. There were many journalists who had come to attempt to understand the situation. Others, like the director of an important American daily newspaper, had arrived with a suitcase full of food supplies. Two porters had had to team up in order to haul his baggage up the stairs. "I was told that at the Metropole it was like living in the jungle, and that there was nothing available," he confessed, "but the fruit here is so delicious that I am going to throw everything away. Would you like to have some of these cans?" As it was forbidden to accept that kind of gift, I gave them to the hotel so that they could be distributed.

In March of 1964, the first American bombings began. At dawn, the planes swept the region of Phu Li, sixty kilometers from Hanoi. The message was clear: should you resist, all the Vietnamese cities will be destroyed just like this one.

One morning, at five o'clock, a family put on the BBC so loud that everyone in the building could hear it. The reporter described the attack in great detail, including the number of dead and wounded. Immediately, our head supervisor appeared: "Reactionaries! Turn off that radio!" But the people counter-attacked: "Be quiet! Let us listen to it. Close your door if you don't want to hear anything." Even if the motto was "We shall overcome," it was difficult not to worry about what was in store for us.

From then on, twenty Jeeps or so were permanently stationed in front of the hotel. The atmosphere was electric. At any moment, I had to be ready to accompany the journalists or the VIPs into strategic zones. One journalist offered me a small tape player with three cassettes of classical music: Chopin, Beethoven, and Bach. Whenever we would leave, especially at night, I got used to listening to the music to calm my fears. I can remember Father Nguyen D. Th., a Vietnamese priest who had come from Paris. We were trapped during a bombardment and our car had been turned over. While waiting for the end of the alert, I put a on cassette. He was astonished: "The Vietcong listen to classical music?" I burst out laughing. "The Vietcong are also human beings." I had trouble accepting the image that had been circulating in the West that the Vietcong fed on its enemies' livers.

Between any two missions, I didn't have much to do. Fortunately, I made friends with Nguyen Knac Vien, editor-in-chief of the *Courrier du Viêt-Nam,* the only newspaper published in French by the Ministry of Foreign Affairs. Sent by his father to study medicine in France, Viet became a member of the French communist party. But as soon as he had received his diploma, the government deported him under the pretext that he was a political agitator. Returning to Vietnam, he enrolled in the Vietnamese communist party and became the director of the *Courrier du Viêt-nam*, and of the publication of works in foreign languages. He was an educated and modest man whose aura struck me from the first time we met. His team consisted of a tightly knit circle of twenty or so people who for the most part spoke French. Vien defined the main lines of the newspaper and signed the editorial, while the others wrote the articles. I learned to type on a Remington whose ribbon had to be refilled with ink. Instead of the ten finger method that was used by practically all my comrades, I adopted that of the "heron jabbing fish," or, in other words, typing with two fingers.

Vien had an easy-to-grasp sense of analysis and thanks to him we began to understand what most of us had never been able to before. In particular, that meant the Party's political line, something with which he did not always see eye-to-eye. He would present his ideas and develop his reasoning, even at the risk of displeasing others. On several occasions, that was exactly what happened, especially when he addressed his twelve points to the National Assembly. The administrative circle dreaded him because with his frankness and his fine reasoning he never left himself open to attack. No one would have said "We detest Vien" or "We are afraid of him." But it was obvious that he was kept away from a great number of the wheels of state. They preferred to contain him in the role of chief editor of the newspaper. He was so morally upright that all the privileges, like fine homes, bodyguards, and official cars deeply shocked him. "The population leads a very difficult existence," he said. "I would be ashamed to reign over a huge house." He lived with his wife in a small room that opened out onto the corner of a quiet street, just across from the newspaper offices. He was a frail man and a yoga enthusiast. In the evenings, he would give lessons in learning how to breathe. In fact, he wrote several books on the subject, as well as many works of reference on historical and philosophical subjects. He was an endless worker and would often repeat, "As it may be, I might not live for long." Next to such a figure, we felt timid and shy. We were afraid of everything—for ourselves and for our children—and it was our very attitude that explained our obedience. Whenever the desire came over us to revolt, we would do it so awkwardly that our action was condemned before it began.

Having studied the recent history of other countries, Vien was persuaded that our bureaucracy would eventually disappear and that we would enjoy, progressively, a greater liberty of expression. "We have everything that is needed to be a prosperous and happy people. It is necessary to begin by analyzing the reasons for our being behind and, from there, organize a harmonious development. But this will take us at least one generation." Having been held to account several times by the authorities, he didn't seem to be particularly affected by it. "Don't worry about it," he would reassure us, "they haven't had the time yet to understand everything that is going on. One day or another, they will realize that I am right." Before the fact of arbitrary arrest and prison camps, he showed the attitude of a wise Vietnamese: Don't get worked up when you feel that it is going to be of no avail. It is better to stay calm and wait for the appointed hour. In the future, history will make us answer for our acts and everything will be brought out into the open.

He taught us—who had been prone to getting worked up over anything and who had debated foolishly about everything—to be patient and to reason wisely. "After the storm, you'll be able to raise your heads. When one is in the midst of the hurricane, it is important not to be uprooted."

Thanks to him, we gained back our confidence. We felt that breath of fresh air that circulated through the offices of the newspaper and considered it as our most precious possession. My comrades suspected me of being in love with Vien. But, like all the journalists who worked with him, men and women alike, I was simply under the spell of his intelligence and his personality. My only regret was not being able to talk about him with my husband. For Hoang, any criticism of the regime was futile and could only lead to trouble.

At the 17th parallel

I had never before heard the name of Ho Chi Minh's friend, Joris Ivens, when the Committee called on me to go and welcome him at the airport the following day. That great Dutch moviemaker, creator of several films on revolutionary movements in the world, had volunteered his services to film life in the most bombed out region of Vietnam—that of the 17th parallel—and I was to accompany him for that task. When Ivens appeared at the door of the plane, I could see a tall and handsome man with wavy white hair. His wife looked quite little next to him: she had bright, red-hair and was wearing a short skirt and boots.

A few hours later in the hall of the Metropole Hotel, we began to select the cameramen. Joris Ivens had already come to Vietnam several times. But this time, the film about the 17th parallel was something of particular emotional interest to him. He told me that he had to mortgage his home for the project. That was a surprise to me as I had always imagined that all film directors were rich!

To get to the 17th parallel, we had to drive down Route 1, which was extremely perilous because of the American bombings. The warplanes arrived in waves and as soon as we heard them we would jump out of the car to seek protection in the shelters that lined the road. One night, a bomb fell just near ours. There were violet-colored shell fragments everywhere. I could make out Ivens, whose hair seemed to have been singed. A cameraman had blood all over his face. All the cars were destroyed, so we had to call for help. We eventually continued on our route in other Jeeps made available to us. Ivens was asthmatic and had a hard time breathing inside the shelters, which were stifling. But that didn't keep him from being ready to begin filming as soon as he got up the very next morning.

We spent three months at the 17th parallel, the greater part of which was underground. On one side of the Ben Ha River was North Vietnam and on the other South Vietnam, run by the Saigon government. Between the two countries lay a moon-like landscape carved by planes unloading 1,700,000 metric tons of bombs, twice as many as in World War II.

Joris Ivens worked with extraordinary willpower, but even more impressive and moving to me was the courage of the Vietnamese. I thought that I had already known war, but it had been nothing compared to what I was seeing there. Every village had an underground network connecting the houses to each other. We filmed hospitals, schools, day-care centers, supply stores—all of them underground installations that allowed people to live almost normal lives. They created incredible gadgets to capture the slightest whiff of air available between waves of bombers. For example, there were cradle-like devices that would be hoisted up to the surface by pulley whenever an alert was over so that the children below could breathe better.

One of the cameramen had fallen in love with a young girl of eighteen who belonged to a team of partisans in charge of cleaning up the road after bombing attacks. Our comrade told us that she had refused to spend the night with him because she didn't want to "become a wife before the wedding." One morning, a bomb blast killed her. The mother cried over her daughter's body, which was intact.

That evening, Joris, realizing just how affected I was, came and sat down next to me. "Phuong, I see that there are many people like you who know how to care for others. But there are not enough filmmakers who deal with war. I think that you have a gift for it. Why don't you try to become a war reporter? It is highly important for your people, and for the rest of the world, to understand what is going on here."

The following days, the checkered raids of B-52s continued. It was hell within hell. It began with a circle of white smoke: the tracer plane was drawing a perimeter for the bomber. There was no use in trying to run away at that point; it was better not to budge. We were all lying on the ground when the bomb exploded. The earth began to tremble, and so did we, like epileptics. Our eyes and our ears filled with dirt. The film studio had given us helmets that we unfailingly used during every alert. As I was getting up, I felt that mine had a hole in the back and I had soil in my hair. I was injured for sure. In fact, we all had holes in our head covers—they were helmets made out of cardboard for the extras.

On the border of the 17th parallel, an enormous Vietnamese flag floated at the top of a twenty-meter mast. Whenever it got too shredded by bullets, it was taken down so that it could be mended by the women and hoisted up again the next day. Joris had decided to place that symbolic image at the opening of the film—something that terribly worried the four bodyguards that Ho Chi Minh had assigned to watch over him. "Don't get upset about that. It's Tuan who is going to film and Phuong will also be with us. Now, if you don't let me do as I wish, I shall go back to Hanoi and complain to Ho Chi Minh." That ended the argument and, on the spot, one of the guards decided to come with us. So, off we went. Joris had a plaid scarf, and an old hat on his head to cover his white hair. I was dressed all in black—pants and shirt—like the people of the region, whereas Tuan, the cameraman, had covered himself with a kind of cape made out of camouflage-colored fabric. When we approached the border, I could see the Saigon soldiers looking at us through binoculars. Did we look enough like peasants on their way to the fields? I was expecting gunshots at any moment. When we arrived at the foot of the flagpole, Joris ordered Tuan to climb to the top of the mast. The poor boy's heart was in his boots: "If I am still alive after that, as soon as I am back in Hanoi I am going to dig a hole for my wife and me and not come out of the shelter until the war is over." Joris and I took refuge in a bomb crater to watch him pull himself up with his camera on a shoulder strap and hidden under his cape. His progression seemed endless. I prayed to Buddha to help him. Half way up, Tuan turned his eyes towards me. He seemed incredibly calm and determined. By the time he reached the summit, we were sure that we had heard several bullets swish by, but he had made it unhurt. Up there, he seemed to have forgotten his fear. Although he wasn't to stay more than five minutes, he was still filming away fifteen minutes later. Then, suddenly, we heard a plane… I don't remember anything anymore of what happened next. Joris's bodyguard picked me up, helped by two other men. I was covered with mud. Joris's face was blackened and a clump of his hair was burned. The bomb hadn't fallen far from us. Tuan climbed down the mast as if nothing had happened.

As soon as Joris had twenty reels of film, he preferred for security reasons to avoid delay and sent them immediately to be developed in Hanoi. Khue was often charged with that mission. One day as he had been waiting for a ferry to cross a river he was killed by an exploding bomb. When the reels were developed, it was impossible to erase the traces of his blood on the film.

Back in Hanoi, after shooting the film, I was not the same person anymore. I felt as though I had no longer the right to complain about my living conditions. At each reception, especially at those which were given in the honor of foreign guests, with tables overflowing with food, I couldn't help thinking of all those heroic people who were surviving at the 17th parallel. Such waste seemed to me hard to bear. It had become urgent that I follow Joris's advice. "You're out of your mind!" my husband said to me when I told him about my intention. "You're not going to give up your position?" Hoang detested all forms of adventure and feared gossip most of all. Why leave a job that provided so many advantages? People would think that I had committed some wrongdoing. Or further still, how could I, in this way and at my age, dare to embark on a new profession of which I knew nothing at all? My children, on the contrary, were enthusiastic, especially my eldest son who was then a student at the metallurgy division of the Polytechnic University where my husband was teaching. "Go ahead, Mom, you're perfectly right. After all that you have endured, you well deserve a chance to do something that you will enjoy."

I still remember the stunned expression on the face of the director of the department to which I belonged at the Ministry of Health, when I announced my decision.

"You don't want to work here anymore? But what do you want to do?"

"I want to make films."

"Don't count on that. It is totally out of the question."

One did not leave such a prestigious employment from personal choice. For months, I returned regularly to push the issue so that I was finally authorized to join the television group and become a director of news shorts and documentaries. My salary was about equivalent to that of a street sweeper.

At thirty-seven years old, I entered the television section of the Ministry of Information and Culture.[1] At that time, there must have been no more than a dozen or so TV sets in the whole city! They were huge, cumbersome, Beryl brand black and white sets from Poland that people watched grouped together. I began to write scripts for films that I would then direct with a team that was, no doubt, more experienced than I was. My first film was about *The Festivities of Mid-Autumn* in Hanoi. The equipment was elementary, consisting almost entirely of Paillard-Bolex 16mm cameras. But it was the film developing that proved magical because we had to keep dipping our hands into the water in order to measure the temperature. From my years in the jungle, I had retained knowledge about how to make bromide baths and that proved useful. Fortunately, too, we had technical books in French and all we had to do was follow the steps of the recipes, one by one.

I next directed *The Churches Accuse*. With footage of damaged steeples, I mixed images of the American bombings. That film brought me my first award: the Silver Dove at the Leipzig Festival. Although I was not authorized to leave the country to receive it, it was a wonderful way of getting back at all those who had criticized me when I wanted to change jobs.

The making of each film was an epic adventure that began with the script. It had to be approved by seven different departments, notably by the television management, by the

---

[1] The first executive staff of Vietnamese television began to be trained in 1964. At that time, only 16mm experimental films were being shot. In 1971, the material and technical conditions for television broadcasting began to become acceptable.

different organizations in charge of reviewing the script, and, especially, by the accounting department. It could take weeks, and a simple veto from any one of the departments meant the project was rejected. The first and foremost quality of a director was patience. For the administration, it was always necessary to stage scenes of victory and unconditional courage. Later on, when I wanted to film *Vietnam and Bicycles*—a celebration of bicycles in times of war as well as in times of peace, depicting Dien Bien Phu and the Ho Chi Minh Trail— the first problem was that the film was found to be too expensive. Next, my head of production refused to show it at the Leipzig Festival. "I'll never understand you, Phuong. At a period of airplanes and satellites, why do you want to show that Vietnam is still living in the bamboo era?"

The summer of 1969 will remain a memorable time for the Vietnamese of my generation. During the month of August, news about the alarming state of Ho Chi Minh's health spread widely. On the evening of September 1st, I was filming the National Holiday festivities with my team. Compared to those of the preceding years, the speech delivered by the Party's General Secretary, Le Duan, in the great reunion hall, was incomparably shorter, his throat hoarse. The faces of the members of the political bureau seemed morose and their applause lacked conviction. There was a strong feeling that a tragic event was in the air and all thoughts were turned to Ho Chi Minh. After the meeting, everybody left the room in silence and the lights were immediately extinguished.

On the morning of September 2nd, my cameraman Trung Viet came over to my house to talk about the filming schedule for the National Holiday. He had barely arrived when my youngest son, Phong, came over to me. "Mommy" he said, "I don't feel well." His forehead was burning-hot. In early August, an epidemic of German measles had started spreading in Hanoi, and ten- to twelve-year-old boys like him seemed to be more particularly sensitive to the disease. My son's torso was covered with small red pimples. Suddenly, he began to vomit blood. Without wasting a second, Trung Viet put Phong on his back and we ran to the Children's Hospital, two kilometers away. There, we confronted an incredible shambles—beds everywhere in the corridors and under the staircases, and several children in each one, all of whom had caught German measles. My friend, Doctor B., a Frenchwoman married to a Vietnamese, immediately put my son on an IV. By nightfall, the vomiting had ceased. Before she left the hospital, however, Doctor B. advised me to keep watch over the child. But the second she left, he started to shake with convulsions and his face turned pallid. Then he fell motionless on his bed. His pulse was scarcely perceptible. With the help of my second son, Phuong, I spent a horrifying night rubbing his hands and feet to warm him up and doing the movements of artificial respiration.

Around three o'clock in the morning, he seemed to come around. He was breathing noisily and spit up a clot of blood. Then, he opened his eyes and, at that moment, I must have fainted. When I came to, two nurses were busy working on my son. He had pulled through.

Around six o'clock, as we were transporting him to another room, the loudspeaker sounded: "Dear citizens, it is with great sorrow and grief that the bureau of the Communist Party has to inform you of our Revered Uncle, Ho Chi Minh's death." From outside, we could hear the surge of great lamenting. Around us, faces were flooded with tears. I took my third son in my arms and my second one hugged in close to us. Those were unforgettable moments.

Under the bombs

The years 1970-1971 in Hanoi were dreadful. We lived in constant fear of the bombings. All the inhabitants who had no particular reason to remain—the children in particular—had been evacuated to the country. My eldest son left with his metallurgy section for the district near Lang Son, on the Chinese border, where some schools had been installed in caves. The other two lived sixty kilometers from Hanoi in a village assigned to us by the Ministry of Foreign Affairs. Situated near a bridge, the area was vulnerable. But we had nothing to say on the matter.

In the city, most of the houses were abandoned and their doors carefully locked, with a wide variety of messages on them: "I have left for such and such province. If you want to see me, do come"; "Mommy, I have returned. You aren't here. I don't know where to find you." Letters nailed to the door bore notices written by the mail carriers: "This letter arrived on such and such day. If someone knows the address of this man, please forward it to him." It happened that men returning from the front found their houses all sealed up.

Soon, my husband left to join our eldest son near Lang Son. I remained alone in Hanoi to continue working. Every Saturday morning, along with friends whose children were in the same village school as mine, we left on our bicycles overloaded with supplies: noodles and rice that had been saved from our rations, fruit, and firewood. When it rained, pedaling on the clay roads became a nightmare. The clay stuck to the wheels; we would slip and slide and not be able to make progress. So we had to walk, carrying the bicycles on our shoulders until the road conditions got better.

With cries of joy, the children would be there to greet us on the wharf at the entrance to the village. Like the other youths, my sons were hosted by peasants with whom they worked in the fields and also went fishing. My second son loved to fish and was able to treat his hosts to his catches. When I arrived, the head of the family would always give me some fish and, inreturn, I shared what I had brought among all the children in the house. I felt the same sort of mutual understanding with the peasants in that village that we had experienced during the war.

In each school, a tunnel was dug out under the benches so that the children could escape during alerts. As soon as the air raid siren sounded, they would put on reinforced straw hats that the committee had ordered the peasants to make and which were intended as protection against bullets. I was astonished to find those youngsters so disciplined.

On Sunday afternoon after lunch, we would set off again for Hanoi. It was a very poignant moment because there was always somebody who would remark: "Who knows if they won't be orphans next week?" It is true that the trip was dangerous, for the road had been bombed a hundred times, but we didn't even pay any attention to that anymore. Thanks to lookouts, the airplanes were always spotted well ahead of time. As soon as we heard the siren, we would throw our bicycles into the ditch and press our bodies against the embankment, with our hands over our ears to protect our eardrums. Once the bombs had exploded and all of us had made sure we were unscathed, we would get back on our bicycles and continue on our way. During that period, Hanoi became a site for repairs. Many cars that had been damaged in the bombings were brought there to be put into working condition again. At night, it wasn't unusual to see a chauffeur sleeping in a hammock next to the car that was being worked on by a mechanic. In that city, which existed under the perpetual menace of bombings, an extraordinary atmosphere prevailed. Whereas most of the young were in the army, many older artists and writers remained. Instead of getting together in one of our houses, it often happened that we would meet in a shelter. We talked about everything and nothing, like in times of peace. When we parted, we would say: "I hope we will see each other tomorrow." Some never came back. But wasn't the simple fact of being able to cross paths again already wonderful enough? In that climate of war, unimportant bickering was not the order of the day. Among all the people who had stayed, a strange interweaving of friendship took place.

The city was bombed regularly. Every night, the siren got us out of bed and we all ran to pile in the shelters. Sometimes we were just too tired to move and we waited with throbbing hearts, wondering where the next bomb was going to fall. Joan Baez was going through Hanoi, as well as Jane Fonda. They had come to meet the American prisoners and try to understand what the war was all about. One night during an alert, we were all together in the shelter that was set up behind the Metropole Hotel. The women were screaming and the children were crying. I then caught a glimpse of Joan Baez, who had also come down. She was pale, trembling, her face dripping with sweat. We had already exchanged a few words in English at the Ministry and she recognized me. I tried to reassure her. "Don't be afraid. Here, we have a saying: 'The bombs won't necessarily fall on us. And if the bombs fall on us, we won't necessarily be injured. And if we are injured, our injuries won't necessarily be fatal. In any case, whatever will happen, will happen.'" But she continued to tremble, so I suggested that she sing something. "No, no, I can't, I can't," she kept repeating. "Try to sing along with me." And I began humming. Some time later, her voice rose above the commotion, rich and magnificent. Then, as if by magic, someone began to accompany her on a guitar... to the deafening background noise of the bombs.

Once the shelling was over, the group dispersed very quickly and we didn't have the opportunity of speaking again. Many years later, in the 1990s, I was in France to participate in the Amiens International Film Festival. A poster announced that a concert by Joan Baez was to be given the following week in Paris.[1] François M., a filmmaker friend of mine to whom I had told the story of our meeting, suggested that I should write to her. Several days later in Paris, there were two tickets for the concert waiting for me when I returned to my hotel.

Joan Baez first sang three songs. Then she said in perfect French: "Now I am happy and moved to know that Doctor Phuong is here. With her, I experienced some unforgettable moments. Where are you, Doctor Phuong?" I found myself on stage next to her under the floodlights. She took my hand. "Thanks to you, Phuong, I overcame my fear. I became calmer and stronger. To my dying day, I will never forget those moments. Now, dear audience, I would like to sing for you this song that Phil Ochs has written in memory of those events and that I am dedicating to Doctor Phuong: *There but for Fortune*." After the last note, the public got up and applauded.

---

[1] November 17, 1997 at the *Café de la danse, des arts et de la musique*.

With Jane Fonda it was different. I had always admired her composure because the bombs seemed to leave her indifferent. At the end of her last stay, she dedicated a photograph to me: "Dear Phuong, I hope that this war will be over soon and that we will be able to see each other again in peace and happiness."

December 24th, 1972 was yet another unforgettable day. No official truce had been declared, but we knew that there would be no American air raids on Christmas Eve. Many people had come back from the country to see their families and insisted on being seen at the shore of the lake, in order to prove that they were still alive and to have news of their friends. Although the Vietnamese have a reputation for being shy, they kissed and hugged each other for quite some time.

A great mass was celebrated in the cathedral that was crowded with non-Catholics as well. The organs vibrated and the bells tolled, just as they used to in times past. I was thinking of my children who had remained in the country.

Past midnight, we were all still outside. It was scarcely one o'clock when the air raid sirens started wailing. The truce was over. Once again, the airplanes swooped down over the city and an entire district was wiped out.

The following day, my team filmed atrocious scenes in the still smoking ashes. There were bodies without heads, and scattered limbs everywhere. All day long, the bombings followed one another. They continued the next day as well, and the day after that, and for twelve more, again. We filmed non-stop the confrontations between the Vietnamese anti-aircraft guns and the airplanes. We filmed the airplanes that crashed and the total destruction of the railroad station, a building that dated back to the beginning of the century.

We listened on the radio to updates on the Paris Conference. Those discussions, which had begun in January of

1969, seemed to us interminable. Then, as if to intimidate us even more, the bombing raids were further intensified, and the ensuing destruction grew worse. American aircraft were shot down and the pilots were taken prisoners in the middle of the city. A plane had fallen just in front of my former clinic and the pilot was led—as all the others had been—to the prison that was located in the north of the city and rebaptized by the Americans the "Hanoi Hilton."

The population showed such ferocious hatred towards these men that they wanted to kill them on the spot. It was the militia that opposed this, in order that the men might serve as a bargaining chip later on. Mr. Peterson, a pilot who had fallen into a rice paddy not far from Hanoi, was one of them. Twenty years later he returned to Vietnam as Ambassador of the United States.[2]

I was relieved that my children and my husband were far from the city. The tension that reigned there had become unbearable. Each day I learned of the death of a friend or an acquaintance.

We lived in the shelters. To encourage the population to continue in its struggle and to give us confidence again, the administrative committee of Hanoi came up with the idea of organizing a parade of the prisoners. Protected by a double row of militia, they proceeded down the streets to cries of hatred and to insults, while women fainted from pain at the sight of those who had caused the deaths in their families.

In Thanh Hoa, I remember having filmed two pilots who had just bailed out of their fallen planes. When the militia made them climb into a cart to protect them from the anger of the populace, one of those young men begged them to let him

---

[2] Former Air Force officer and three-term Florida Congressman Douglas "Pete" Peterson was appointed American Ambassador to Hanoi in 1995 by President Clinton and served with distinction to January 2001.

get down to be able to relieve himself. There he was, squatting by the shoulder of the road, hanging his head, half naked, with his pilot's outfit down to his knees, trembling under the insults of the peasants. I could not help feeling pity for him.

At the central prison, where I organized numerous television interviews with the prisoners, I was continually torn apart by mixed feelings of hatred and compassion. A short time later, all these pilots were dispatched to various other sites out of fear that a bomb might fall on the building. The English-speaking radio station kept on broadcasting with its famous anchor, Madame Ngo, nicknamed Hanna by the prisoners and then Hanna Ngo by everyone else.

On January 15th, 1973, the very moment when the loudspeakers announced the end of air raids over Hanoi, an extraordinary phenomenon took place: the ceaseless roaring of the planes came to a stop and there was total silence. Immediately, the people crowded together along the edge of the large lake, crying and laughing as though they were insane. Then they dispersed very quickly again for they had to go and get those who were in the country. Life could finally get back to normal. A new time of peace was approaching, something that we had not experienced for a long time.

The southern route

Hardly had I returned to Hanoi when my eldest son made the decision to commit himself to becoming a war correspondent in South Vietnam. In college, his father had made him choose a different field from his own out of fear that others might accuse him of partiality towards his son. As a result, Phuoc had always been bored to death with his studies in metallurgy. My husband went to great pains explaining to him that the country would be in need of engineers in metallurgy and his professor urged him to go on. But in no way did such coaxing change Phuoc's interests and he continued to be bored. A short time after I had decided to give up everything and become a director, he started up a conversation with me one evening, seated in front of the house. "Mom, I want to do as you did—I want to work in an area that I like." "Obviously, your mother's madness is contagious," my husband interjected. But his comment didn't take into account Phuoc's stubbornness.

First of all he needed a letter from his professor, authorizing him to leave the Metallurgy Institute to study at the Film Institute. The teacher in question said to me "I'm quite afraid of your husband. If he talks to me about this affair, I will pretend that I don't know anything about it." My son didn't dare look at me as the teacher wrote the precious letter. Three years later, Phuoc brilliantly finished the program at the Film

Institute, receiving a "red diploma," which enabled him to continue his studies abroad. But, beforehand, he still had to complete an internship with a team that was filming on the Black River. The Russians had helped us finance the construction of a dam on this river north of Hanoi and I was on site there to film the exodus of the local families. These were dramatic times, especially for the minority ethnic groups who had been living at different altitudes in the same place for generations: the Dao at two thousand meters, the Muong, at a thousand meters, and the Cao Lan in the valley.

Before leaving their villages, the inhabitants pulled up the fruit trees, and opened the tombs to carry away the remains of their ancestors.

My son was also filming there with his group of apprentices. At the end of the day, I must admit, we would share our experiences with one another in a jovial mood despite the tragic scenes that we had been witnessing.

After that internship, Phuoc was authorized to leave for the film school in the Soviet Union. I was proud of him and very happy about the idea. But three weeks later when I returned home, he sprang out of the house. " Mommy, I'm not leaving for Russia anymore. I'm joining up as a volunteer war correspondent in South Vietnam. I want to serve my country, just as my father and mother have done before me."

Knowing him well, I knew that he had thought seriously about it and that nothing could deter him from his project any longer. For once, my husband—bless him—made no effort to hide his satisfaction: his eldest son was getting ready to take over the reins. The evening before his departure, we organized a farewell dinner with all his classmates who were aslo leaving for the South. At the end of the war, there were only five left, out of twenty-seven. All the others had been killed. But what I remember most about that meal was the pile of dishes that I had to wash afterwards.

Before leaving for South Vietnam, the volunteers had to go through a six-month internship in Hoa Binh, situated sixty kilometers north of Hanoi in a mountainous zone. There, they were put through intensive physical training in preparation for the hard reality of the Ho Chi Minh trail, as well as psychological training—just as intense—to teach them how never to confess that they were from the North.

South Vietnam was divided into several zones: B3, B4, and B5. All that I knew was that my son was assigned to B5, to which Hue belonged. Perhaps it was because he had family there.

After his departure in 1973, I no longer had any news of his whereabouts. When the radio announced fighting in Hue, I remained awake all night wondering where he was and if he was still alive. I could not speak about it to anyone, not even to my husband.

But my trials were not yet over. Since 1969, the Committee for the Reunification of Vietnam had been recruiting young people with the intention of training future officials for the South. One morning we were visited by one of the Committee's delegates. He informed me: "Your second son, Phuong, has just passed his baccalaureate exam. We are going to send him to study in a socialist country. Which one would you like? Poland, Hungary, Rumania, or the U.S.S.R?" Phuong jumped at the chance. "Which country is the most free?" Out of fear of our inquisitor's reaction, I quickly added, "Comrade, tell us, rather, in which country is French most spoken?" "Poland" he answered. "In that case, I choose Poland," my son cut in. It was apparently because of the fact that my older son had been to the front that my second son was being given this chance. A few days later, he flew off for

Poland to pursue his studies in mechanical engineering, specializing in refrigeration. My third son, fortunately, was still attending school. In spite of my all-engrossing work, I had a great deal of trouble living the life of a soldier's mother. Even in the midst of the jungle, I had never been afraid. One night, a violent pain shot through my belly. I couldn't breathe and began to suffocate. At three o'clock in the morning, I found myself wandering aimlessly in the deserted streets. The following day, something made me jot down that incident in a notebook, which I rarely ever did. Two years later, I would understand the reason why. One evening in 1975, someone knocked at my door. A man in rags was on the threshold, leaning on a stick. He was bald, his face was pale and he had a swollen stomach. He was a beggar, no doubt. "Wait a second, I will get you some rice."

"Mommy, don't you recognize me?" I stood there speechless. My son, that athletic boy with a bright future ahead of him could not have become that old man, incapable of standing on his own feet. "It is me, mommy. Don't cry. I am alive." During a mission in the jungle, Phuoc had contracted a pernicious abscess. There had been a total absence of hygiene in the cave that sheltered the hospital, with three or four patients to a single mat. Pressured into having to move the hospital because of the menace of the American air raids, the nurses had transported my sickly son, and two others in equally pitiful condition, to the edge of a stream. My son had heard them pronounce farewell words: "Rest in peace. We cannot take you with us. The day that we come back, be assured that we will take your remains with us." As soon as the sun had set, the water began to rise. When my son woke up with the daylight, he was almost totally immersed in freezing water. His two companions were dead. Rescued by a soldier who was guarding a medication depot nearby—equivalent to the rice depots—he was then sent to a military hospital in Hanoi. "Do you remember what day they abandoned you by the stream?" It was the precise day that I had experienced the belly pains.

In order to buy the medication necessary for my son, I had to sell as many things as I possibly could, one of which was a wardrobe that I had brought home to put an end to the perpetual disorder. Phuoc remained in the hospital for two years, and for two years we had to survive on practically nothing in order to feed him. Once he was rehabilitated, he could finally begin to work again at the Studio for Documentary and Scientific Films about Vietnam.

When the news spread that the South was falling apart and that the liberation army was about to enter Saigon, Hanoi was in turmoil. It seemed to me out of the question not to participate in that event. "It is extremely dangerous," objected the television chairman when I announced my plan to him. But the next day I, with five other members of my team, got into a Romanian Jeep that was equipped with an extra fuel tank of a hundred liters of gas set onto the back seat. A civil servant, working for the television and originally from Hue, also wanted to come along. Before leaving, each one of us was outfitted with two khaki fatigues and a fabric helmet: it was preferable that one could recognize immediately which side we were on.

As soon as we were outside of Hanoi, the road became merely a succession of military trucks and cars. When we crossed over the 17th parallel, we were deeply moved just thinking about all those lives that had been sacrificed in that area. We stopped to observe a minute of silence in memory of those dead, among whom were my friends who had worked for Joris Ivens's team. Then we set off again, heading for Hue. My heart was throbbing at the thought of seeing members of my family.

Little by little, the landscape began to change. We could see small houses with gardens and women in *ao dais* and conical-shaped hats, just as they used to wear in times gone by. The inhabitants seemed to be terrified of us, and fled. We had no idea why. At that period, like most of the people in the North, we were ignorant of the horrible massacres of 1968.[1] In the city, most of the houses looked abandoned. The streets were strewn with military uniforms, shoes, and bundles left there by the Saigon soldiers. It was often necessary to get out of the Jeep in order to clear the road of its obstacles.

We arrived as well as could be expected at the Reception Committee in Hue where we began to film the chaos. Then we got back into the car and went on twelve kilometers further to Thuan An. All along the road, the state of disorder was just as indescribable, with suitcases and clothing, television sets and motorbikes, everywhere.

In Thuan An, the tracks on abandoned tanks were still rotating. There were dead bodies floating in the water. Far out at sea, we could see American ships. After having filmed those apocalyptic scenes, we returned to Hue. For lodgings, all we had to do was enter a hotel. Anyone wearing a uniform of the North was housed and fed free of charge. We took rooms at the Hotel Morin. There were still a few waiters at the restaurant who looked ill at ease. The food was very good and copious, but we hardly had time to take advantage of it for we were there to work.

---

[1] During the Tet offensive of 1968 by the North Vietnamese, close to three thousand civilians in Hue were massacred and their bodies thrown into a common pit.

In the officers' homes, the drawers remained half opened, the wardrobes full of clothing, and the tubs still full of bath water. The streets were strewn with corpses.

On the third day, when I wanted to go and see my family, I realized that I no longer knew which route to take to get to Eo Bau, the village where I was born. At the market, I questioned a merchant. Worried about it, she said, "Why do you want to go to Eo Bau?" "Because I am originally from there." "What? A Vietcong[2] from Hue?" Hearing the conversation, twenty or so people gathered around us, touching my arms and my cheeks. "This Vietcong has real flesh." In the South, it was said that the soldiers from the North were so skinny that seven of them could be lined up on one branch of a papaya tree.

Thirty years had passed since I had left my family. I was returning to the shady trails of my youth. Eo Bau had not changed much: the water buffalo ruminating in the shade of the banyans, the scent of the grapefruit flowers that floated all the way up to my grandmother's house. There were the same inscriptions in Chinese letters on both sides of the door. Suddenly, I could not go on. I was hearing my brothers' and sisters' laughter and I could see my mother in her vaporous silk *ao dai*. Where were they now? My legs gave way and tears blocked my view. Without saying a word, my two cameramen each took an arm to hold me up. I was at last in that orchard that I had so often dreamed about and I called out: "Grandma, grandma!"

It was my ninth aunt who came out of the house, my mother's youngest sister who looked so much like her. "Is that really you, Phuong?" Together, we broke down into sobbing. The cameramen, as well, began to cry. My grandmother then approached, leaning on a stick. Slowly, her hands recognized

---

[2] A Viet communist.

my face: "I prayed to Buddha so much for your return. It is thanks to him that you are here at last." At eighty, she could hardly see, but just enough to be able to recognize me. As for my aunt, she could not stop crying: "Phuong is here, Phuong has come back!" Then, without wasting a second, she dashed back into to the house to bake some cakes: it was well known that the Vietcong were starving to death. We had to wait for her to finish at least one before we were able to talk.

While waiting for me, my team went for a walk in the garden. It was paradise for them. They couldn't get over seeing so much magnificent fruit, and, furthermore, they had forgotten that a family like mine could exist. "How could you have abandoned everything here to go live in the North? You are really quite heroic!" one of them cried out.

Seated on the porch with my aunt and my grandmother, I learned that my father and my mother were living in Saigon with my sister, Xuan Nhan. My awful mother-in-law had been killed in 1968 during the events of Tet. A bomb fragment had penetrated the interior of her house and hit her in the head. The other members of my family were also in Saigon, except my brother, who was in command of the Air Force at Da Nang and based on the island of Son Tra.

Exactly two days later, we received a call from the information service at the Da Nang front. Da Nang had just been liberated and we were needed for filming there.

Along the hundred kilometers that separate the two cities, the road offered a nightmarish vision. Dead bodies were piled up on the shoulders of the roads and Jeeps were abandoned. Our driver stopped at each one to collect the keys, as if he were in charge of their distribution. During his collecting, we did our best to keep our eyes off the corpses.

When we arrived in Da Nang, we were welcomed by the Liberation Committee, which consisted of top-ranking army officers who had come out of hiding and taken over the running of the city after the departure of the soldiers of the South. In that chaos, resembling the end of the world, they had much to do. Apparently, we were the first journalists to penetrate into the city since its liberation. We were lodged downtown at the Hotel Orient, a luxurious establishment, which had been miraculously spared in the midst of the shops that were still burning after the widespread sacking that had taken place.

Secretly obsessed by the idea of finding my brother, I didn't have any reason to stay in the city and we left immediately for China Beach. Although I hadn't seen Phat for thirty years, I was sure that I would recognize him. Uniforms were strewn about the ditches on the side of the road, abandoned by the soldiers of the South who had attempted to pass for civilians. At China Beach, several detainment camps were set up where all those who could not flee were being held. The men were exhausted and their faces expressionless.

The guards let me through and I tried to find the officers. "Who among you would happen to know Col. Xuan Phat, my second brother?" One of them finally answered me: "Yes, I know him. It was he who commanded the Air Force here." "Do you know where I can find him?" "No, I haven't seen him for three days." That was March 29th. All day long as we were filming, I repeated the same question.

Under the direction of a high-ranking official in Da Nang, the officers of the South repeated the Vietcong songs. Officially, they were not prisoners, but "regrouped officers." Every evening, a political commissioner came to explain to them why the imperialists had left and how, from then on, we were all brothers. I examined the faces in vain, for it was impossible to find Phat. However, as we were filming a group of officers assembled in a house, a young man addressed me:

"You are Phuong, aren't you? You lived in Eo Bau?" "Yes, how do you know?" "I am your cousin." An Air Force captain, he piloted helicopters under my brother's command. I learned that Phat had first helped to evacuate all the members of our family before being able to leave Da Nang. He was one of the last to board a helicopter whose pilot had been bribed by another of my cousins working at the airport. My father and my mother, my brothers and sisters, and all the members of my immediate family were then able to get out on one of the last American airplanes that left Saigon.

Relieved by that information, I could then go back to Da Nang. The buildings were still aflame. Looters were seen coming out of abandoned houses carrying furniture and refrigerators. Thanks to a commander of the army of the North whom I had known during the war, my cousin could then be liberated from the camp. He had to return to Hue to follow the obligatory three-day "study" for all the sergeants of the North, before fading away into the crowd as an ordinary citizen. Only three days were required for the sergeants to listen to a political commissioner explain the Party line, but many more for the officers. Some of them, particularly the information officers, would be boarded there for ten years.

I spent a week in Da Nang, in what was an apocalyptic atmosphere. By day, as by night, there was an ear-splitting commotion of the comings and goings of people and trucks. Nobody knew who was who and nobody understood anything anymore. The soldiers from the North systematically searched the buildings to find the Saigon soldiers who were hiding out there. I witnessed unbelievable scenes, like the looting of the huge rice depot: at least five hundred square meters packed with rice piled up to the ceiling. Since the doors had remained wide open, hundreds of people rushed inside. Suddenly screaming could be heard. The sacks on the tops of the piles were no longer balanced properly and tumbled down crushing several people under their enormous weight.

It was impossible to sleep at night. Shots could be heard throughout the city and, in the morning, still more bodies were collected. The sight was horrifying. Fortunately, we also witnessed moving scenes of people who were finding each other again. Like me, numerous soldiers of the North were looking for their families from the South. One of them let us follow him with our camera. He asked any passers-by where he could find Madame X's house. Finally, a neighbor took him to the spot. Before our eyes, the son fell into his mother's arms. After so many scenes of horror, it did us wonders to be able to film such an instant of happiness.

Nha Trang had just been liberated and we were asked to go there. The route that led out of Da Nang went through several high passes. We crossed an uninterrupted caravan of vehicles. The people who had fled out of fear of the fighting preferred to go home.

The shops were burning in Nha Trang, too. As the Northern forces approached, the Saigon soldiers looted the city and then set it aflame. Men attempted to put out the fires by throwing buckets of water and we filmed non-stop. The next evening, in the lobby of the Hotel Nha Trang, where we were staying, I was approached by a young girl in *ao dai*. "I am your half-sister, Huong," she said to me. I looked at her, flabbergasted. "You don't know me," she continued, "nevertheless, I am your sister. If you like, I would like to invite you to come to my home."

In the little room where she was living, on the ground floor of a prosperous house, she told me about my father's second union, one with her mother who had adopted his name, Can. She showed me photos. She called my mother "Mother" and hers, "Mommy." "Our mother had left for Hue," she resumed, "so papa took mommy." Then she led me to see her brother, Long, who was living a few houses away. In spite of the obvious resemblance they both had to my father, I couldn't get myself to feel anything for them. The next day, they invited me to dinner with their mother at a house behind a shop in the center of Nha Trang that was supposedly built by my father. "My child," she said as she welcomed me. But I didn't leave her a chance to continue. "No, please, call me Phuong, or your niece, that is enough. I don't want to be your child. I can't have two mothers."

She was a tall woman, with a nice face and white hair that was tied in a bun, and she was wearing a jade necklace and a matching bracelet. During dinner, I finally understood why my father and my mother had been separated for so long. I also understood that she was afraid of me because, in her opinion, I was a Vietcong and she knew nothing of my intentions.

In 1976, when I was able to correspond with my mother, who was in California, I received a fifty-page letter from her, like a small package, wherein she explained the whole story to me—down to the smallest detail—and begged me to cease all contact with that woman whom my father had married without her permission. In any case, I had not the least intention of seeing her again.

We stayed in Nha Trang for three days before setting out for Saigon, where we were to film the progression of a tank division. The night preceding our departure, none of us could sleep. We had dreamed of the reunification for so long. The hotel was full of Vietnamese journalists who were as excited as we were. One of them confessed that the reporting there marked the crowning of his career.

On April 29th, we were five kilometers from Saigon. As we approached the city, two volunteers, a man and a woman, came to take charge and guide the driver. The young girl was dressed in light colors and smelled lovely. The chauffeur remarked: "They're not like the girls from the North, always dressed in black and white." Shortly, a commander blocked the road. "It is impossible to enter the city at the moment. The tanks are crossing the Saigon Bridge and we are fighting hand to hand. You must stay here until tomorrow." He assigned us to a tailor's house that was on the side of the road. Obviously terrorized, the man of the house waved and called us "*Monsieur*" and "*Madame*." "Call us comrade." "No, I don't dare do that. Do you want something to eat?" The house had five rooms, which were well furnished, with fans everywhere and a huge refrigerator in the kitchen. We found piles of clothing in all sorts of colors in the bedrooms.

The tailor told us that his father was from the North. He had taken advantage of the three hundred days of free migration in 1954 to move to the South. The proud, old man came over to greet us. "You are too determined, you people from the North," he said to me, "There is no way to get rid of you!"

The meal was like a feast to us. I had trouble eating because I was so very moved. Next, I went into the bathroom. In the large mirror that was over the sink, I perceived a strange face with feverish eyes and hair plastered down from the heat. I took a bath rapidly to let my companions take theirs. In the evening, we ventured out to the bridge. There, I witnessed a scene that I would never forget: a tank was advancing and a very young Saigon soldier threw a grenade at it. The grenade did not go off, so he darted out to block the road. The tank did not halt. Going back to the tailor's house, I asked myself what the war was all about? I imagined the pain of the mother whose child had just died.

Ho Chi Minh City

The afternoon of Wednesday, April 30th, 1975, we entered Saigon. The orders were very strict. We were all in uniform, with our soft-rimmed hats, and we were very excited, but very moved, as well. As in Hue, as in Da Nang, the chaos was indescribable, with shoes and South Vietnamese uniforms strewn everywhere on the sidewalks. People watched us pass by with certain indifference. Many of those were wearing armbands with a yellow star, as if to say, "We are truly with the Vietcong." Cars with loud speakers called for everyone to keep calm. Henceforth, Saigon was to be called Ho Chi Minh City.

The last Americans had left that morning. On the street in front of their embassy were mounds of suitcases and more uniforms of South Vietnamese soldiers. It was a very beautiful day and very hot, but all the doors remained closed. The plan had been to have us stay at the Hotel Caravelle. Upon our arrival, the staff was ill at ease. But, for us, it was paradise all over again. Imagine the first evening: there was even cheese on the menu and the waiters could not get over the fact that I was familiar with it. Later on, in the room, I was to discover a real bed with white sheets and a bathroom for me, alone! We stayed on for several days, enough time for all the units to regroup and the work to be organized.

On May 7th, we were finally taken to the five imposing buildings used for television broadcasting. In the courtyard, we met other groups from North Vietnamese television. Emotionally worked up, we cried and hugged each other.

Television had been placed under the responsibility of Colonel Hoa of the Saigon army, who warmly welcomed us. The installations seemed to be intact. Our technicians were dumbfounded in front of ultra-modern equipment that they had trouble identifying. In the corridors, we came across graceful young girls whose appearances contrasted enormously with our own.

From there on in, we were to be lodged behind the television buildings, where several sheds formed a semi-circle. The chairman in charge of television for the North arrived about the same time as us and soon began giving us our orders: it was forbidden for those who were natives of the South to visit relatives, to sleep in the city, and to share information with the inhabitants of Saigon about the exchange rate of money in the North, about the standards of living there, or what could be found in shops. For an entire month, we weren't even allowed to go out at night. During the day, we were free to go about filming, but as soon as the sun set, we were to return to the "Castle"—such was the name we had given to the television buildings—and not leave again until morning. There were about sixty of us who were placed under this regime and life got organized around it rather happily. The sheds were transformed into dormitories. We were given sheets, but everybody slept on the floor and we used the lavatory sinks to wash ourselves.

I began at once to conceive of a scenario entitled, *When the Cannon Go Silent*, wherein I evoked the early hours of peace. With my cameramen, we filmed the cleaning up of the mounds of garbage which were piled everywhere, the burial of the unknown dead near the river, the designation of the administrative committees, and all the different changes that occurred in the city. The former television staff developed the films and I took care of the editing. At noon, I noted that it was always the same boy and girl who brought us our lunch. Finally, I got curious and asked why. "Because you don't go out, we don't go out, either," the girl said to me, with the expression of a startled wren. "But there is no reason to do so. We are under orders to remain here, not you. 'Now, off with you and don't come back until tomorrow.' In the meantime, I will have finished my editing." Since our arrival, those youngsters had stayed in the editing room around the clock. Their parents brought them what they needed for subsistence.

"But aren't you a Vietcong?" she inquired anxiously.

"Yes, we are, all of us."

"In that case, why is your accent less pronounced than the others, and the way you speak less brutal?"

"Because most of us are intellectuals. You haven't had any contact with the others and that is why you are scared of them."

We had to reckon three days from the time we did the shooting to projection of the films. The chief editor was in charge of the commentaries. Films from other places were also brought to us. For that reason, we were able to see the great festivities that marked the victory in Hanoi, as well as the ones in the Mekong Delta. The news programs followed one another on all three channels and the people stayed glued to their sets.

Three days after our arrival, the chairman came to ask me to go to the Reunification Palace to film the former Minh government. I knew that my husband's younger brother had been at the Ministry of Information, in charge of the recall of people from the North who were willing to work for the Saigon regime of Ngo Dinh Diem. Perhaps, I would meet him there.

The park of the former Palace of Independence was crowded with tanks and armed soldiers. In the great reception rooms, at the top of the stairs, everything seemed in order. I caught a glimpse of huge elephant tusks, armchairs upholstered in red brocade, and superb carpets. Several delegations were waiting, comprised of fifty or so people and, it seemed to me, a few of them were French. Seated behind a large table were the representatives of the provisionary military government of Saigon. When a North Vietnamese general stood up, everyone stopped talking. "I invite you, all of you who are here," he announced in a solemn tone of voice "national press and international press, to witness the resignation of the South Vietnamese government."

At the top of the great staircase, two officers appeared and started walking down. Then, one by one, all the members of the former Saigon government of General Duong Van Minh followed, pale and exhausted from having been confined to the Palace for several days. My brother-in-law did not seem to be among them. They approached the large table. It was the first time that I saw General Minh. He was tall, well built, and looked like an intellectual. Whereas the others were very elegant in their suits, he was dressed in a khaki uniform. I felt great admiration for the courage he had shown in staying until the end, instead of fleeing abroad, as so many others had done. Someone introduced the members of the former government, one by one. Next, Duong Van Minh took a piece of paper out of his pocket and read in a mournful voice: "We have unconditionally surrendered and, as of now, we place all our power in your hands." The general who was presiding the meeting then took over: "You are all going to return to your homes. From today on, I am asking you to show complete cooperation with the new government." Once again, I had the feeling that I was witnessing an historic moment: after the abdication of Bao Dai, that of the South Vietnamese government. The only difference for me between the two events is that I can now relive the latter by watching the films that my two cameramen had shot.

Hardly had I left the Palace when I heard a voice calling my name. It was Hue, one of my two maternal uncles whom I had not seen since my departure in 1946. We threw ourselves in each other's arms. After having retired from the *PTT*,[1] he had started a business in trading grain and had opened several stores, mainly in Hue and in Saigon.

"You must come to my house," he insisted as he wrote down his address on a piece of paper.

"Do you know where my parents are?"

"The whole family left on April 29th." As for himself, he had not wanted to abandon his property.

By the end of the month, we were finally allowed to visit a member of our family and to dress in normal fashion in shirts and black pants. At 336 Tran Quy Cap, Uncle Hue was living in a five-story house, where other distant members of my family from Hue and Da Nang were regrouped in the hope of leaving for the United States. There were fifty or so of them camping together, occupying rooms throughout the house. Not having enough money or the right connections, they had not been able to get away and were waiting now for the outcome of events.

As soon as I entered, my aunts pranced on me and drowned me in kisses while crying, "We have nothing left." "They burned everything," one of them said.

"Not at all, auntie. I've been to Hue and nothing has been burned."

---

[1] *Poste, Télégraphe et Téléphone*—the former name of the national post office system, which ran the mail, telegraph, and telephone services in one centralized organization.

"Oh, yes, my girl. You don't know about it." I insisted that the villagers led me to their houses and not one of them had been destroyed. Suddenly relieved, my aunts broke out into laughter and went away to prepare the meal. Taking advantage of that, my uncle went to invite in my cameramen who were waiting outside in the Jeep.

Curious people assembled around the vehicle. My uncle introduced me: "Here is my niece who has returned from the Resistance." Then, he turned to me: "With the Jeep in front of the house, no one will come and bother me." Another of my cousins, living in the area, then arrived. She was my uncle's daughter, too young at the time of my departure for me to have known her. I was seeing a beautiful young lady come towards me wearing a blue, Saigon-fashion *ao dai*, heavy make-up, and long fingernails with red polish.

"What am I to do, Phuong?" she whimpered. "I won't be able to go out anymore if I am not allowed to wear make-up. Is it true that you are going to cut off long, polished nails and shave penciled eyebrows?" Because of my surprised reaction, she continued: "I read in the newspapers that the soldiers of the North yanked out polished nails."

"No, not at all. Calm down! Don't change anything of your appearance. Besides, it's very attractive."

"It is? It is?" she repeated, relieved.

Those were strange moments. Each person, in turn, flooded me with questions. Unfortunately, I did not have answers to everything and, even worse, I could not reassure them about their future. What I had gone through in Hanoi had taught me a lesson and I preferred to be cautious. Anyway, whatever I would have said, I knew well what they were really thinking: "More Vietcong propaganda."

As my uncle kept on insisting, I ended up by going to live in his house along with my cameramen and my chauffeur.

The governing authorities allowed us to do so because living at the "Castle" had quickly become impossible. My uncle gave us a huge room with beds against the walls and chests underneath for our belongings, which was far more than adequate considering we only spent nights there. Every evening, he insisted on showing us the city. In the Chinese district, I discovered a sort of immense appliance store overflowing with refrigerators, electric cookers, and a whole bunch of gadgets that I never could have imagined. My uncle seemed to be seized by a mad shopping spree. He confessed that he was afraid of devaluation. "If money isn't worth anything anymore, I can still re-sell all this merchandise."

A few days later, I finally decided to visit the house that my parents had lived in. Although I had been dying to do so ever since my arrival, I realized that I had preferred to postpone the moment. My sister Xuan Nhan was living in a large building, several stories high, on rue Yendo. "You are the elder sister?" the French caretaker asked me immediately. "Your grandmother talked about you often. You look so much like the rest of your family. Wait here a moment." When he came back, he held out a fat envelope. "There, that's for you. I know you don't have much of anything. At this point, there is nothing that I really need for myself anymore." It was a wad of bills, more than I had ever possessed. Then he gave me a small revolver. "Here, a present from me. Maybe you'll need it one day." Carrying arms was strictly forbidden but, like the money, I didn't have the heart to turn it down. I would get rid of it later on.

The interior of the house was impressive, with marble everywhere. My aunt had told me that it had been built by an Italian architect. The pharmacist, the laboratory technicians, and all of my sister's collaborators continued to work in the lab that occupied two floors, as if nothing had changed.

"Where is my parents' bedroom?"

"On the fifth floor," a voice answered. In the room, everything seemed intact. It was apparent that my parents had left unexpectedly, leaving all their belongings behind. On the ancestral altar I found a snapshot of myself when I was five years old. For all those years, I was officially declared dead. Going through the closets, I recognized my father's suits and my mother's *ao dais*. I could smell her perfume; I would have liked to stay there forever. I quickly picked up the numerous family photos that were strewn about on the floor. In the mirror, I spotted faces staring at me with curiosity. As soon as Saigon was liberated, a law had been promulgated confiscating all the houses whose owners had fled the city after April 25th. It was totally out of the question that I could live in my sister's home.

Soon, I met one of the comrades with whom I had done my mid-wife studies in Hanoi. Shortly afterwards, she had left the Resistance to become personal secretary to Madame Ngo Dinh Nhu and, later, take on the direction of a big insurance company. As soon as she had heard that I was in Ho Chi Minh City, and that I was allowed at last to leave the enclave of the television studios, she invited me to an evening party with other former classmates. My director and cameramen friends, as well as the poet, Phan Vu, another of my friends who had come from Hanoi, were all excited at the idea of going with me. Arriving in the courtyard of the house at 80 rue Hong Thang Tu, we first thought that we were at the wrong address. Full of American and Japanese cars, it looked more like a meeting of diplomats. My friend greeted us at the doorstep and, inside, the house was swarming with people. The men were in evening attire and the women were dressed like princesses, with sparkling diamonds. But it was our own dress that created a huge stir: the military outfits and Ho Chi Minh sandals. No sooner had we taken our seats than people were snowing us with questions.

Among the elegant women, I recognized a few of my former friends. I was impressed with their hairstyles, their make-up and their well-cared-for hands. Their charm worked on the men who accompanied me. They wanted to know everything about us—why we had signed up with the Resistance and what happened during all those years. But it was they who answered their own questions. Phan Vu recited several poems that he had written, himself. I guessed that the lives those women had led seemed quite dull compared to ours. It was as if one of my friends had understood what I was thinking when she suddenly remarked: "We have a good life here, but then again, nothing ever happens to us." Two women passed around some dishes. In the North there were no longer any servants like them.

My friend pulled me along to her bedroom. Lining three of the walls, there were closets in which I discovered a profusion of dresses, handbags, shoes, and jewelry. When I asked her whose wardrobe she was keeping, she thought that I was making fun of her. "All this is mine. I wear most of what is here, and the other things I keep here for the pleasure of looking at them."

The atmosphere during the evening was very warm and relaxed and I had not the slightest notion of what time it was. I had the impression that affairs were brewing among my former classmates and my companions. It had been so long since I had experienced such moments. When we took leave of each other, one of my friends told me, "If our past had to be summed up, it would not take long: We left to pursue our studies in Switzerland or in France before coming back here in order to try hard at accumulating as many riches as possible."

On May 15th, the television chairman asked me to go to Dalat to film an important meeting. I was thrilled at the idea of seeing my childhood city again, with its magnificent pine trees and Great Lake.

The road was all uphill for three hundred kilometers, crossing forests and passes lined with inns that had re-opened. In Blao, tea could be purchased again, as had been the tradition. But civilian cars were not yet authorized and, halfway there, a man motioned at us and the chauffeur stopped. I recognized one of my former classmates. "Can you give me a ride to Dalat?" I had just begun to understand that people felt more secure with the North Vietnamese.

As we came to the waterfall at Prenn which marked the beginning of the rise towards Dalat, two black silhouettes darted out of the side ditches of the road and aimed machine guns at the car. "Stop!" They were quite young boys, sixteen at the outmost and extremely worked up, like the ruthless ones I had seen in the past during the land reform. The one who seemed to be the leader yelled out: "Who are you?"

"We are a team from Vietnamese television, heading for Dalat where we are to do a documentary."

"Let me see your papers!" He turned our pass in every which direction. I was surprised: "Don't you know how to read?"

"How do you dare ask such a question to a revolutionary?" He got even more nervous and waved his rifle under my nose. I tried to stay calm: "We, too, are members of the revolution."

"You're lying." Then he turned towards my friend. "This one is a former colonel from the Saigon army." "Perhaps, but now, he is no longer a colonel. He belongs to our team." "I have orders, so I'm going to put you all in jail." The chauffeur whispered to me to keep quiet: "Not a word more because he is going to shoot us. These guys are like the red guards—they don't hesitate." Without wasting a second, there they were, hopping on to the running boards and ordering us to advance.

The situation was extremely ironic: I had struggled the greater part of my life to be able to return freely to my native city and here I was being led in as a prisoner, held as a target by boys scarcely the age of my own sons. Hardly had I the time to recognize Dalat when I was locked up in a house in the center of town. "I'm going to draw up a report for my superior officer," the leader declared. But suddenly, he whipped around, grabbed a stick that was in the corner of the room and began slashing my friend. "Traitor, spy, there, that's what you deserve!" I attempted to bring him to reason: "Stop. You have no right to do that." My intervention served no purpose because he pushed him into the adjoining room to carry on beating him. We could have jumped out of the window into the street, but I feared not knowing where to go. Monsieur Luong, commander in charge of the military administration of the city, was a friend of my family and a former student of my father's. Therefore, I could have confidence in him. I decided to write him a letter and gave it to someone who was passing by. Three hours later, around eight o'clock in the evening, a car stopped in front of the house. The door opened and Luong held out his arms to me. "Big sister! Why didn't you tell me that you were coming here? I would have come to welcome you. What is happening?" I told him all about our adventure. In the meanwhile, the two boys had disappeared, abandoning my unfortunate friend in a lamentable state.

My first few days in Dalat, I recognized nothing. The city was in the hands of looters. Students roamed from house to house to collect all the writings in foreign languages that they could get their hands on and entire libraries fed the huge bonfires on a hillside. My parents' house, which had already changed tenants several times, was falling into ruin. The buildings of the *Couvent des Oiseaux* were unchanged. Its park was as beautiful as it had always been, but the church was closed and most of the nuns had returned to France. There was only a Mother Superior and one sister left who did not cease repeating to me: "How could a girl from the *Couvent des Oiseaux* ever have become a Vietcong?" I saw the lake again and the market but the atmosphere was stifling. It was obvious that the inhabitants were afraid and preferred to clam up. Although people seemed friendly enough to our faces, I knew very well that as soon as our backs were turned, bitterness welled up in them. How many of their relatives had left Dalat and had not as yet sent any news? We could have been happy—the Americans had departed, and the war was over, but not the one dividing the Vietnamese.

Back in Saigon, I returned to my uncle's house. Within just a few days, the city had changed quite a bit.

Soldiers had been quartered in beautiful, unoccupied homes and such a sight was often depressing. The tank crewman who had come with us was living in a judge's house. Along with his friends, they had completely looted the place, taking pictures and objects. They slashed the mattresses and did not even know how to handle the faucets. They built fires in the garden with the furniture and planted cucumbers and red peppers in place of the rosebushes. There was ignorance in their acts, for sure, but a desire for vengeance, as well. Elsewhere, the soldiers turned a swimming pool into a fish hatchery. But how could they be blamed? Just a short time before, they were still peasants.

One evening, my uncle wanted to take me to dinner in the Chinese district. "You're going to meet an extraordinary person," he told us. In Cholon, all the shops were open, overflowing with goods. On the ground floor of a house, in a large reception room decorated in the Chinese style, we found ourselves in the presence of a man in his fifties, dressed in a long black brocade robe, with lavender sleeve lining, patent-leather shoes, and a soft, black hat. Surrounded by four or five bodyguards, Monsieur Quang was smoking a water pipe and seemed to ignore our presence. After bowing before him, my uncle introduced me: "Here is my niece. She has been away at war for thirty years. Now she works for the television." With those words, the other seemed to wake up. "Very pleased to meet you. Come, we're going to dine together." Two American cars were waiting for us outside.

Fortunately, my cameramen had accompanied us and I felt less alone. We soon arrived at a restaurant called "The Baghdad." Monsieur Quang spoke in Chinese with the boss. We were led to the back of the room. "Duck your heads," the man said. We entered a room whose walls were built up with aquaria. The impression was extraordinary, with all those brightly colored fish undulating about. "Put two gold taels[2] on the table," Monsieur Quang ordered to one of his bodyguards. The owner of the restaurant picked up the gold and bowed so low he was touching the floor. That was understandable: two taels were worth around four hundred dollars. The meal was sumptuous and the table was too small to hold all of the dishes that arrived, one after the other. "Just wait, this is not all there is," my uncle whispered. A yellow curtain that was hanging in front of one of the sides of the aquarium spread open and revealed two young girls in Chinese brocade dresses, one quite tall, all in white, and the other smaller, in black. They both had old-fashioned hairstyles, which were exquisitely beautiful. "They are characters from *The Pink Pavilion Dream* who are

---

[2] The tael is a standard Chinese weight equal to 1.2 troy ounces or 0.1 pounds. In 1975 gold was worth an average of about $165 an ounce.

going to interpret for us the story of *The Veranda of the East,"* Monsieur Quang announced. The moment was magical. "He had brought back these young girls from China to have them transformed according to photos," my uncle whispered. What a contrast there was between that social status and the rest of the country, where blood had been spilled for so many years! I left the dinner behind me, like my companions, sickened at the thought. We would have preferred to be spared such an invitation.

Most of the people still living in Ho Chi Minh City were mainly just working people—those who had not been able to leave. On the whole, they showed a rather kindly attitude towards us, but I supposed, behind the facade, they, too, were afraid. On the other hand, the film editors and the sound engineers were always eager to invite us to their homes. Each time, the meetings were convivial and offered the occasion for us to note the comfortable standard of living those families enjoyed. In that circle, all the children had a reserved place to study, the houses were well kept, the women wore carefully ironed *ao dais*, and people were polite with one another, saying "good-bye" and "thank you." I realized to what extent I missed order and stability. I was nostalgic for a well-organized society.

After having spent several weeks in Ho Chi Minh City, I was to return to Hanoi. The ditches at the sides of Route No. 1 were still cluttered with abandoned trucks. Even the least important building hoisted a red flag. At the 17th parallel, the bridge was transformed into a checkpoint. Everyone was searched. The wads of fabric that I was bringing back at my friends' requests were unfolded and all mixed up. I couldn't remember which one was for whom. Back in Hanoi, I returned to my family and my house, where nothing had changed. Through long conversations, I shared the historic events I had just experienced with my friends and I went from school to school to talk about them. My husband was beside himself when I told him what I had seen in Ho Chi Minh City.

All things considered, I was then determined to leave Hanoi for the South, and too bad that my husband had strongly affirmed that he, personally, did not like its commercially oriented culture. But I had endured our restricted living conditions for too long a time—the interminable waiting lines for water and for the toilets, the smells from the kitchens, and the screeching from the loudspeakers. He wound up by telling me: "If you really want so much to live in the South, go ahead. As for me, I'm staying in the North." One evening in 1983, I came home totally exhausted from work and found everyone already in bed. I took my mattress and climbed up to the roof. There was a full moon that night and it was cold. I started rambling out loud: "Why go on like this? I can't take it any longer." The next day, I wrote a letter to the television chairman, asking him to find me a new position.

As I was born in Hue, I was first offered a position there, as might have been expected. I was not at all against such an idea, especially since my eldest son was living there with his wife—whom he had met in the city—and their child. Nevertheless, I preferred to spend a few days there before committing myself any further. At first sight, the television studios seemed rather small compared to those in Hanoi. I would have to get used to that. But even worse, three days later my aunt's house—where I was living—was invaded by other members of my family who had stayed on in Hue. For the most part, they were officers of the Saigon army: "Don't you remember me? You haven't forgotten your niece, your cousin?" All were obviously waiting for me to provide work for them at the television studios in Hue. "You must welcome them with open arms," my aunt said, "if not, they will say that you are a heartless communist." I had to greet them, smile and listen to them, one after the other, knowing that I could not hire a single one of the lot. They hadn't the least experience whatsoever, and no technical training. They were there simply because I was their aunt or their cousin. I made my decision on the fourth day. I could not accept that job. I had too many relatives living in Hue and they would create far too many problems for me that were impossible to solve. Therefore, I returned to Hanoi, to its six months of drizzling cold weather. Nothing had changed, except me. I knew at that point that it was possible to live differently and that many of my convictions had proved wrong. Whether my husband agreed with me or not, we had to get out.

At the television studios, a short time beforehand, a journalist working for tourism had told me that executives were needed in Vung Tau (the former *Cap Saint-Jacques*). Commercial activity had begun developing due to the offshore drilling being carried out by foreign companies. The moment was just right. My sons could work in Vung Tau while I could find a job with the television in Saigon. The prospect enchanted them, especially Phuong, my second son, who had a particularly difficult time readapting to our kind of life after having spent three years in Poland. I had already evoked the possibility to Phuoc, my son living in Hue, and he was ready to join us.

The Vietnamese Director of Tourism, whom I had known for a long time, seemed enchanted with the new recruits. From one moment to the next, my sons were promoted to head administrators of tourism in Vung Tau. "Tomorrow," he told me, "we have trucks that are heading there. Do you want to take advantage of that?" Without a telephone, I could not even let my husband know, so I wrote to him. By evening, our suitcases were ready. The next morning, the 27th of May, I believe, we left. In Hue, my son, my daughter-in-law, and their son joined us and we continued on, first towards Saigon, and then to Vung Tau. There, my sons were given a well-furnished house with electricity. What a dream!

Upon arriving in Ho Chi Minh City, I first had to obtain a residence card, an indispensable document without which I could not permanently stay on. The city administration began by refusing to give it to me. "Your husband is in Hanoi. Why do you want to stay here without him?"

"He is very fond of Hanoi. As for me, I have to first think of my children who are in the South." But the civil servant played dumb. All I could then do was plead my cause to the city's vice-president, another of my war friends. "If I had known when I joined the Resistance that I would be treated in such a way... Why hadn't I been warned that I would have to live where the government chose for me to live?"

Five days later, my residence card for Ho Chi Minh City was delivered.

I lived for a while with my cousin, Hoa Quang, the one who had polished nails. Later on, the television organization found me an apartment in an out-of-the-way neighborhood, but I preferred to use my own means to find one in the center of the city. On top of my usual work, I began promotion films for the Vietnamese Tourist Service. For compensation, I was given a room at the Hotel Bong Sen, in the former rue Catinat, re-baptised Dong Khoi, which means "uprising," after having been named "Tu Do" or "liberty" by the South Vietnamese. I spent a year and a half there, and began to put aside a little money. Once or twice a month, I took the overcrowded bus to Vung Tau to see my sons. From time to time, as well, I went to visit my husband in Hanoi. In spite of my sons' begging, he swore that he would never join us in the South.

Three years before retiring, I finally found the house of my dreams on rue Catinat and I am still living there today. I have a duplex apartment with four bedrooms on the first story, and three more upstairs leading out onto a terrace. I had two second-hand American appliances, a refrigerator and a washing machine. What luxury compared to Hanoi. I even had a woman come in to cook and clean. At last, I recovered the feelings of my childhood, those of finding pleasure in coming home to a well looked-after house. Even if the street was full of soldiers and the political atmosphere more and more stifling, the enormous vitality that the city generated remained contagious.

There was just one thing left for me to do. I had to get my eldest son transferred to the Ho Chi Minh City Audiovisual Center where he could eventually be in a position to replace me. After 1980, it had become exceedingly difficult to settle here. The City Committee screened applications and accepted only college graduates. With my son having graduated from the Film Institute, his hiring by the Audiovisual Center was not too much of a problem. At first, my daughter-in-law refused to leave Vung Tau. Then, she eventually had to admit that leaving her husband alone in this city was not a good idea and she relented. I encouraged her to study English and to find an independent profession. I was seeing too many people who were counting on the state to provide jobs, and therefore had to be satisfied with measly salaries.

Once a month at the television studios, we attended a compulsory meeting during which the political line that had to be followed was defined. In a given month, there were to be five broadcasts produced on the subject of rice. In another, we had to report nationalization of factories. Each one of us chose the subject we were most interested in and I selected to be in charge of social affairs: drug-addicts, prostitutes, illiteracy, and water problems. I also directed numerous films for a series entitled "Vietnam, Our Land." Those broadcasts brought me huge stacks of mail: the audience wondered why a country with so many resources could be starving. "You deliberately managed to lead people into asking themselves such questions, haven't you?" the chairman asked me. Of course, I had done it on purpose. When I considered the deprivations that the people at the 17th parallel still had to endure in order to make the soil produce a bit of manioc, tears welled up in my eyes. In Tonkin, at Thai Binh where I had been filming, the population density—one thousand three hundred people to the square kilometer—was such that one could reach out the window of one house and touch the wall of the next. The peasants had nothing but a tiny patch of land. They had no fertilizer except whatever alluvial deposits were left by the river, and they used them to grow, at the cost of superhuman effort, every single clump of rice plant. The more I traveled across the country, the greater grew my admiration for its people.

A Vietnamese in Paris

In 1975, I was terribly disappointed to learn that my family had just left for America. Since that moment, I never ceased dreaming of the day when I would be reunited with them. But in the years 1985 and 1986 one had to go through a nightmare of administrative red tape to get permission to work abroad. It was necessary to climb a ladder consisting of seven rungs, that is, obtain the right from seven successive authorities—beginning with my own head, who would, in turn, start the process with the police and other authorities that would be most likely to grant me a passport. It seemed so hopeless I might just as well have given up before even trying. But it was through Thien Tich—"Heaven's Benediction"—one of my uncles from Hue who had been living in France for some time and who had been begging me to come and see him, that I was allowed in 1986 to fill out my first application. Officially, I was to travel to see my uncle, but actually my intention was to get to see my mother by transiting through France. That same year, I was also beginning to prepare for my retirement. The day that I would no longer have the status of civil servant, the formalities for departure would be less complicated.

An entire year passed before I was summoned by the police. "It is difficult to let you travel because all your family is in America," the man in charge told me.

"In other words, *you* don't want me to leave. My whole life has been spent fighting for my country, and you don't even trust me."

"On the contrary, we do trust you, and it is for your own protection that we are telling you this." It was not worth insisting. It was better to wait for my retirement and I continued to work as usual. But it was more and more difficult for me to bear the stifling atmosphere that had spread over the country. We were allotted thirty minutes of international news on television, provided it came exclusively from socialist countries. We were ignorant of events in other nations and we were not allowed to talk to foreigners. Even I was prohibited from exchanging words with them in the street, and was restricted to communicating exclusively at a hotel. Like all officials, I had a police file that I knew by heart: "Too independent—knows too many foreigners." A member of the Party's Central Committee in charge of the journalists told me one day: "You are too disobedient."

At the end of 1986, the head of television personnel summoned me: "Sister, you have attained the age of retirement. As you have an excellent work record, we would like to keep you on for five more years. I am ready to sign a new contract which would allow you to earn your retirement pay as well as a salary that is twice the sum of what you are earning now."

"I thank you very much, but this is out of the question. I really want to retire."

I did not even hesitate. Nothing anymore was more important now than seeing my mother again. "You know that by retiring, your salary will be decreased by thirty-five per cent. How are you going to live on that?" "Never mind. I have thought it all over quite seriously." The same day that I signed my retirement papers, I went to ask for my visa as an ordinary citizen. My former superior waited for six more months before issuing a certificate attesting to my work.

"When you leave the country, don't talk too much about all that is not going well in Vietnam," he recommended to me, as if what was happening here went unnoticed abroad! Permission for me to leave the country finally came through in the beginning of 1989. Before that, I had to write numerous letters describing my family members, how many there were, their whereabouts, and their activities. Giving all those details was not in the least problematical since I had always told the truth. Then, finally, I had to obtain authorization from the French embassy. "You are no longer very young," one said to me. "Your uncle, who has filled out the housing certificate, is living in a retirement home and does not have the means to put you up. Consequently, we regret the fact that we can not issue you a visa." "I have enough to live on in France all by myself for three months. Why are you refusing to deliver the visa?" "You must petition the ambassador, himself." Actually, my uncle had lost a lot of money at the races and, fearing loss of face, he did not want his family to know about it. By chance, over the years, I had also made many films for the new foreign investors in Vietnam, besides the work I had been doing for television. Alain L., chief executive for a French naval construction company, did not hesitate one second to vouch for me and agreed to guarantee a place for me to stay in France. It was a gesture of generosity that I would never forget.

Alas, hardly had I obtained the precious documents needed for leaving the country, when a sad event compelled me to postpone my departure. My friend Nam, whom I had not lost sight of for one second since my return to Hanoi, had developed liver cancer. Because of the lack of hospital facilities in the North, my husband suggested that we help him obtain care at the Reunification Hospital in Ho Chi Minh City. There, he would be cared for in the best conditions possible and his wife could spend nights at his bedside. I made sure that there would be a nursing service to give him massages. I went to see him every day when I was in the city and, in the beginning of 1989, Nam passed away in my arms. Just before dying, I heard him pronounce my name. "Phuong, thank you for everything you have done for me. Now, I am going away." After the funeral, I experienced a feeling of great loss. I wanted to return to Hue alone to revisit the places that we, Nam and I, had known together. Once more, my husband proved to be very generous in letting me leave. In Hue, I floated through a week of wistful daydreaming. I wandered the paths that we had rambled over in days gone by. I went to see our school, the house where Nam had lived and the pagodas that we were wont to visit. It was a parting pilgrimage—a way of putting remembrances into order. Then I spent two days in a pagoda, in the company of nuns. Emerging from my withdrawal from the world, I felt much better, having rid myself of that haunting pain that had been oppressing me since the death of Nam. The moment had come to leave and seek out how I was to occupy my free time, to complement my twenty-dollar monthly retirement allocation with a means of earning a living.

My trip to France would certainly expand my horizons. What I wanted more than anything else was to create my own company, be my own master, do everything I had ever wanted to without having to ask permission from anybody. I had spent my life depending on others and obeying them. I had sacrificed all that I had for the benefit of a collective society. I reasoned that the moment had finally come for me to live for myself. At that time it was still impossible, however, to imagine how on earth a private enterprise functioned. The state was omnipresent. It is true that people had the right to set up their own businesses but, after fifty years of collective work, the obstacles that the authorities imposed—the laws, the contracts—were endless. Most of my friends feared seeing me getting involved in such a project. "Look at us. We are living a comfortable life with our pension. We don't need much and we have no worries which prevent us from sleeping at night."

On the eve of my departure for France on July 12th, 1989, my husband, my children and all of my friends accompanied me to the airport. I chose to wear a simple grey pants suit—my best outfit—and someone lent me a suitcase. I was deeply moved having to leave my family behind, but also excited at the prospect of leaving the country and at last making new discoveries. I will never forget the moment when the Air France flight took off. The two French people sitting next to me were astonished at how well I spoke their language, considering the fact that I had never been to France. At the stopover in Bangkok, I could not believe just how grandiose the airport looked compared to the one in Hanoi. It was all the more surprising for a people that the Vietnamese had always considered as being inferior. When we landed at Charles de Gaulle Airport, I was flabbergasted by the gigantic installations. I felt totally lost. Not knowing how to redeem my suitcase, I followed the other passengers. While I was waiting for my baggage, I could see people on an overhead viewing area waving at the arriving passengers. My uncle, Thien Tich did not appear to be among them. It was out of the question that he had not come to get me! I also put aside the idea that I would not recognize him after forty years of separation.

At the exit, among all the Vietnamese, I immediately saw a man who resembled my mother. He did not notice me, though. That was not astonishing, since the last time he had seen me, I had been sixteen years old and now I was fifty-nine. "Is that really you, uncle?" We were both deeply moved and he took me in his arms. My aunt, who was Chinese and whom I had never met, also hugged me.

We left the airport and, once more, it proved a great shock encountering the multitude of cars and the traffic jams around the buildings. The sight of such wealth made me feel our daring fight with France was totally incongruous. I felt like a heartland farmer who leaves her village for the first time. My uncle drove quite fast in his Fiat and stopped at the first bakery in sight: "It is early. Let's buy some bread and go home for breakfast."

It was the first time since leaving Dalat that I found myself in a French bakery. It reminded me of my youth, except for the size of the shop, which was far larger and sold not only bread, but croissants, raisin bread, and all varieties of pastry, as well. The fragrance went to my head. I could have tasted every thing. My uncle bought a *baguette* and, in the next-door grocery, some cheese. Then, off we headed toward *St Michel-sur-Orge*.

Thanks to my brothers who had sent him money, my uncle had reserved a hotel room for me. That was fortunate, as I would have felt like an inmate in his retirement home, where one had to be careful to prevent doors from making any noise when being opened or closed, to walk on tip-toes, and to whisper rather than speak, lest someone inevitably yell: "Be quiet!" The retirees went to fetch their platters and took them back to their rooms to eat. Most of the time, nobody came to visit them. No matter how comfortable the home was, I wouldn't have wanted to be put in a position of having to live like them, and that particular kind of solitude of the elderly was one of the first things that struck me in France. At home, there would always be some relative to care for them. When I asked my uncle why he would not go back to Vietnam where he still owned a house and had aunts who would take care of him, he answered that he would never return because he was too frightened of the mosquitoes!

Late that afternoon we called my mother in California. Not having yet been issued her green card, she could not leave the United States, so I was the one who would have to make the trip. Our agreement about the solution was quickly reached. At the American Embassy I had to stand in line outside on the sidewalk. A huge soldier, holding two ferocious-looking hounds on a leash, kept walking back and forth in front of us, and this made me feel quite ill at ease. Once inside, I showed my passport to the official who was sitting at his desk. "You are Vietnamese?" he asked me in French. "Yes." He carefully examined my passport, page after page. "Sorry," he concluded, "you come from an enemy country. You cannot be given a visa." There was nothing left for me to do but wait until my mother could come over. Immediately after my arrival, I had also tried to contact Joris Ivens, but to my dismay he had died just a week prior to my visit.

From St. Michel-sur-Orge, I had to take a train to get to Paris. The first time I used the automatic ticket dispenser, coins came cascading down into the receptacle bin below. When I conveyed my surprise to the station attendant, he just laughed and explained that the machine was simply returning my change.

In Paris, everywhere I walked I had the strange feeling that it was all very familiar. I felt that the French culture that I had absorbed ever since my very earliest childhood was resurfacing. The people's carefree attitude was enchanting to me and I was fascinated by the abundance of goods in the shops. In the *Prisunic* department stores I could spend hours in the stationery sections. I looked at the enormous assortment of bags and supplies children could choose from before going back to school. I compared the beautiful white pages of the notebooks with the ugly, black-straw studded paper that my children used to write on. I would roam the aisles from top to bottom of *Le Bon Marché*, reminiscing about the orders we used to place there from Dalat. Very soon, I realized that in order to make plans for my future I would be much better off living in Paris, rather than in St. Michel-sur-Orge. My sister sent me a thousand dollars, which enabled me to survive for quite a while. Besides, I renewed acquaintances with several French people whom I had met in Vietnam in the mid 1980s and who had offered to help me if I ever came to Paris. Stéphane R. came to fetch me in his Peugeot and put me up at his place. Soon, I moved on, first staying at his friend Jean-Pierre N.'s place, and then at Bernard P.'s studio in the St Sulpice district: "Here's the key; the telephone is on me. You can stay as long as you like." Being able to explore this district without the least restriction or constraint, and seeing all the magnificent shops I felt as if I had become a student once more. Everyone introduced me to his or her friends and I was invited all over. In the course of conversations and when making new acquaintances I came to realize just how limited most people's knowledge about Vietnam was, and especially of its fine arts. People knew only about the war. At the Vietnam House on *rue du Cardinal-Lemoine*, many French people bought books and art objects and showed interest in a few mediocre silk screens that were on display, as if they were worth something. Thus, the idea came to me of creating a company that would blend tourism and art. When I wrote to my sons telling them of my project, their response was enthusiastic and they were ready to work with me.

From then on, I spent a lot of time in the travel agencies of the 13th district to see for myself how the Vietnamese operated. I took down notes that I sent to my sons. A pharmacist, Roland R., who had worked in Saigon with my sister until 1975, introduced me, in turn, to some other friends of his who were interested in Vietnam and the Vietnamese arts. Soon I became convinced that I could succeed in this field. But for the time being I had to wait for my mother, who could still not make it to France.

My prolonged stay in Paris also helped me to forget somewhat the years of hardship. My meetings with Vietnamese people made me realize that they fell into two categories: the fierce anti-communists and the no less fierce pro-communists. When I was invited to anti-communists' homes, they would start criticizing me as soon as they heard that I was from the North. I could not engage in even the most rudimentary discussion with them because, for the most part, they had lost everything—family members, wealth, and status. There was nothing left for me to do but to remain silent and try to avoid them. On the other hand, I met other Vietnamese who eventually became dear to my heart: a lawyer Toan, one of my brother-in-law's friends and former Minister of Information under the Diem government; a lieutenant in the military secret service who had been promoted to vice-president of the Vietnamese Patriot's Association and whose son, Maurice C., was a famous physician working in acupuncture; and Dr. T., who was my former superior at the Cultural Relations Committee. These latter, on the contrary, invited me over almost every week so that I would feel less alone in Paris. With them, I chose to avoid delicate subjects of disagreement. All the more so as their way of thinking was very positive, with clear ideas and realistic projects, something which would be of great help to me. In Hanoi, we never really used to know what was going to befall us from one day to the next—be it that one single bomb would land in the wrong place and everything would be over. Thus, it was very difficult for people to know what they could achieve and difficult for them to make plans. Whereas here, I saw people everywhere launch into endeavors and succeed in their professions—for example, a former colonel who had bombed Diem's palace was now an executive at the famous food shop, *Lenôtre*. He knew absolutely nothing of my preoccupations, but I never tired of hearing him describe his work methods and I took careful note.

However, in spite of their success and their comfortable lives, I realized that all those Vietnamese were nostalgic for Vietnam, and for their friends and their relatives who had been left behind. Most made a good living, and their children were going to the best schools. But often they did not even speak Vietnamese and the character of their family relationships was utterly different from that of those who still lived in Vietnam. One Sunday, one of my friends wanted to take me outside Paris to see his son who was a doctor. He rang the bell of a very beautiful mansion. At the window, we could see a young woman sewing. "Who is it?" "It's Daddy." Yet, nobody came. My friend rang the bell again. At long last, the woman came to open the door. "What do you want?" "Meet my friend Phuong. We just wanted to spend the day away from the city." "But I didn't invite you! Why didn't you phone first?" We left, and to save the day, my friend's wife suggested we have lunch in a little restaurant nearby. Then we went for a little walk. "You see," my friend said, "this is the way the Vietnamese live abroad." But his own intention was to go back to Vietnam as soon as he could.

Ba, my pediatrician brother in America, had a pharmacist friend, Mr. Bui, who, along with his wife, would be instrumental in helping me understand France. Amidst all those friends, I sensed that time was flowing by faster. Every month my mother wrote to me: "Wait for me a few more weeks." At three-month intervals, I renewed my visa; and two years went by in the course of which I traveled all over France. In the meantime, I had become the quasi-official interpreter for the Vietnamese Embassy, which called on me every time a Minister was visiting. This allowed me to take advantage of all the official receptions and to enjoy exceptional privileges, such as the incredibly luxurious room at the *Hôtel Crillon* in which I wallowed for ten days waiting for a delegation member who had been unable to leave Vietnam.

I also subcontracted translations, and the money I thus made went towards obtaining more pleasant amenities of life. As soon as I was paid, I would begin by filling up the refrigerator. Afterwards, I was able to spend my days in museums and libraries. I immersed myself in the poetry of Prévert and also gobbled up accounts of how some people had achieved their success. Evenings, I would go to the movies. I never seemed to tire from my recovered freedom. It is hard to imagine how intoxicating it is to be able to walk the streets without anyone paying attention, to be able to move about without any hindrance, to be able to make a living in any way one wants or even become rich thanks to one's work.

The announcement of my mother's imminent arrival in the company of my brother came through a call from my sixth sister, the one born in 1951 while I was in the jungle. My little sister was already in Paris with my third sister, Xuan Nhan, but preferred to wait there for our mother before we all got together. From then on, I could not sleep at night. Memories kept flooding back to me. I saw my mother, by my bedside, with her long hair and light-colored silk pajamas. Would we surely recognize each other, wouldn't we? When we got to the airport with my uncle, Thien Tich, my third sister asked me to stay a little behind them, so that my mother would not undergo too much of a shock at seeing me anew.

From a distance, I immediately picked her out from among the passengers. At eighty-two years old she had not changed much and seemed quite young for her age. She was as elegant as ever. I heard: "Where's Phuong? Where's Phuong?" "Calm down, mother. She'll be here soon. There's no need to hurry," my sisters answered. At that point, I could not hold back any longer and went up to her.

"Mother, here I am." She looked at me but there was no recognition.

"Who are you?"

"It's me, Phuong. Don't you remember me?" I could not stop the tears from welling in my eyes. She stared at me, still reluctant to recognize her eldest daughter. Then, all of a sudden she came closer and took me in her arms, crying out: "May Buddha protect you! I can see how much you've suffered. We all prayed so much for you while you were living in constant danger!"

Time seemed to have come to a halt. People stopped right in the middle of the aisle to stare at us, aware that something important was happening. Curiously, I did not recognize her fragrance. She used to smell of betel, I thought, and now it is more like *Chanel N° 5*. But the hands that were caressing my face were still just as fine and soft. As we were leaving the airport, my mother told my sisters: "Mind Phuong, don't let her stumble." To her I was still the sixteen-year-old girl she had lost.

At the hotel in St. Michel-sur-Orge, we spoke for a long time of the past, and of my father's death. He had died from kidney problems on May 7th, 1981. Despite all that, my mother was happy and laughed constantly. It was an immense joy for all of us to be together again, just as it used to be. My sisters and brothers whom I had left when they were kids had become adults. Each of us told his and her story, but to avoid inflicting too much pain upon our mother I refrained from giving too many details of my adventures. She told me of her anguish when, in Saigon, she had heard about the bombings in North Vietnam. She could not sleep. She prayed to Quan Am, the goddess of protection, thanks to whom I was now still alive.

Such reunions went rather badly for many families, but not for ours, not even when I showed them some of my films. Among them was the one about the Ho Chi Minh trail.

"This is communist propaganda," said my younger brother, who wanted to stop the cassette player. The others protested: "No, we want to watch it." There was a feeling of immense love amongst us, regardless of what had happened.

We spent three days in St. Michel-sur-Orge, and then four more at the apartment that Jean-Pierre N. let me use on *rue de la Gaité*, before my family's departure for the United States. They had a hard time understanding how a foreigner like me could have such nice housing—I was lucky to have such good friends. Those few days went by too fast; we had so many stories to tell one another, so many giggles and tears to share. My second brother, the pilot, had been nostalgic for bread since his student years in France, so we kept him endlessly supplied with *baguettes*.

My sisters and brothers left as scheduled a week later. My mother was to stay a full month. But then it was imperative for her to return to the United States if she did not want to forego the pension to which she was entitled as a widow. In the morning she would ask me, "What would you like to eat?"

"I'd love you to prepare glazed fish, just as you used to. I've never had any that even came close to yours." Every day she prepared a new dish. That was all we did: we cooked and talked.

After her departure and thanks to Joris Ivens's wife, I was able to attend the Cannes Film Festival. Eight films a day!

It was heaven for me. I could not get enough. One evening I sat next to Roger Moore, and another evening I had a long conversation with Akira Kurosawa. Those were unforgettable encounters. When I got back to Paris, I felt that the moment had come for me to return to Vietnam. My bad memories had receded little by little and I was ready to try my luck.

Before leaving, I still wanted to put together an exhibit of Vietnamese paintings in order to try and assess the reactions of amateurs. In a room provided by the City Hall in Paris's 1st district, I assembled canvases that I had sent for from Vietnam. Several were by Hoang Sung, my son's father-in-law, whose lacquers I admired very much. My sister in America, Nhan, decided to come especially for the occasion. The Vietnamese Ambassador opened the exhibition and it met with a good measure of success, notably with the "old guard from Indochina," who rediscovered this traditional painting with a great deal of nostalgia. I had even to bar my son's father-in-law from conceding to an art dealer for two hundred dollars per month the exclusive rights to his entire work. By the time the exhibition was over, I was certain that Vietnamese art abroad had good prospects ahead.

The Lotus Gallery

When I arrived in Ho Chi Minh City in December of 1991, my son Phong had already created our company under the name ATC—Art and Tourism. He was a little frightened when I announced my projects because he thought that we did not have the necessary funds. When I spoke of them to my husband he did not criticize me, but he did not encourage me, either.

After being away for two years, I had the impression that things had not evolved very much in Vietnam. It was not my son's opinion: even if most people still had dreadful living conditions, he found that the country was more open to the world, that there were fewer restrictions, and that relationships with foreigners were more relaxed.

I had earned two thousand dollars with the sale of paintings in Paris. The sum was enough to rent a small shop that I called "The Lotus Gallery," where painters could leave their works on consignment. I needed authorization from the Cultural Service, which I got without too much hassle. I had decided to exhibit only painters from the North, whose art is more traditional, more moving, as well, and appreciated by people who truly care about Vietnam. On occasion, I was able to buy this genre of painting very cheaply from the State galleries, whose curators were letting the works accumulate without taking the least interest in marketing them.

Before each exhibit, it was necessary to photograph the paintings, put together a dossier, and submit it to the proper office for authorization. If any of the works was considered inappropriate, we were bluntly told that it would be advisable to substitute another. By avoiding naked figures or anything regarded as truly decadent, censorship was kept minimal.

Foreigners began returning to Vietnam. A few days after the opening, two Frenchmen bought four paintings, which was an encouraging sign. At the very same time, a huge state-run gallery that was just across the street from mine decided to get rid of its entire stock, amounting to a good hundred pieces or so. I succeeded in buying all of them on credit, at a dollar each. The sales got off to a good start. In one single month I had recuperated my two thousand dollars and could then purchase other pictures. During that time, my sons and I had the idea of renting cars in order to offer visitors guided tours.

In the beginning, I played the role of the guide, myself. At the airport, I would go up to travelers arriving on Air France flights and offer our services. My son would drive and I would do the speaking. As I knew the country so well, the people were quite satisfied and, in turn, addressed their friends to us. By the end of three months, we had expanded to renting three cars instead of one and all my French-speaking friends were called in to help because I had to spend my time at the gallery.

In France, I had learned that in the beginning a gallery must aim at promoting young talents whose works are inexpensive. Therefore, I traveled all over the country looking for unknown artists. One day in Hanoi, my friend Sung, a painter, told me about an exhibition devoted to a certain Truong Dinh Hao. The name did not ring a bell. On the third floor of the gallery in question, I discovered a series of magnificent paintings. They were not complex works, but powerful, and almost all done on newsprint. A man could be seen dozing on a chair in a corner of the room.

"Excuse me, but I would like to see the artist, Truong Dinh Hao."

"You're looking at him," he said to me.

Hao lived in a mountain village three hundred kilometers from Hanoi with his wife and his three children. When he had graduated from the *Institut des Beaux-Arts* he was not free to paint as he wished, so he turned to taking care of costumes for a song and dance company. At fifty-two, Hao had practically renounced practicing his art. His house was a miserable hut that leaked from all sides. The interior was dark, being badly lit by two petrol lamps. I saw him climb into a clay oven, where one usually stocked wood and coal, and pull out piles of newspapers.

When he unrolled them, I had a shock. It had been a long time since I had seen such beautiful works executed with so much humaneness. Hao, his wife, and his children assembled in a corner of the room. They looked at me, happy to see that someone was finally showing appreciation of these paintings done on newspaper, the only material available. There were about three hundred in all and I could not afford as yet to be so extravagant as to buy all of them. However, I also realized that I would never find works of such fine quality again.

The sum that we agreed upon very quickly was enough for him to have a decent little house built. I took the works back to Hanoi, escorted by Hao and one of his sons, so that I could hand them over the money to the wide-eyed dissatisfaction of my family.

When I organized my first important Hao exhibit, my friends from the *Association des Beaux-Arts* were astonished.

One of them who was an influential figure told me: "It is my opinion as a seasoned critic that Hao's works have no artistic merit," he insisted, punning on the word "Hao," which means "prosperity," but also "two cents," as in "two cents and not one cent more."

"Excuse me, but I feel that he is prosperous, rather. In any case, let me remind you that this is my gallery and it is a private one. If I lose money, it is no one else's business but my own." A large painting with immense begging eyes hung on the wall in the middle of the exhibit.

"Why do you have this picture as the center of attraction? It is so sad one can feel how tortured he is!" my friend exclaimed.

"I, too, am tortured. Nobody here is happy except yourself, for you are such an extraordinary man. In the name of what can Hao not openly express his misery?"

"It is obvious that he is criticizing the regime," he continued.

"That is what you think. There is nothing to prove so."

The Hao Exhibition was a huge success. I showed Monsieur Blanchemaison, the French Ambassador, the painting that had brought me so much criticism. He found it magnificent. Besides, it was sold during the first days of the show, just like a third of the canvases that were shown.

Some time afterwards, in a gallery on *rue des Tambours*, I was drawn to a small lacquer painting of young girls bathing at a creek that was signed Dinh Quan. I questioned the woman who was in charge of the gallery: The artist was a young man who had just left school but, in her opinion, his work had no intrinsic interest. I insisted on meeting him. She refused. "If you like this picture, buy it. I do not know the whereabouts of the artist." I got the same answer at the *Association des Peintres*. Then, someone finally recalled that he had left school the year before and could be found four kilometers outside of Hanoi.

I located Dinh Quan in a tiny room where he was living with his pregnant wife on the fourth floor of a building. He showed me a number of rough pastel sketches on paper, all of which were small in size due to the fact that he did not have sufficient space in the room to stand farther back from his work. All of his paintings were there because he had to wait for the sale of one in order to buy what was necessary to produce the next. I told him that I was ready to purchase an entire year's work in advance under the condition that he grant me exclusive rights to his production.

"What kind of paintings would you like?" he asked me.

"It is not for me to decide what you must do. You are the one who paints. If you want to execute lacquers from all these sketches, that's all right with me because I like them very much." I also advanced him money so that he could buy gold and silver for his lacquers, after which we agreed upon a certain sum that I would give him for the year. In the beginning, he would phone me all the time to ask if he should put gold in the backgrounds or not. I had to be very firm with him so that he would understand that it was he who was the artist and not I. Having been led around on a leash for so long, people had lost the habit of taking initiatives.

In a very short time, Quan brought me his first paintings, ones that I sold immediately. Today, Dinh Quan has built a three-story house and he exhibits in America.

On a street in Ho Chi Minh City, I came across Doan, whose paintings I had already seen in Hanoi. "I am living here now," he told me.

"Would you like to work for me?" He accepted without much coaxing, and told me about a painter without talent, who had asked him, along with other artists, to come and work at his home. They would paint and he would sign his name to their works. As Doan needed money badly, it was an offer he could not refuse. "From now on, you are free to paint whatever you like and to sign your own name." Soon, my gallery presented nothing but quality works and was a success. I had more and more faithful collectors from France and Japan. In 1994, I managed to take along several of my artists to France, to have them exhibited there. Hao had never been outside of his village and had never flown before. For that matter, neither had the others. When I accompanied them to the Louvre, they all thought that it was "criminal" for such an institution to close at five o'clock in the afternoon. We pursued our visits, from the Luxembourg Gardens all the way to the *Chateaux* of the Loire. Hao laughed continuously and kept repeating: "Now I can see that there exists another life in this world."

The huge exhibit of lacquers that I put together in Dijon was a success beyond all hope. I no longer needed to take out a loan in order to pay back the trip. I could even consider beginning to introduce my painters to other countries.

From 1994 on, I would organize exhibits all over the world on a regular basis: in Belgium, Holland, Germany, Japan, and, once a year, in Singapore. It was there that I was fortunate to meet Patrick R., an enthusiast for Vietnamese painting. Therein, a close friendship grew between him and my artists.

On his own, my son developed the tourist agency with the same measure of success as my gallery undertakings. My retired friends could not understand why I kept on working so much and why I arrived so often late to our meetings. I would have long discussions with them, particularly with the military doctor. At that time, she was not doing much anymore and was satisfied with her meager pension as an ex-colonel. Her only wish was that nothing disturb the norm. Others were fed up with playing nursemaid to their grandchildren. Whenever I suggested to them to take time out to read or to go for walks, they would sigh and say: "What am I supposed to do? I have no money left. At present, my children are the ones who feed me so it is natural that I work for them."

Beyond fifty, women in Vietnam are considered old. They would dress any which way, saving their nice clothes for visitors and not taking the least heed of their looks under the pretext that death was near. One of my aunts, who had come to see her eighty-nine-year old sister in Saigon, refused my gift of a plane ticket back to Hue. For her, the train was quite sufficient. I had to agree to take the flight with her before she accepted my offer. I tried my best to explain that it was not a question of luxury, but a commodity that saved time and helped avoid unnecessary fatigue. Even in the end, I was not sure that I had really succeeded in convincing her. Having left my family so young, I had the feeling that I always led my life as I saw fit, even if the price I paid in sacrifices was enormous. Moreover, I had the intention of doing everything I might have missed out on during my youth.

My last commercial adventure dates back to 1995. In spite of my retirement and having other demands on my time, I would still, on occasion, return to film directing out of my passion for movies. I would often do so with my own money and the help of my friend, Alain L. One film, for example, was about Pasteur's collaborator, Doctor Yersin, after whom the *lycée* in Dalat had been named.

In 1995, then, having the opportunity to film the visit of the Party's First Secretary to the island of Con Dao, I was enthralled by the savage beauty of the wilderness there. Con Dao, or Poulo Condor, was the former penal colony during the French occupation and is located forty-five minutes from Saigon via helicopter. During the visit, the First Secretary showed us the cells where he—like most of the other Party members—had once been imprisoned. I was both quite moved by being in a place so laden with historical implications, and immensely charmed by that magnificent island with its fine, sandy beaches, its emerald-colored water, its abandoned art deco houses, and its virgin forests invaded by giant creepers that harbored red-faced monkeys. While working there, I also had the chance to discover the fourteen neighboring islets. At night, giant turtles came to lay their eggs on a beach and, elsewhere, thousands of birds nested on huge rocks. Since the North Vietnamese prisoners were released in 1975, the deserted island was allowed to return to a state of wilderness and was henceforth under the authority of an administrative committee.

Welcomed by the head of that Committee, the Party's First Secretary was astonished: "Why do you leave Con Dao in such a bad state?" "We don't have any money," the other answered. I then heard the First Secretary suggest: "There is no reason for not renting out these plots of land."

First we leased one thousand six hundred meters of coastline that was lined with a few French houses. Then, when I realized that there was fresh water on the island, I added four acres to plant fruit trees. In the beginning, a renewable lease was established for fifty years, whereas, today, it has been extended to ninety. But fifty were quite enough for me. Saigon-Tourism—in other terms, the State—occupied the rest, where a dozen traditional houses still existed but were soon to be razed and replaced by atrocious all-white edifices.

As for me, I preferred to try and save the housing where the French prison staff had lived. In Hanoi, I made sure of procuring the services of artisans who specialized in renovating temples and pagodas, and who assured faithful restoration, down to the most minute detail.

Another time, when I was in Hoa Binh, two thousand kilometers from there, I saw Thais ready to demolish their magnificent century-old pile house in order to replace it with a construction in brick. I was so disappointed in seeing such beauty on the brink of destruction that I asked them to sell it to me. They accepted the offer and I arranged to have it moved to Con Dao. During the next two years, I procured two more Thai-style dwellings that I rent out to tourists. But, in the future, I intend to devote an entire village to examples of minority people's houses, which otherwise are in the process of going extinct.

Since the state had invested in Con Dao, the roads were widened, a harbor was built, and, soon thereafter, an airport was opened. From my house, I have a magnificent view of the sea and I often spent my weekends there. In a few years time, I'll really retire and live there year round.

The changes that my family has undergone are the same that are felt by Vietnamese society, in general. Today, one of my grandsons, Anh Vu, is studying in Sydney, and the other, Phuoc Minh, in San Diego, where he is housed by my little brother and his wife. Just before Phuoc Minh's departure, Anh Vu explained that he wanted to remain in Australia for five years in order to study and make some money before returning to Vietnam.

While we were all re-united in my eldest son's house, I recollected feeding him manioc and sugar cane juice, trying to protect him from leeches. My grandson said to me: "When I am in America, we'll correspond by e-mail." And before his departure, my oldest son slipped me a word: "Thank you, mommy, for giving him permission to leave."

My five brothers and sisters are living in California with my mother. My third sister, Yen, died of leukemia in 1995. I still have eight aunts and two uncles. Under the former regime, their children worked in banks, or were engineers or aviators. Many numbered among the "boat people" and now live in the United States, Canada, or Australia. Most of them are still afraid to return to Vietnam—like my mother, who remains violently anti-communist and refuses to believe my "Vietcong words." My cousins from Australia came to visit for the Tet festivities only because I was there to "protect" them. I am fortunate: we have never had misunderstandings among us. They have understood that I am not a hard-liner, and that I have suffered as well. We have great affection for one another even today.

My husband has gotten used to things. He is passionately working on memoirs about the Vietnamese army and talks only about the past. He refuses adamantly to get into a rickshaw. He travels by car or he walks, but cannot accept that a man might put himself out for him. Furthermore, when he sees all the nightclubs that have opened and the people who sing on television, he suffers tremendously. He takes everything to heart, for he does not want things to change in any way. As for me, I am lucky insofar as I have always had an enormous capacity to adapt.

Voyage to America

On April 4th, 2000, I received a call from Nga, my sixth sister. My mother was asking for me. Her health was declining. On the 5th, I completed a visa application at the American Embassy. On the evening of the 7th, I took off for America. The trip lasted eighteen hours, but I could not manage to sleep. I harbored a certain anxiety at the idea of discovering the big country that had so tortured our people. But at the same time, I could not wait to see my brothers and sisters in their own homes and, especially, I was impatient to see my mother. I was so afraid that she might die before my arrival. Landing in Los Angeles, I had trouble realizing that I was at last, really and truly in America. My fourth sister, Sun Yen, greeted me at the airport. Yes, mommy was still alive. We then drove off in her Mercedes to her son's lavish mansion, fifty kilometers away where she was living. She had prepared a room for me that was enormous, with flowers everywhere. My nephew and his wife were pharmacists. The house was entirely contemporary, with Vietnamese paintings on the walls. As soon as I arrived, the telephone started ringing non-stop. The next day, my second brother, the colonel, and his wife came to see me, followed by my third brother, the pediatrician, and my sister Nha, who had a leather goods store on Sunset Boulevard. There we were, all reunited for dinner. The meal was a combination of American and Vietnamese food. We spoke in Vietnamese. It was decided that we all go to visit my mother the next day. Since her visit to France in 1989, we had been writing to each other very often. Although my aunts and I had tried many times to coax her back to Vietnam, she had always refused out of fear of the communists, even if, as her letters indicated, her deepest desire was to "eat the water weeds of her village of Eo Bau." She had not been able to walk for two years. The house where she was living was a two-hour drive from my nephew's. The whole family had pitched in for the rent so that the children of my third sister—deceased in 1995—could live there and take care of their grandmother. Seeing how they lived, I could better understand the long way they had come since 1975. Having arrived in the United States after a brief period in the Philippines—except for my brother, the physician, who, in 1975, had an internship in the United States—they had had to fend for themselves in order to earn a living. Today, thanks to their efforts and their unrelenting persistence, all their children went or are still going to college and are doctors or engineers.

In her room, my mother lay on a bed, wrapped in a sheet. Above her head, there were flasks and an oxygen tank. Her face was puffy, her eyes closed and her long, white hair was spread out on the pillow. I sat down beside her and took her hand. When she opened her eyes and we exchanged looks, they were full of tears. I felt her hand trembling and thought I could hear a murmur: Phuong, Phuong. Two years before, she had had a stroke and could no longer speak. My brothers and my sisters stepped out of the room and I remained alone with my mother in silence. Two hours passed, she dropped my hand and stared at the door. I called in my nephew, Giao. He told me that she had to be changed every two hours and that she did not want anybody to see her.

The following days, I took turns staying with each one of my brothers and sisters. With Phat, the Colonel, we never brought up the subject of the war in Vietnam. Former South Vietnamese military personnel, or civilians working for Americans and authorized to settle in the United States, often came over to chat or play cards. When they were there, I did not feel brushed away. I really think that this page of history has been turned.

When I went to my father's tomb, I was surprised to discover that his name had been engraved in a marble wall on the grounds of a magnificent mansion, decorated with works of art. My brother explained that our father's coffin was set inside that very wall. It was only at that moment that I noticed other names inscribed, as well, on the sides of the room. Then I understood why my sisters had hesitated ever so slightly before entering the edifice. My second brother had brought offerings of oranges and apples, along with incense sticks. I placed them on the floor, in front of the wall. I put the sticks in a glass and whispered to my father that I had returned.

After three weeks of lovely get-togethers, the moment had come to leave again. When I went to say adieu to my mother, she took a hold of my hand and did not let go. She stared intensely at me and tears flowed down on her cheeks. Then, she released her hand and followed me with her eyes as I inched away.[1]

Before going back to Vietnam, I stopped over in Washington, where one of my husband's nephews was living. There, I had the opportunity to visit many places—like the White House—that I had read about in books. But I also went to that soft green lawn which blankets a hillside, where the wall commemorating the American soldiers who had fallen in

---

[1] Phuong's mother died in July 2002.

Vietnam is erected. It is a long slab of black marble, with letters engraved in alphabetical order by date of casualty, in front of which the crowd slowly files past. Large books hold the names of the soldiers, with the dates and places of their deaths. Small children come with their dolls, and grown-ups with bouquets that they lay on the ground in front of the wall. I saw a very old woman touch a name. The pain on her face was so intense that I had to turn away.

I returned to Ho Chi Minh City with a heavy heart, knowing deep down that I had perhaps said farewell to my mother for the last time. But, after having been away from everyone for a half a century, the mere possibility of now calling my brothers and sisters at will, of being able to express my sad as well as happy feelings, and of listening to their private thoughts, was still almost beyond my comprehension and was of deep comfort for me.

Whenever I am asked if at any point I felt the urge to emigrate, I can answer that the thought never crossed my mind. During the Resistance days, I never even really knew what the world outside was about. Furthermore, even if in the 1980s everyone around me was trying to get out and at the slightest pretext my social origins were looked upon with suspicion, I still felt no desire to leave my country. Often I quote Erich Maria Remarque: "The uprooted are never happy."

The presence of my husband and my children help me enormously, but I have always been confident that Vietnam would become the country of our dreams. Even if, today, injustices and unacceptable living conditions prevail for many, it is for the Vietnamese, themselves, to determine their destiny.

I have also kept in contact with many of my old friends from the Resistance who are living in the provinces throughout Vietnam. Some are ministers or generals. Others are shopkeepers, and still others have spent time in prison because of their divergent ideas. Whenever we get together, opposing viewpoints disappear. We are united through our strong affection for one another—one more intimate than amongst the members of a closely-knit family. Having been through so much together has created bonds between us that nothing will ever alter.

Epilogue

All about Phuong and me
by Danièle Mazingarbe

I had always been attracted to Asia. As a student, during holidays, I spent three months in India, Nepal and Sri Lanka, traveling all around by train. Later, I went to China during the Cultural Revolution, and twice more afterwards. As a journalist, I reported about the Cambodian camps in Thailand. But I had never been to Vietnam. Like everybody else, I had read a few books about the war in Indochina, and later watched the now so familiar TV images of Kim Phuc, the little girl burnt by napalm, and those of the fall of Saigon. I did not want to go there as a tourist, like many French people do. However, in 1995, when my employer, the Paris newspaper *Le Figaro*, offered a tour of Vietnam, I thought I should go along. We landed in Hanoi, and I was immediately taken by the sweetness of the air. Our guide was a young man whom we learned later was the son of a Party member denied the right to go abroad. He came across as bitter, and commented constantly on our clothes. Not at all pleasant, he insisted that we keep together as a group. But with my husband, Ralph, we managed to escape on our own and have a dinner that included a tasty pho, the typical Vietnamese soup of beef and lots of herbs. People were very friendly, the night was warm, and the experience, delightful. The tour continued, classically from north to south, to spectacular Halong Bay, where people were anxious to show us Catherine Deneuve's room during the time she was there filming *The Lover,* based on the book by Marguerite Duras. Of course, you could not help noticing how polluted the sea was, and the extremely poor condition in which families were living on the sampans. Then we went to Hue, Danang, and so forth. Everywhere, hordes of adorable children tried to sell us goods, from fake silver dollars to embroideries. And we saw women working in the rice fields, feet in the water, and muddy villages, and police and soldiers lining the roads. In Ho Chi Minh City, we had a wonderful elderly guide, who knew La Fontaine by heart and was very proud of his French education. The towns, the climate, and, of course, the atmosphere, are very different from the North. You can still feel the American influence. The whole trip lasted ten days; but I returned very frustrated at not having truly met a single Vietnamese.

The occasion for making a new trip was offered to me the following February. Paris was going to host an exhibit of Vietnamese painting called *Le Printemps vietnamien* (The Vietnamese Spring) and the people organizing this event took five journalists to Vietnam to meet some of the artists whose works were to be shown in Paris. I delighted in returning to Hanoi, this time being able to meet all sorts of people and to go to workshops and see "the real life," a life that was difficult, yet active and highly creative for artists. After Hanoi, we went to Ho Chi Minh City and met even more artists. The French Consulate gave a party to present *Le Printemps vietnamien.* There, I noticed a very energetic elderly woman, who rose to say in perfect French that it was very unfair to present, in Paris, Vietnamese artists working in Vietnam—that is to say, in extreme hardship and poverty—while at the same time presenting artists of Vietnamese origin working in Paris. For instance, the most famous photographer in Vietnam had no money to have his photographs printed. I thought it was a most interesting and fair remark, so I went to her and told her so. She told me to come and visit her in her art gallery the following day, where she would be happy to show me the work of some of her artists.

The Lotus Gallery is located on one of the main streets of Ho Chi Minh City, Dong Khoi, the former *rue Catinat*. It exhibits many artists whose works are either lacquers or paintings executed in styles ranging from classical to contemporary. Among them was her very famous Hao. She offered me tea, and I started the interview I wanted to write for *Madame Figaro* (the Sunday women's supplement to *Le Figaro*). Almost from the beginning, she said: "When I was in the jungle ..." "When you were in the jungle?" was my reply and that's how my adventure with Phuong began. She mentioned a film being made about her.[1] I asked: "No book?" She replied: "No, we could write it together." Fifteen minutes later, I left to catch my plane for France.

The following day, I had lunch with a friend working at the Paris publishing house, *Editions Plon*. I told him about Phuong and the next day I was in the publisher's office signing a contract. I did not know what Phuong would decide. In the meantime, I had sent her a letter telling her about me, and why I wanted to write a book with her: that is, to understand the momentous choice that she had made, her dedication to the cause, etc. A month later, her contract came back, signed. We could start our work.

Nevertheless, I did not know much about Indochina, where Phuong was born in 1929, nor about Vietnam. So I

---

[1] *Phuong le phénix* (Phuong the Phoenix), a film by François Maillart, produced in the year 2000 by INA and EFM Productions, France.

started reading and reading, buying all the books I could find. We talked on the phone and decided I would go to Vietnam for a week in November to start recording her memories.

Phuong lives in a room at one of her sons' houses—a very Vietnamese thing to do—and we started working on a rooftop terrace there. The story she began to tell was like a fairytale: a nice little girl from a lovely family going to war to defend her country, living in the jungle like Robinson Crusoe. We were interrupted all the time by phone calls; she was pleasant about it but we could work only three or four hours in a row. The rain started to pour after five o'clock each day and I had to stay in my hotel room. But she also took me all around the country to show me where she had been in the jungle, and to where she had lived in Hanoi. I met some old gentlemen, who had been her companions during the war: young generals of mandarin origin who were discharged from the army after Dien Bien Phu. Upon my return, I had my tapes transcribed. The result was a mountain of disorder and it was obvious there was an enormous amount of work yet to be done. I went to Vietnam again the following February, for Tet. We visited all her relatives. There, I witnessed the Vietnamese tradition of families living together under strong-willed grandmothers reigning over their lovely granddaughters watching MTV and exchanging e-mails. Once back in Paris, however, I realized that the stories I registered on the tape recordings I made sounded too romantic. Therefore, Phuong agreed to come during that summer of 1999 to work with me for three weeks at my country place south of Paris.

By the time she arrived, I had collected a hundred or so books, was familiar with what had happened during the Vietnamese revolution, and understood all its ambiguities.

The plane landed at Charles-de-Gaulle Airport, north of Paris, at five in the morning. We picked up Phuong—who was fresh and lively as ever—and went to our summer place. I showed her all around the house. We went to my office. She saw all my books about Vietnam. "You know, Phuong, when you met me, I knew nothing about your country, but now... Look at all those books. Maybe we should revise what we have done together to make the text stronger. People in France are very passionate about Vietnam, as you know, and when the book is published I do not want you to face too much criticism." She went to her room to take a nap and that afternoon we began a new story. She also seemed very different: more relaxed, and freer to relate what she had undergone. I went back again to Vietnam. She came back again to France, working hard on the book, organizing the 2,500 pages of our conversations, and—for political reasons, of course—cutting out a lot of her recollections from more recent times. It was obvious that she really trusted me. By this time, she had become part of our family, teaching me how to cook Vietnamese dishes and prepare the delicious Pho.

I rewrote the book once, twice, and a third time during my Christmas vacation, even after having already delivered the manuscript. *Ao Dai* was published in Paris in April 2001. Phuong came and stayed three weeks for the interviews. She also met with many Vietnamese moved by what she had accomplished, and got in touch with friends from the *Couvent des Oiseaux*. Then Phuong returned to Vietnam, where I know that she must still keep a low profile for political reasons. But at least she is back to doing the business of exhibiting her Vietnamese painters all over Asia, and she is as prosperous as any Vietnamese could be.